STILL

You know that time is passing and you seem to be getting nowhere.

You know your chances of advancement are blocked in your company, or perhaps you want to move into a different field.

You know you are capable of handling far more challenging tasks and assuming more important responsibilities.

But you don't know how to begin to look for a better job—and are unsure of those vital things that will get it, from sending in a résumé that will impress that unknown person who reads it, to putting your best foot forward with the stranger who will be interviewing you.

This book was written to show you
HOW TO GET A BETTER JOB QUICKER

RICHARD A. PAYNE holds an M.B.A. from the Harvard Business School and has worked in important marketing positions with several major companies. For more than a decade he has conducted courses in job-finding for such groups as Harvard Business School and MIT graduates and corporate clients like GTE, Citibank, and Benton and Bowles.

MENTOR Titles of Interest

HOW TO GET A BETTER JOB QUICKER

New Expanded Edition

Richard A. Payne

A MENTOR BOOK

NEW AMERICAN LIBRARY

NEW YORK AND SCARBOROUGH, ONTARIO

NAL BOOKS ARE AVAILABLE AT QUANTITY DISCOUNTS
WHEN USED TO PROMOTE PRODUCTS OR SERVICES. FOR
INFORMATION PLEASE WRITE TO PREMIUM MARKETING DIVISION,
NEW AMERICAN LIBRARY, 1633 BROADWAY,
NEW YORK, NEW YORK 10019.

New Expanded Edition

Library of Congress Catalog Card Number: 79-90050

MENTOR TRADEMARK REG. U.S. PAT. OFF. AND FOREIGN COUNTRIES
REGISTERED TRADEMARK—MARCA REGISTRADA
HECHO EN CHICAGO, U.S.A.

SIGNET, SIGNET CLASSIC, MENTOR, PLUME, MERIDIAN and NAL BOOKS
are published in the United States by
New American Library,
1633 Broadway, New York, New York 10019,
in Canada by The New American Library of Canada Limited,
81 Mack Avenue, Scarborough, Ontario M1L 1M8.

First Mentor Printing, February, 1980

9   10   11   12   13   14   15   16   17

PRINTED IN THE UNITED STATES OF AMERICA

Contents

To Judy, my loving wife,
who has helped and encouraged me
in so many ways.

Preface

The interview went great. We had a few things in common and actually had a couple of laughs together. I really thought I was going to get an offer from this outfit. But a month has gone by and I've heard nothing. I must have blown it some way.

For a while I was relying on a particular employment agency to help me land my next job. In the beginning this agency was great—sent me to about half a dozen different interviews in three weeks. But none of the jobs they sent me to was really what I was looking for. Then the agency stopped calling. After three weeks I realized you can't rely on anyone but yourself to get a good job!

About eight weeks ago I spotted an ad for a job which must have been made for me. Honestly, the 'ideal candidate' in that ad sounded like it was me they were describing. So naturally I wrote and sent my resume. Silence is all I got. The worst part is that since it was a box-numbered ad, there's no way I can reach this company to sell myself to them.

Maybe you have heard job-seekers say things like this. You may even have heard such things from good people who you felt should have been able to land a great job with no problems at all. Or perhaps you have made comments like these yourself. It wouldn't surprise me. In the seventeen years I've been helping job-seekers to get better jobs, I've heard hundreds of comments like these . . . again and again. Frustration is commonplace during many job campaigns, even among top-level executives, the kinds of people who have already demonstrated that they are "winners" and shouldn't have any trouble finding a market for their talents.

9

The fact is that many of the frustrations of job search can be avoided, and many job-seekers could secure better jobs in less time if they were only better buttoned-up in the techniques of selling themselves in the job market. A lot of job-seekers may have trouble believing this statement. "Getting a good job is largely a matter of luck" they claim. Maybe it is part luck. But it's also knowing what you're doing. For instance, if someone gave you a 34mm camera with no instructions on how to use it, you'd expect to take fuzzier, less well-exposed pictures than if you had some basic directions on how to operate it. The same holds true in job search. If you know the rules of the road—the things that work and the things that don't—it stands to reason that you have a better chance of getting the position you're looking for sooner and with less frustration than otherwise.

Strangely enough, the great majority of job-seekers "go it on their own" without such direction. Perhaps it's because they feel that they're good in their own field and that should be enough to get them the job they want. (They forget that competence and knowing how to sell competence are not one and the same.) Maybe it's a matter of pride. (Many who seek me out initially feel self-conscious about asking for help.) Maybe it's because they just don't realize how much competition they're up against. (The fact is there's plenty.)

A survey several years ago showed that the average job is sought by nineteen people. That means you are, in all probability, competing with eighteen others. Your resume will lie on a desk with a stack of resumes of men or women with qualifications fairly similar to your own. Your prospective employer will look at nineteen people dressed in their neatest attire—each talking fast and hard, each seeking to impress the person behind the desk that he or she should be the one.

What are the people like who will compete with you? There's a good chance that some will be more distinguished or attractive than you. Some will speak more eloquently and fluently on their feet, some will have gone to a "better" school. And, to make the game just a little bit more difficult, you don't know who your competition is. You don't know what weak spots they might have that you could match yourself against. You've got to play the game on your own.

Furthermore, your prospective boss is not eagerly awaiting you. Chances are he will look over your resume at the end of a hard working day. Even if you make it past round one and, on the basis of your resume, are invited to cross the threshold of your prospective employer's office, the sledding won't be easy. You have to be on your toes throughout every phase of your job search.

No job-seeker today should take the luxury of learning the hard way. Those who try it on their own in a hit-or-miss fashion are most often the ones whose searches take longer, or who settle for lesser titles on the next job than they had on the last. They are the ones who so often take the *wrong* job because they didn't know how to get the *right* one.

The fact that you opened this book suggests you're not the type of person who starts a major undertaking without counsel. In going after your new job, you want some help. There are lots of reasons why you might want it. You may be thinking about changing jobs for the first time, or for the first time in a long time. You may have been trying to get a new job for many weeks or months without the success you thought you should have. Whatever the case, you've recognized that you can do a better job of selling your talents with some practical, down-to-earth guidance, and you have the initiative to seek it out. If this is the case, read on. This book deals with how you *can* get the job you want *quicker,* and with *less frustration.*

A tough promise to meet? Yes. But a realistic one, because this book provides you with plans and tools that *work.* It's based on the experience of literally thousands of job-seekers who have shared their job-search problem with me, and those who have worked with me to develop strategies, plans, and tools, not only to overcome personal obstacles but to avoid the basic pitfalls common to job searches. How can this book help you reduce the frustration so many job-seekers feel when they go after a better job? In two ways. First, by identifying those obstacles you may confront in your search *before* they arise, so that when a problem comes up, you can do something about it before it gets out of hand. Second, by providing you with *practical* solutions that have been developed and tested over the years. So you avoid both the time and energy needed to develop solutions on your own by "trial and error." Many job-seekers insist on reinventing the wheel. But that's the hard way. With this book your search doesn't have to be a hit-or-miss proposition.

While the techniques in this book have helped thousands of job-seekers reduce both the frustrations of job search and the time it takes to get a better job, it's a mistake to think that because you read it once you'll get precisely the job you want without a good deal of effort. Thomas Edison once said that genius was 1 percent inspiration, 99 percent perspiration. The odds in job search are not quite that steep. Knowing what to do and what not to do can account for a good deal of your success in landing a better job in less time and with less effort. But plain hard work is still a critical factor. You can't get away from that because only you can adapt the plan and tools provided by this book to your own situation. Is it worth doing a job search "by the book"? Only you can answer that. But keep in mind that for thousands of job-seekers the techniques in this book have spelled the difference between getting "a" job and getting "the" job—one that is the most satisfying of their lifetimes.

Introduction

In the Preface you just read, I promised this book would provide you with the tools and plans to get the job you want next quicker and with less frustration. And it will! From the very first page of Chapter 1 you'll be introduced to proven job-search strategies and techniques that you can adapt to your own campaign. There's one important thing, however, that you've got to get done before you can make any of the tools in this book work for you. You've got to decide just what the next job you want really should be. If you don't know your target, all the best strategies in the world won't get you your next job in less time and with less frustration. It's like being a soldier in the dark who has no idea of the range of his enemy. Lobbing artillery without knowing the target is more often than not a wasted, time-consuming effort. There's no way around it—you've got to identify the *better* job that you want to aim for right at the start.

For most readers, deciding on what a better job really is will be a snap. All you really want is to find a company where you can do what you've been trying to do in the company you're now in. But, unlike your present company, you're looking for one that will support you in getting your mission accomplished; one that will recognize your contributions and reward you accordingly; one that with time will give you the opportunity for advancement that you don't see in your own company.

For a few readers, deciding on what that "better" job really ly should be won't be quite so simple. Perhaps you really don't know what you want to do next. You may be wondering what the best way is to the top—taking into account where you are now, and where you'd like to be in ten or twelve years. Or, quite possibly, you've reached a point in your life in which you have come to a decision that you've "had it" with your current career, and you are pondering a totally new one. (This happens to an awful lot of good people in their late thirties and forties, so don't be concerned if you're having doubts of your own.) Chapter 15 deals with the relationship of your current job search to your career goals, but that's not the major thrust of this book. I've assumed that most of you have a pretty good idea what you want in a "better job," and this book deals with how to go about getting it.

Even if you have a pretty good idea of what a better job is in your case, though, I'd like to suggest that you try to *pinpoint* as precisely as you can five major factors about that next job before you go on to Chapter 1, and start learning the tools of job search. Pretend for a moment that you are a pilot. Deciding on what city you'd like to land in really isn't enough. You've got to choose the airport—LaGuardia or Kennedy in New York, for example—and the exact runway, if you're going to have a successful landing. To locate and land your own "better" job, you've got to zero in on just that precisely by considering:

☐ THE JOB TITLE YOU ARE WILLING TO ACCEPT On the surface, perhaps a job title doesn't seem all that important. "It's the job function, money, and opportunity that count" say many job-seekers. But if the job you take doesn't work out, the job title you secure is terribly important since it can affect the next job you go after. If you accept a title in your current search that's not as good as the one you now have, for example, it may put a real damper on securing better positions throughout the rest of your career.

☐ THE MONEY PACKAGE What you are willing to accept as minimum financial compensation for your efforts can have a big effect on the timing and style of your job search. If you insist on a great deal more money than you make in your current job, your job search will probably take a lot longer than if you are willing to settle for just about as much money as you are now making. Your circumstances should dictate a realistic money objective. If you are currently employed, for example, and have all the time in the world to get your next job, you can afford to establish a high money goal for yourself. But if you're out of work (or close to it), you really don't have that option.

☐ LOCATION If you are willing to move anywhere, including Timbuktu, there are many more potential employers. Naturally, your job search should take less time than if you insist that the next company you work for be within four miles of your present home. (Believe it or not, this is precisely what one out-of-work job-seeker I counseled demanded in considering any new position. As you might expect, his search lasted close to a year!)

☐ THE TYPE OF COMPANY YOU'D LIKE TO WORK FOR Many job-seekers have, somewhere in the back of their minds, a feeling about certain types of companies. "Too small for me to grow," thinks one. "Too much infighting," thinks another. "Too large and impersonal," thinks a third. You should decide long before you take your first interview what type of companies you could happily work for. If you do, you can eliminate wasted responses to ads and needless interviews. Not only do you streamline your search and use your time more effectivey, but more important, you increase your odds of being happy and successful when you do land a job!

How can you decide what type of environment you want to work in? Consider your current and past experience. What type of company did you like best? What kind of organization were you most successful in? Weigh what friends and family say about you and the type of company they think you'd be happiest in. Job-seekers who go willy-nilly after any company without matching its personality to their own are inevitably the ones who are back in the job-search market sooner than they otherwise need to be. Why conduct a job search twice when once should do it!

☐ JOB SATISFACTION More than anything else, you need to define for yourself before you answer a single ad what makes a job satisfying for you. How much responsibility must it have to keep you happy? What type of a boss can you live with? What advancement opportunities would it take to please you in the long run? Jobs with the exact same titles can be very different from one company to the next. A "product manager" at one company might have genuine profit-and-loss responsibility. At another company the same title might define what is primarily a staff function. *Unless you know what you do want, there's always the chance you'll get what you don't want!*

In addition to considering these five specific objectives, there's one other factor you ought to decide on before you read further in this book. And that's the job search timetable you can live with. Obviously, if you are out of work, and your resources will last only for six more months, you know precisely how long you have to get the job you want, and in developing your job search tools and plans, you have a goal against which you must work. On the other hand, if you are now happily employed with no presssure on you, and you're reading this book because you might like to "test the water," you could decide to take two years and find the "perfect" job. The point in asking you to decide on a timetable before you start your search is this: the amount of time you can devote to your search will affect the tools and strategy you need to use. Do you, for example, have the time to conduct a discreet, narrow-based campaign, or do you have to fire all your guns at once, and go down every possible avenue towards that "better" job? The situation you are in will undoubtedly have an impact on how fast you take action on the tools that this book will reveal to you, and may well temper each of the specific factors you take into account in zeroing in on what you decide is the right job for you to take at this time. It only takes a moment to establish a realistic target date for yourself—one that you can really live with. But doing so can affect the success of your campaign. So do it now—then turn to Chapter 1, where you'll learn the secrets of self-selling.

One

How to make the world want you: four principles of self-selling

At one of my classes on how to conduct an effective job search, I asked each person present to come forward and tell the rest of the class why we should hire him. A gray-haired, vested, distinguished-looking gentleman in the class offered us this answer:

> You should hire me as your next plant manager because I'm responsible for all phases of manufacturing in the company where I am now, including production, purchasing, scheduling, plant engineering, and industrial engineering. I've been involved with computerized inventory control, production-control systems, warehouse-locator and inventory systems, and budgetary control systems. And I've had a total of fifteen years' experience with four of the leading companies in my field.

On the basis of his presentation, I asked the class whether they would hire this distinguished candidate. The first few classmates to speak said, "Yes," perhaps because of the gentleman's appearance. And then one member of the class said, "No. I know the kind of experience he's had. But I'm not sure he's any good at what he's been doing." This classmate was right! Looks aside, for all we knew, this distinguished gentleman may have bungled every assignment he ever had in the many areas of manufacturing in which he'd worked. We knew he had fifteen years of experience with four companies. It's possible he left each of these just as he was about to be fired. What was missing from this distinguished gentleman's presentation that could have convinced us to hire him? Some evidence that while he was on the job he did specific things that helped his company in some way or another. We know from what he told us that he was involved in a lot of different activities. But we have no idea from what he told us of how *valuable* he was in each of the jobs he held.

There are four basic principles in selling yourself. The first and most important principle is this:

1. Your prospective boss doesn't care what you did between nine and five—he only cares what happened as a result of your being there

In a word, it isn't a laundry list of job functions that turns on the people who might hire you. It's what *specific* things you were able to get done that in some way improved your company's situation that counts, because they are practical demonstrations of your worth.

At the very same class, another, somewhat younger manufacturing executive told us why we should hire him. His reasoning was altogether different. Here's what he told us with a great deal of enthusiasm.

> You should hire me because I've got tremendous machine and fabrication know-how. I'm thoroughly familiar with a wide range of metal, plastic, and fiberglass tooling techniques. And I've got genuine administrative perception. I have a full grasp and working knowledge of a broad cross-section of manufacturing and planning controls. And I'm a real morale and productivity builder. I'm adept in planning and organizing, scheduling and follow-through to make sure we get the job done. Not only that, I'm a profit producer. I can help any manufacturer beat the cost squeeze.

At the end of his speech, a few people in the class volunteered that they'd hire this bright-eyed, bushy-tailed young man. But most of the class felt differently. Most, like me, wouldn't have hired the second executive either. The reason: because, while he told us he was good (damned good, I might add), we had only his word for it. As someone said to me after the class: "Not only did his speech sound extremely boastful, but I really didn't know whether what he was saying was fact or fiction."

In point of fact, none of us in the class that night knew

whether the young, animated man's evaluation of himself was accurate. It's possible—perhaps probable—that his opinion of himself was a biased one.

The second important principle of self-selling, then, is this:

2. Your prospective boss isn't interested in your opinion of yourself

He doesn't know you. He doesn't know how well you evaluate yourself. What your prospective boss wants is evidence that you are the best person he can hire. How can you provide this evidence? With results. With illustrations of what you did on the job that, in and of themselves, are indisputable evidence of your worth to the companies you worked for. Things that you did that the other eighteen candidates with whom you compete didn't do, or couldn't do. Your prospective boss needs to be convinced. The one thing that will convince him most is specific examples of your ability to contribute something worthwhile in situations that might have a bearing on his particular problems.

"That's all well and good," you say, "but how do I know that the results I achieved on my old job, or my last several jobs, are the kind of results my prospective boss is seeking? Is my experience relevant?" Obviously you don't know this, but it probably isn't the deciding factor. On the priority scale, your prospective employer must rate specific experience secondary to your ability to do whatever job you have in such a way as to help improve the situation. And you can prove your ability to get *results* by describing the things you achieved at the job you now hold, or previously held. Don't get me wrong. It's nice to have the exact experience your prospective boss is looking for. But it's not essential. If you've done well at whatever you have done, you're far better off than the persons who may have the "exact experience" but who have done nothing on their current jobs to prove they have the ability to take on the one they're going after. To put it in its simplest terms, if you have demonstrated your worth on a smaller job, you can handle a bigger job. Believe it because it's true, and go after the bigger job.

If you doubt that experience is secondary to what results you achieved in whatever you undertook, consider this example. A number of years ago a friend of mine, then a sophomore in college, wanted to apply to Harvard Business School.

He wrote to the dean and asked what subjects he should take in order to get accepted at this, the most famous business school in the country. The dean wrote back, "It doesn't matter which courses you take, just do well in what you elect to study." My friend majored in, of all things, philosophy—because he liked it. He ended up with honors in his field and a Phi Beta Kappa key. To no one's surprise, he was accepted at Harvard Business School even though he had never taken a course in marketing, finance, or economics! But he had proved along the way that he was a cut above the others he competed with.

When you stop to think about it, it's quite natural that tangible proof of your worth on the last job is more important than precisely the right experience. Why? Because in a year's time what you have learned on the new job will be infinitely more important than what you learned in five years on the last one. In point of fact, you may need to overcome some of the experiences you picked up at your former company simply because they don't tie in with the procedures and systems that are in effect at the company you hope to join.

Even more impressive to your prospective employer than one example of what you accomplished on the job are a number of examples, particularly if they show you helped improve the situation in a series of positions, each with more overall responsibility than the last; and particularly if each successive example demonstrates your *growing* value to the company over time. I know a man who is today the executive vice-president of a major health-aids company. He is responsible for the worldwide marketing of fifteen famous products with multimillion-dollars sales. How this gentleman moved into the marketing field is proof of the importance of demonstrating your increasing ability to secure positive results in whatever positions you've held. He began his career in the accounting department of an appliance company. His first job was in accounts payable, first as a junior accountant, then as an accountant, then as senior accountant. All in the space of three years. At this point in his career he decided he was more interested in marketing than in accounting. Thwarted in his attempts to get into marketing at the appliance company, he decided to seek employment elsewhere. He managed to secure a fairly senior job in the advertising department of the health-aids company he now presides over. How? By selling both his rapid rise in responsibility and progressively greater contributions in each of his positions within the accounting department of his former company. This leads to the third principle in selling yourself:

3. Consider your career in terms of a series of progressively more important demonstrations of what you have accomplished for the organizations that hired you in the past

Some specific instances of your value to your company may be minor, others major, in terms of the new job that you seek. Organize your contributions in such a way as to show this growth quickly. Help your prospective boss to know that you can be counted on for personal growth. Make him believe you are a person on the way up, one with potential for growth in the next job.

At this point many of you may be experiencing doubts. I have stated that the first and most basic principle of self-selling is that you sell your experience or your self worth. I then asked you to sell these demonstrations of your value in a progressively more important manner, whether in a resume, an interview, or letter. Now you may well be wondering what so many others have wondered: Is it boastful to talk about those instances in which you did something worthwhile for your company? I confess that when I first considered the concept of offering illustrations of positive results I helped to achieve for the companies I worked for, I was afraid it might appear I was bragging. I knew very well that I wasn't the only one responsible for the successes of some of the business ventures in which I had participated. And I felt awkward saying, "I saved the company thousands of dollars," or, "I introduced a new product line that increased company sales by two million dollars." If you have pangs of conscience (and it wouldn't be surprising), let's move on to the fourth basic principle of self-selling.

4. Selling your prospective boss specific examples that prove your worth on the job is not bragging if you present each problem you faced and your solution to the problem in a factual, honest, and straightforward fashion

Here are some specific examples that demonstrate what

businessmen and women achieved in their respective jobs. See if they sound to you as if the authors are bragging.

> For four years sales had declined on product "X". To counter this I developed, then recommended to management a new package concept for this product. Management accepted the recommendation, and the purchasing department secured the package ′for us. Nine months after the new package was introduced, product "X" sales were 8 percent ahead of the previous year, with no increase in advertising or sales promotion expenditures.

> The cash balance at our company was extremely low, and our management contemplated a major bank loan. After analyzing accounts receivable, I recommended a cash discount for prompt payment that I thought would alleviate the problem. Management bought the idea. The new discount improved our cash position to the point where a bank loan became unnecessary.

> We had a label-sticking problem in our plant so I recommended utilization of a new glue formula. This suggestion increased labeling speed by 20 percent and reduced machine overhead by an equivalent amount.

Wouldn't you think seriously about hiring the people who demonstrated their worth with the specific illustrations that appear above? Do you think they were bragging? The first person told us there was a packaging problem with his company's products and that he recommended a change. Obviously, his boss, and perhaps his boss's boss, had to buy his recommendation. The change wasn't his alone, and he never claimed it as such. Yet he was instrumental in the change, and his contribution obvious. The second example came from a financial person and the third from a production engineer. None of the statements sounds boastful since they are businesslike solutions recommended by the people involved.

Concrete illustrations of what you have done in each of your jobs to overcome problems and obstacles are basic to the success of your job search. You can use them to your advantage throughout your campaign—in your resume, letters, interviews. As such, we'll refer to this device on many occasions throughout this book. Rather than bore you by repeating such statements as "a specific example of your contribution to a problem your company faced" over and over, I'll refer to this idea as a "worthpoint." It's a word one of the people in my class coined a half-dozen years ago. It stuck throughout each session and I've been using it ever since. Some people refer to these examples as "accomplishments" in their letters and resumes. Don't! This word is a turn-off today, a self-serving phrase that seems to suggest you are about to start lauding your own efforts. Think rather of "worthpoints" as your private word that describes the factual examples of what you did on the job that led to productive results. Let the person to whom you relate your worthpoints realize for himself that each was a significant accomplishment. Don't cram accomplishments down his throat.

Even if you accept that a well-spoken or well-written worthpoint is not bragging, you may have one further doubt. It might express itself like this: "My job is the kind of job where I haven't made any contributions, and I can't make any contributions." You will never convince me of that. Let me tell you a true story that explains why. A man who worked for one of the world's largest advertising agencies came to see me one day. He had spent fifteen years in the media department, and in a management shuffle he was fired. We went over the idea of describing his value to the agency by the use of worthpoints, and he said the same thing you may be thinking: "I have none that I could use." I wasn't convinced, so we sat there for two hours, with me firing questions at him to try and stimulate his thinking. "Absolutely no worthpoints," he maintained the entire time. "None."

And at the end of two hours, just as my patience was beginning to wear thin, I noticed that he was wearing a Little League tie clip. I asked him about it. He told me he had started a Little League in his home town in New Jersey. He started with only two teams. Now there were ten. He persuaded someone to donate a ball field and someone else to donate the lights. He organized a parents' committee. He had done this all himself. After talking about the Little League, I pointed out to him that he had revealed a number of worthpoints as he talked about each of the obstacles he had faced and overcome for the pint-sized Babe Ruths. Talking about them in a matter-of-fact way wasn't bragging. And then the floodgates broke loose. Not all his business worthpoints were great. But they were clear, concrete examples that revealed his true value to his present employer, and to his future ones as well! Once I got him over the initial hurdle of talking about them, he was psychologically ready to talk about them in interviews. And in no time at all he found a better job at another advertising agency.

There you have it. The four basic principles of self-selling:
1. Don't sell what you did between nine and five, but rather what the results were of what you did.
2. Don't place a value on your own worth. Let the results of your efforts speak for themselves.
3. Sell your contributions in such a way as to show personal growth.
4. Tell the incidents that demonstrate your worth in a factual, anecdotal form and they won't sound like bragging.

We could stop this book here. You have the guts of the matter. But as we go on, I will try to show you how to apply the "worthpoint" approach to your resume, how to utilize it in your interviews, how to fit it into your letters.

Let's turn from theory to a practical matter. How are you going to uncover and organize the many worthpoints that are part and parcel of your career in such a way that they provide the basis for selling yourself? It isn't easy. You may spend an hour for every year you've been in business. But it has to be done. You can't write a truly good resume without them! So the time to start is now. List every incident in your career where you faced a problem of some sort and came up with a solution, even if it was only a partial solution. *Every* worthpoint is important. It doesn't matter if you saved your company $10 or $10,000. It makes no difference, as long as you tried to save money and succeeded. Maybe you located a single customer for your company. The fact that you went after the customer and succeeded in getting him is what counts—not how many customers you went after. Maybe you created a design that won an award. That's a worthpoint and your prospective employer should know about it. So now is the time to stop reading this book. Pick up a pencil and start writing down your own worthpoints at each of the businesses with which you've been associated. Write each as a story. First state the problem, and, finally, state what happened as a result. Keep your stories short. In the chapters on writing resumes and planning interviews we'll take up some special refinements that will make your worthpoints sell even harder. For now jot down each of your specific contributions as they come to you without worrying about style. It's the demonstration of your worth that counts, not your writing ability.

One word of caution when you write up your worthpoints: make sure they sound believable. Don't claim to have done the impossible single-handed. It's easy to make yourself stand out, even as part of a group responsible for a project's success. To do so, just follow these two suggestions:

☐ Put your worthpoints in its proper perspective. Here's an example:

> Freight charges at our company were hurting profits since we couldn't pass them along to our customers. I initiated a program to switch from metal to lighter-weight plastic containers for our products. This change (in conjunction with a reduction in labor which the plastic containers made possible), increased net profits 28 percent the year following the shift from metal to plastic.

☐ Give credit to others, where appropriate:

> At one time we were not able to determine which of the 23 product lines in our division were most profitable. As a member of the president's financial task force, I conceived a new costing system. This system was adopted as part of the overall financial program recommended by the task force to top management, and is in use today in three company divisions.

HOW TO RANK THE SALES POTENTIAL OF YOUR WORTHPOINTS

If you have done your homework between the sections of this chapter, you have written down a number of most important worthpoints in your career. And what you've said you've done is believable. No one will accuse you of being boastful or of being Superman. By this time, your spouse or a friend may have read over your paragraphs to make sure what you contributed during your years in business is clear. But there is another key question that has to be answered concerning your worthpoints. Are they relevant to the needs of your prospective boss?

Obviously, without knowing who your prospective boss might be, it is difficult to make sure the worthpoints you describe to him or her are what he or she is looking for.

There are, however, several kinds that are more important than others in the eyes of most executives. These are outlined below. As you look over this preferred list, keep your own worthpoint roster in mind.

☐ PROFITS If there's one common denominator all business people understand, it's profits. Quite possibly you were reluctant to mention your contributions to profits because they may have been small ones. Mention them anyway. Not every person is in a position to add a million dollars in profits to the company's coffers. I know of a woman who, after seven years with a company, could report that she had saved her company only $17,000 in excess-interest charges. The size of your personal profit contribution is less important than your ability to recognize an opportunity to increase profits at all.

☐ INCREASED SALES You don't have to be a salesman to have helped increase your company's sales. You may have introduced a potential client to your firm. You may have corrected a pricing error which could have cost your company the loss of a customer. As a result of your production ideas, you may have contributed to a decrease in product cost which in turn resulted in a lower price to consumers. That lower price may have resulted in increased sales. You may have engineered a product improvement that helped the sales of a product. It doesn't matter whether you are in production, finance, marketing, or research, etc.; you have opportunities to help your company increase its sales. Your prospective boss should know about your contributions, no matter how small. Because, in the end, increased sales (with profits) are the aim of every business.

☐ REDUCED COST As with increased sales, reduced costs are not the exclusive franchise of any single department. If you are a process engineer, chances are you reduced the cost of a manufacturing system. If you are in purchasing, you may have made an extraordinary buy that saved your company money. If you are an office manager, you may have improved an administrative procedure so that you didn't hire an extra clerk. Prospective employers are looking for people who know how to save money. Because, ultimately, reduced costs become increased profits. If you've saved your company money, let it be known.

☐ ESTABLISHMENT OF NEW OBJECTIVES AND STRATEGIES I know a man who joined a great old New England company that produced a limited line of five products. Within a year after joining, this man had persuaded management to introduce three new product lines. Three months later this person decided to leave in a dispute with management over the introduction of additional new products. At the time he prepared his resume, results were not yet in on the success of the three new product lines he had introduced to the trade. He could not, therefore, refer to increases in sales and profits on his resume. But his resume was strong nonetheless, because he said in it: "Introduced three totally new products for the XYZ Company, the first introduced by this company since 1933."

☐ SUCCESSFUL PERSONNEL TRAINING A woman who attended one of my classes complained to me that she wasn't getting anywhere. As a claims supervisor in an insurance firm, she had trained no less than four men who had gone on to become vice-presidents of the company. Yet she herself remained as a claims supervisor, with no corporate title. As she discussed her future, I suggested that she focus on her ability to train. Her resume now sports this worthpoint: "Developed successful training techniques which have resulted in advancing careers for four key insurance company officers." The ability to develop people is an extremely important asset that can increase the profits of the corporation for whom the trainer is employed.

☐ RECOGNITION OF OVERLOOKED PROBLEMS Recently I came across a resume that said: "Analyzed costs and selling prices of three sizes of paints sold by the ABC Company. Discovered price structure, in effect for ten years, resulted in reduced profit to firm on larger sizes. Recommended price changes that increased profits on larger sizes while making it worthwhile for consumers to trade up to the bigger packages." This candidate scored well not only for his contribution to profits, but also for his curiosity, which led to the profit increase.

THE WORDS THAT SELL

Not all words create excitement. Take the difference between "hitting the ball" and "walloping" it. Certain words are active words; others are passive words. In talking about your career, try to use words that are exciting and active. Nothing annoys me more than a memo from one of the people who work for me saying, "Per your request, this document reviews . . ." I would much prefer the person to write instead, "Here are my recommendations concerning the pressing problem . . ."

So when you review your worthpoints let the words you select reveal your initiative, your extraordinary interest, your ability to move mountains. In this respect, there are several kinds of words and phrases you should try to incorporate into your interviews, resumes and letters. These include:

☐ TAKE-ACTION WORDS Some to consider for yourself are initiated, developed, conceived, planned, created, formulated.

☐ TAKE-CHARGE WORDS Like directed, organized, supervised, administered, managed, took responsibility for, presided over, led.

☐ GET-RESULTS PHRASES Some you may want to use are resulted in, led to, contributed to, demonstrated that, reduced, saved, increased, provided.

There are other active, exciting words. The sampling above only gives you an idea. Choose your own. But make sure each evokes a positive interest in you.

As a corollary, avoid words that suggest someone had to push you to do the job or that you were only following orders ("was asked to prepare an analysis" instead of "analyzed"). Show your prospective employers that you are a person of initiative and action by using action-oriented words. You may feel that selection of words is a small point. Maybe. But for some job-seekers it has made the difference between "No" and "Welcome aboard." Don't be a runner-up.

Two

Fifteen questions
to ask yourself

This chapter is dedicated to helping you write down your worthpoints. It is a short chapter, but it may take you longer to get through than any other in the book. Because now you take over, you do the work. If you have already written down all the contributions you've made in each of the positions you've held and are satisfied that your prospective boss will be interested in them—if you are certain you have gone over your experiences for the best examples you can offer of your value to the organization you'd like to join—you can skip this chapter. If not, read on.

This chapter includes fifteen questions and a commentary on each. Before you read the questions, however, let me warn you that you may not be able to answer all or some of them. To put you at ease, let me tell you a remarkable incident that occurred in a class I gave for a group of job-seekers nearly a decade ago.

Shortly after I handed out to the class a mimeographed sheet listing the questions I'm asking you to answer, one member (a tall blond man in the back row) raised his hand. When I acknowledged him, he exclaimed, "Your course on how to get a better job can't help me!" "Why?" I asked. "Because," replied the tall blond gentleman with a strong foreign accent, "I can't answer any of your questions." I asked the gentleman to be patient and listen to other members of the class answer some of these questions. Throughout the class he remained silent, sullen, and unconvinced.

After others in the class had answered one or more of the questions, I asked the tall blond foreigner if he felt any differently. "Not at all," he replied. On the spur of the moment I said to him, "You have a strong accent. Where are you from?" "Czechoslovakia," he replied. "How long have you been here?" "Three years." "And who taught you English?" "I learned it myself." "How?" "Well, I learned it while I was on the job." "Did you speak English at all before you arrived?" "Not a word."

I pressed on. "Tell me," I asked, "how did you get out of Czechoslovakia?" "I escaped," the man answered. "Did you come alone?" "No. I managed to get my family out." "How?" I asked. "Well, I devised a scheme. I built a rubber life raft in my home. The Russians were very careful about where one traveled, but they allowed people to go to Yugoslavia for their holidays. My wife, two children, and I went to a resort town on the Adriatic, just across from Trieste. I had the rubber life raft, deflated, in a fake compartment of my suitcase. In the dead of night, I inflated the life raft and we floated fifteen miles to Trieste."

I turned to the class. "This incident tells a lot about this man. It tells us he has courage to start life anew in a foreign country with no knowledge of the language. It tells us he is creative. It tells us that he can organize and succeed."

Someone in the class suggested applause for the gentleman from Czechoslovakia and this gentleman, who thought he couldn't accomplish anything, received a standing ovation.

The point of this story is simple. If you can't answer one or two or three of the fifteen questions in this chapter, don't be alarmed. It may be that you can answer other questions that are equally important because they show that you are a person who can accomplish difficult, if not impossible, things.

Now on to the fifteen questions you should answer as best you can.

1. Did you help to increase sales?

How? How much? Be specific in your answer. By what percent did you increase sales? How many dollars? What were the circumstances? What was your contribution? Did you help someone else to increase sales? What was your part in the sale? Specific dollars are the most convincing evidence you can offer. Use percentages only when revealing the actual dollars would mean giving away sensitive or current information that a competitor could use, or when the actual numbers are less meaningful than percents.

2. Did you save your company money?

What were the circumstances? How much did you actually save? What was the percentage of savings? Was your ability to save your company money greater than that of the person before you in your job? Of other people in your company?

3. Did you institute a new system or procedure in your company?

Why? What was the situation that led to your instituting the change? Who approved of your change? Did your procedure compete with any others? Why was it selected over others? What happened as a result of the change in procedure that you initiated? Has your procedure been adopted elsewhere in the company? Where? In other divisions? Departments?

4. Did you identify a problem in your company that had been overlooked?

What was the problem? What was the solution? Why was the solution overlooked? When you answer this question, you prove that you have the capacity to dig deeper than the next person. And this is important. Let me illustrate. One of the men I coached worked as a market researcher for a company that markets a well-known women's bath powder. Over a few months he discovered a number of complaint letters concerning the powder's new fragrance. Yet the company had conducted a wide-scale fragrance test, and the new fragrance in the product was the one women greatly preferred over the previous one. Still the letters came in. Then he went digging. He found out that the fragrance in the powder was not the same as the one that had won the test! What had happened was that an overzealous purchasing agent had talked to a different fragrance house, which promised him it could produce "an exact duplicate of the winning fragrance for about one-third the cost." On his own, the purchasing agent had substituted the so-called duplicate. Unfortunately, the duplicate broke down over time in the powder base. Hence the complaints. This story was a major factor in the market researcher's ability to get a better job. Have you demonstrated your capacity as a supersleuth? If you have, let all your prospective employers know it.

5. Were you ever promoted?

Why did your boss promote you? Was there some one thing you did that your management thought stood out? How long (or short) a period occurred between this and your previous promotion? How much more responsible was your new job than your old? How many more people reported to you? The phrase "was promoted" is the only passive verb that is worth a damn in a resume. It's proof that a third party thought you were better than your competition, that you had potential for growth. If you have been promoted several times by several different third parties, it is substantive evidence that you have potential for growth. Your prospective boss wants and needs to know this.

6. Did you train anyone?

Did you develop a training technique? What was this technique? How long was the training time by your technique as compared to the old one? What happened as a result of your training technique? Is your training technique being used by others in the company? It's a well-known truism that executives don't get promoted until they've trained a replacement. Employers are always on the lookout for people who know how to train someone to succeed them. If you're one of them, let it be known.

7. Did you suggest any new products or programs for your company that were put into effect?

What were they? Why do you think they were adopted? Did they result in extra sales to your company? Did you win any incentive awards? Did you develop any patents for your company? Did you win any industry awards for your company with your suggestions? Did you receive any extra bonuses for your product or programs contributions? Did you represent your company at any industry-wide symposia at which your suggestions or programs were presented? Have your ideas for programs been published in any industry magazines or journals? Think hard for your contributions in this area. I'm unaware of a company that doesn't want to meet people who know how to innovate.

8. Did you help to establish any new goals or objectives for your company?

Did you arrive at these goals by any new or unusual thought process? Did you convince management it should adopt the goals you established? An executive I once knew was asked by management to take responsibility for integrating a newly acquired firm into his current company's operation. After six weeks' study of the methods of distribution of the newly acquired firm, the executive recommended that the new firm not be integrated into the operations of the parent company. He reasoned that both the customers of the new acquisition and its methods of distribution were sufficiently different to make integration a hardship on both the acquisition and parent company. Management bought my friend's recommendation.

As a result of his personal goals, my friend decided to leave the company shortly after he wrote this report. Because of the timing of his move, he was unable to write on his resume that he had "succeeded in building the sales of the newly acquired company." My friend's resume, however, did include a statement that he had evaluated the acquisition policy of the parent company and recommended strongly to management that it operate the newly acquired firm independently. Management endorsed his recommendation. In this instance my friend sold prospective employers on his ability to evaluate and his ability to convince top management of the wisdom of his recommendations.

9. Did you change, in any way, the nature of your job?

Why did you redefine your position? How did you redefine it? Have other persons in jobs similar to your own had their positions redefined per your definition? Have there been any significant responsibility changes as a result of your redefining your job?

Whenever I think about the importance of redefining a job, I can't help remembering a young woman in one of my classes. She was a college graduate, an economics major. She graduated with honors. She wanted to work on Wall Street but was unable to get a job. (This took place twenty years ago before women were accepted in executive positions in this field.) And so she accepted a job as a clerk in the personal trust department of a large New York bank. Each day she added up figures, on the instructions of her immediate supervisor. One day, after a week on the job, she asked her supervisor why she was adding up the columns of figures. He told her. Then she said, "If that's what you want to find out, you're going about it the wrong way." She explained to her boss how she would approach the problem. A week later her title was changed from clerk to departmental statistician. Not surprisingly, at the time we met her in our class, she was head of the bank's personal trust department. The essence of her case history is this: If you were able to redefine your job, broaden your responsibility, widen the scope of your authority, your prospective employer will be interested in knowing how you did it. Companies are continually seeking leaders. People of sufficient ability to assume leadership positions don't come down the pike every day. If you possess the ability to shoulder more responsibility than other people in your position, let it come to the surface.

10. Did you have any important ideas that were not put into effect?

What were these ideas? What effect would they have had on sales or profits? Would they have led to extra savings? How did you develop these ideas? Why weren't they put into effect? The idea behind this group of questions is to turn each of your lemons into lemonade. Let me give you an example. A young man who worked for an advertising agency included on his resume the fact that a product he helped to promote (a spray starch with silicones) did enormously well in test markets and would have been introduced nationally, were it not for a prior commitment on his client's corporate funds. A part of his resume read like this: "Helped introduce a new spray starch brand into test market. After four months, brand secured first place position in this growing marketplace. Results were so well received by corporate management, tentative decision was made to introduce spray starch nationally. Limited funds, however, delayed national introduction." The fact of the matter is that the delay in introducing the product nationally was disastrous. The company's major competitor reproduced the spray starch with silicone formula and copied the advertising word for word and idea for idea, and the competitors product was introduced nationally, but the original brand died in test market. Despite the sad ending, the man's contributions to the test marketing of a new product made good reading for his prospective employers. The fact that his plan wasn't used except in a test was only a small handicap to selling his original efforts.

Obviously you are better off using positive worthpoints—examples in which management went along with your recommendations and achieved the results you said they would secure. But if you can't come up with any positive worthpoints, keep the negative ones in mind as a last resort. A woman who was formerly a vice-president of a leading New York brokerage firm left this firm because she was unable to convince management to go along with her recommendations as to when to sell certain stocks during the recession several years ago. In her resume she reveals that, had her "sell" recommendations been adopted, the firm's customers would have saved hundreds of millions of dollars. She sold her talents to a major bank that realized she had ability to contribute if stumbling blocks weren't put in her way.

11. Did you do anything on your job that you thought you couldn't do?

Over the years this question has sparked many job-seekers to come up with items of real worth in their experience. One analyst told me how he completed a two-hundred-page report on a company that his firm was considering acquiring in just ten weeks. Even he thought the assignment was impossible. How had he done it, I asked? "By working twenty hours a day," was his reply. A salesman told me how in six months he had sold a customer that no other person in his firm had been able to sell in fifteen years of calling on this prospect. How had he done this? By asking the prospect *why* he had always refused to buy. A general manager told me how he had taken over the direction of a company that was ninety days from bankruptcy. By finding a purchaser for its most unprofitable operation, he actually saved the company. "It was a lucky break" he confided to me. "I might have waited ten years for a buyer who needed that sort of operation and who thought he could make it profitable. As it was, one came along in six weeks." If you have done the impossible in your current or previous position, your prospective boss might expect that you can do the impossible again for his company!

12. Did you ever undertake an assignment or project that wasn't part of your job just because you were intrigued with the problem?

If you have, you are the sort of person who is totally involved with his work. Any such project you undertake is proof of your interest in increasing profits. Prospective employers will be interested in this kind of dedication, particularly if this "extra" assignment led to significant results for your firm.

13. Did you ever do anything simply to make your own job easier?

Did you ever do anything to lighten your own load with no thought of its value to the company you work for? A very shy person once took my course. He was a supervisor in the costing department of a paint and chemicals company. When I asked him if he had done anything for his company he said "no," emphatically! The class wasn't satisfied that in ten years with his firm he'd done nothing of value at all. After a while his classmates prodded him in an encouraging way to reveal a single worthpoint. Finally I asked him the question about making his own job easier. And I guess it got to him. He told us how he became fed up when he discovered again and again that the people who worked for him had unknowingly processed duplicate cost requests. This happened frequently because several salesmen would ask his department to analyze the very same formula within weeks of one another. In order to avoid this needless extra work he came up with a way of cross-referencing cost requests by individual component. As a result he and his staff eliminated costing out all identical formulae that had been costed out within six months. I asked him how many requests he was able to avoid costing: "About one in five," he told us. I prodded further: "Did this save your company any money?" "Well," he told the class, "we were eventually able to let one of our six people go, and we still get out the work faster than before." The point of this story is simple: anything you do to streamline your own job probably will result in saving your company money, or helping it to increase sales. Or both. Did you do anything to make *your* own job easier?

14. Did something so good ever happen at the office that you had to come home and tell somebody about it?

A project that worked out particularly well? A compliment from the boss? A suggestion you had that was adopted? Maybe the news was so good that you invited your spouse or best friend to go to dinner with you! Review this question with your family and close friends. They may remember those "exceptional" days better than you do.

15. What would you say would be the most important qualities of the "ideal candidate" for the position you seek?

Put yourself in the shoes of your prospective boss when you answer this question. Decide on the half-dozen most important characteristics you would look for in a candidate if you were in a hiring position. When you have zeroed in on these qualities, think back over your own experience. Look for examples that would *prove* you had each of them. Don't just say to yourself, "Yes, I am conscientious." Instead, jot down specific worthpoints that demonstrate you have these characteristics. These illustrations will do a better job of convincing your prospective employers you have what they are looking for than any "claims" you make for yourself in your resume or interviews.

CAUTION: Don't read any further until you promise yourself to answer these fifteen questions. And put your answers down on paper. Don't take a chance on forgetting them.

Three

Your resume is your calling card

When you think of the job-search "tools" available to you, chances are you think first of a resume. It has to be the most important selling document for the vast majority of job-seekers. Considering its importance, the ways job-seekers go about writing resumes is enough to make you cringe: all too frequently, a job-seeker borrows a resume from a friend who is conducting a search and uses it for style. Or he pulls his old resume (from five or ten years ago) out of a file, adds a paragraph to bring things up to date and has it typed up without looking critically at the resume's previous portions. Or, worse still, he reaches into an office desk drawer, pulls out his job description, and plagiarizes it to create a description of himself. Saddest of all is the time frame in which countless resumes are written: the job-seeker is fired in the morning and feels compelled to "get something out" in response to ads that night. So the document that serves as the backbone for a job-search campaign is whipped out in a matter of hours. As you might expect, it inevitably suffers from a too-short period of gestation.

Your resume is too important to you not to be the most effective personal selling document you have ever created. It is a tool that can turn on executive recruiters—get them to recommend you to their clients—or turn them off. It is often, though by no means always, the only document available to present your case to prospective employers who receive literally hundreds of responses to their blind newspaper ads. The two or three pages you write about yourself have got to help you survive the "cut" as the hundreds of resumes are reduced to perhaps a dozen "worthy" individuals who will be granted personal interviews.

Your resume can be valuable in other ways: it is the best document any job-seeker has to "guide" interviews; it is the only practical "leave-behind" for the person who interviews you to use in selling you to his superiors. In short, your resume has to be the most *compelling* summation of your worth that you can possibly provide.

Fortunately, effective resumes—those that get you in the door and sell you up the line—are not difficult to write. But there are two things you must keep in mind:

☐ First, that your resume *represents* you. The way it is written and the way it looks are a reflection of you as a writer and executive. The style and format of your resume create an image of a professional in your field or something less than that. The impression you create with your personal document is as important as the impression you create with the suit or dress you wear to your interview—if you get one!

☐ Second, the content of your resume has to convey quickly and convincingly that you are not "just" qualified for the job—after all, as suggested earlier, almost everyone applying for a job will be to some extent qualified for it—but that you are *better* qualified than the other candidates with similar backgrounds. In short, your resume has to be able to communicate your real worth in writing in a way that will be both read and *understood* by your prospective boss.

This chapter reviews the critical elements of *style* that time has shown are necessary to create the right first impression of you. The next chapter covers the three critical elements of *content* required to make you stand out positively from other not dissimilar competition.

HOW TO BE LIKED WITHOUT BEING KNOWN . . . HOW GOOD DOES YOUR RESUME LOOK?

Like it or not, your resume is in the hands of your prospective boss long before you have a chance to sell yourself in person. Since you're not there to defend it, your resume must impress your prospective boss favorably or you'll never get a chance to do so personally. Your resume is prima facie evidence of your writing ability, your organizational ability, and your approach to business problems. Just for a moment, then, let's pretend you're someone in a hiring position and together let's look at some real-life resumes to determine what kind of people wrote them, and whether you want to meet them personally. For the moment, disregard the contents. Let's evaluate the candidates based solely on the appearance of their resumes.

☐ THE OVERLONG RESUME   Winston Churchill was once complimented on a speech that lasted one hour. He was asked how long it took to write it. He replied that it took two hours. "Amazing," the interviewer interjected. "Not really," said Sir Winston. "I could have written a half-hour speech if I'd had four hours to write it." If you are long-winded in your resume, your prospective boss must assume you will be long-winded at the weekly executive committee meeting. Unless you are in your fifties with a career involving a great many job changes, two pages should suffice—at the outside, three pages. Resumes as long as five and six pages are a bore. Almost no prospective boss will read beyond page two or three, but will throw down your resume in disgust and move on to the next one. Worse still, he may not read it all, thinking to himself: "If he can't summarize his own experience, how can he summarize our key business problems?"

☐ THE OVERDETAILED RESUME   One reason resumes sometimes get too long is because they are too detailed. Consider the first page of Resume 1. The writer suffers from verbosity. He fails to *isolate* the significance of his background. He includes excess verbiage because he doesn't have the time or skills required to cull out the important things in his career. A resume that is overdetailed is, in point of fact, insulting because it assumes the prospective boss who read it has little or no understanding of the scope of the job to be filled. If you are applying for a job as a plant manager, you shouldn't need to describe every piece of equipment that you've ever dealt with. It's the scope of your operation that is going to be evaluated: how many people you worked with, what kind of industries the plants you managed were in. Give your prospective boss credit for being able to realize the details of your current operation and sell him on the breadth of your experience.

What kind of people write overdetailed resumes? As a prospective employer you might well assume that they are involved with minutiae, probably unable to communicate broad, basic generalizations. When you prepare your own resume, make sure your background is simple and broad-brush. Don't be thought of as thinking small, or you may never have the opportunity to think big.

☐ THE "IRRELEVANT-FIRST" RESUME   The author of Resume 2 takes you through his education and early jobs before you find out what's happening now. The author of Resume 3 did just the opposite. He lets you know what he did yesterday because it's most relevant to your performance tomorrow. As a rule of thumb, your most recent experience is ten times more important to your prospective boss than your experience five years ago. Not only should you talk first about it, you should talk most about it too. As a guide, if you've held four jobs, you might well devote 40 percent of your resume to your current job, 30 percent to the previous job, 20 percent to the job prior to that one, and 10 percent to the one before that. Only in exceptional circumstances should you vary that format. The obvious exception is the instance in which you desire to secure a job in a position more similar to your previous job than to your current one.

☐ THE SLIPSHOD RESUME   When you consider that first impressions of a resume can convey as much of a message about the job-seeker as his or her personal history, you would think twice about sending out anything but the most professional-looking document possible. Still, less-than-professional resumes arrive daily in executive recruiters' offices and on the desks of prospective bosses. For the record, here are some of the more common symptoms of nonprofessionalism that create a negative image of the candidate before one word of his resume is even read:

1. *Overcrowded pages* with next to no margins—looks as if the author was too cheap to run off a second page. (Resume 4)
2. *Difficult-to-read copies* that were undoubtedly duplicated in

the back office for nothing—and are worth about that much.

3. *Typographical errors* that glare off the page. You've all heard about the person who asked to be "excepted as a candidate" in his cover letter. He was, and he deserved to be!

4. *Paragraphs and words that don't line up*—the probable result of home typing on a beat-up college portable, or pasting and clipping last year's resume to this year's update. If you look carefully at the first page of Resume 5 you may note that the last paragraph doesn't have the same typeface as the ones above it. And also that the sequence of jobs is out of order. Quite obviously the author used the space at the bottom of his last resume to type in his most recent experience. Not quite the professional you'd hire to be your next chief engineer.

5. *Blurred letters.* Your reaction has to be: Doesn't this person have any pride? (You wish you had some fluid to clean the keys.)

6. *Changes in format,* spelling, and style between paragraphs. You wonder why the individual doesn't spell the same word the same way twice, why he or she switches margins, indents paragraphs differently with no apparent rhyme or reason. Is the candidate the sort of person who simply can't organize? The kind of person who can't think through a job from first to last?

In words of one syllable, the people who send such resumes are slobs. Would you want a slob working for you? Do you think your prospective boss wants a slob working for him or her? The answer is "no" to both questions. You just can't be cheap with your time or money when it comes to making your resume look good. Make sure it's typed professionally, with plenty of white space so the elements in your resume show up. Check for typographical errors. This may be more difficult than you think. If you have your resume typed by a resume service, they'll expect you to approve the master sheet at a moment's notice after it has been typed. Lose a day. Take the master home with you. Check it thoroughly. There's nothing more amateurish than a resume with typos in it.

☐ **THE BURIED-TREASURE RESUME** In recent years a number of resume counselors have suggested that "accomplishments" be included in resumes. Unfortunately, for one reason or another, these counselors haven't made any firm recommendation as to how to include accomplishments in the resume itself. Thus, all too often I read resumes with accomplishments literally squeezed in at the ends of paragraphs, hidden from all but the most persevering reader (Resume 6). Unfortunately, the prospective employer may never discover them. If he skims your resume, his reaction may well be that the resume is from a mediocre candidate. Had you punched home your worth by putting the same information in a separate and visible paragraph (Resume 7), the prospective employer might have had a vastly more positive reaction. Because few prospective bosses will persevere, it will pay you to separate your worthpoints from your brief job description so that both stand out, as the same writer has done in revising Resume 6.

☐ THE MAKE-DO RESUME   The number of people who have the audacity (or stupidity) to send last year's resume for this year's job is mind-boggling. This fault is not limited to neophyte job-seekers, either. I have received numerous resumes from senior executives, prepared for a distant time in the past and supplemented with an addendum or overriding letter. The executive receiving such a resume has to question the sincerity of the job-seeker in applying for the position. It costs no more than $20 to have a resume updated. If you really mean business, surely it's worth that much to turn out a *current* selling sheet about yourself.

Last year's resume with addendum attached is not the only kind of make-do resume. Another is the resume written originally to go after a particular job, such as engineer, but sent out in response to ads for a totally different kind of position, such as production supervisor. Frequently its author underlines the one or two relevant paragraphs in the otherwise nonrelevant background, lest they be overlooked. The attitude of prospective bosses to such make-do resumes is likely to be this: If the candidate in question really wanted to be considered seriously, why didn't he rewrite his resume, stressing his experience, however limited, in the field where he is now applying for a job? Tidbits, even underlined, are not enough!

☐ THE GLAMOUR-PUSS RESUME   It is prepared by a one-flight-up resume-writing firm. You can spot this kind of resume a mile away. It may have a gold or blue border. It may be printed in maroon or green ink. It may use a very bold IBM typeface. It may be printed on a stock so stiff it can't be folded. Anything to stand out. And it does—as a resume that was not written by you. Your prospective boss is interested in what you have done—not anyone else. And that includes the ability to organize your career in a meaningful way to him. If you can't write your own resume, why should your prospective boss expect you to be able to write an effective two-page summation of a business problem? And just as important, if you are too lazy to write your own resume, just how energetic will you be on the job?

☐ THE BUFFOON'S RESUME   A remarkable number of jobseekers must believe that if they can devise a way to make their own resumes "jump out" of the pile of resumes submitted in response to ads, it will insure an interview, so they go to great lengths to make their resumes do just this. I've seen resumes printed on heavy posterboard stock, on 8″ × 14″ paper. (They literally stood out until someone folded them in half.) I've come across resumes printed on a rainbow of colored stock, in colored inks, in booklet form, in binders, etc. The prospective boss with any professionalism isn't fooled by this sort of thing. He asks himself: "Did a sincere, businesslike person write such a document, or was it written by a 'promoter' who probably didn't have all that much good to say about himself?" As proof of the pudding, my friends in executive recruiting send me these types of resumes for my collection; rarely do their writers get picked to meet with the prospective employer! Instead, your resume should be well printed on the best-quality white or cream bond that money can buy. After all, it is a reflection of you, and it ought to be the best there is.

The message these less than perfect resumes bring is obvious: Your resume is your calling card. It has to demonstrate your ability to organize your career; to think and present clearly; to be concerned with style; to be produced by someone who is conscious of quality at every point if it is going to create a positive impression with your prospective employers.

Quite possibly you are wondering if there isn't an "ideal" format that does just this—say, margins set at one and one-half inches, triple spaces between jobs, etc? I doubt it. Effective resumes come in a variety of forms, reflecting the personalities of their authors. The one thing they have in common stylistically is that they look (and read) as if the writer is a person who always travels first class.

Edward J. Lowenstein
                                        1449-71 Mosholu Parkway
                                        Brooklyn, N.Y. 11243
                                        (212) UL-9-4172

OBJECTIVE

To hold a position of responsibility commensurate with my experience
where I can successfully guide people and give direction to the
profitable manufacturing of products.

1968 to present

Director of Manufacturing of a medium-sized company engaged in
the manufacture of dermatological products, ethical and proprietary.
My job is to schedule production dependent upon the needs of quarterly
supply. I am responsible too for all purchasing from raw materials to
finished product. I coordinate all purchasing with production requirements, keeping a reasonably smooth flow of material into the plant and
no back orders. (When I first arrived at this company, the back order
collection on some items was six months.)

Because my machinery experience is so extensive, it is my duty to
decide on the purchase of new equipment to suit the special needs of
these very special formulas.

For the first time in the history of the company, because of the
employment of my production techniques, the company has assay proof
products. (All products sampled at any point in production pass inspection based on label requirements.)

In addition the fill requirements for tube, bottle or jar are
exactly as required. This is important particularly in bottle fill
production. Some formulas are very light and full of air and conse-
quently the bottles are passed through without being entirely filled.
To offset this some firms use larger bottles (in length and diameter)
...this means changing problems all the way down the packaging line,
such as boxes, etc. The company used to rework the packaging line,
(heat to fluidity, etc. so as to be able to fill into bottles.) This
is no longer a problem. They can now take stored material at room
temperature and fill without reworking.

The company's most valued product ingredient used to be trouble-
some. A precipitate would develop in whatever product it was incorporated...such as hair tonics and suntan lotions. Using the method I
introduced, the precipitate is removed from the distillate fraction
before it is stored for incorporating into the various products. I
might add that filtration did not work. At first it appears to be
sufficient, but after a week of standing it becomes obvious that the
material is so fine it passes through even the finest of filters.
(Experiments proved.)

These accomplishments, in addition to the daily routine of
assigning job work to the people are a sample of the nature of the
way I work.

JOHN H. GREERSON
1140 Camino Flores
San Jose, California 90412
213-437-6051

Age 39.   165 lbs.   Health excellent.

B.A. degree - San Fernando State, 1953

Sept. 1953 - Feb. 1958 - Collegiate Drug Company

3 years Sales Representative.
2 1/2 years District Manager.
Left Collegiate to go into packaging business, 1 1/2 years.

Feb. 1961 - Nov. 1965 - Joined Murphion Corporation to head
new Industrial Division. Moved to Assistant to General
Sales Manager and then to Regional Sales Manager.

Nov. 1965 - Nov. 1968 - National Sales Manager - Developed
sales and sales force. Sales force grew to 60 and 4
brokers. Sales doubled.

Nov. 1968 - Promoted to head up new USA Test Market and
moved to Cleveland, Ohio. Responsible for sales in Michigan,
Ohio and New York areas - 17 brokers, assistant and 1 D.M.
and 9 salesmen.

Jan. 1968 - Test market successful and moved to San Jose. As
Regional Manager 10 Western States. Company built new facility
to sell packaged instant potatoes. Hired 4 brokers to start
and grew to thirty salesmen and 3 District Managers covering
California, Utah and Arizona. Obtained solid distribution of
company products in all retail outlets.

SUMMARY

Experienced in   - Hiring and training salesmen, district
                   managers, brokers.
                 - Sales to supermarkets, drug stores and
                   department stores.
                 - Setting up sales territories, programs,
                   coverages, etc.
                 - Budgeting, forecasting

Proven record of success

Compensation open for discussion, currently in low 30's.

JAMES AUBREY ROBINSON
471 Old School House Road
Dobbs Ferry, New York
(914) HU-7-1578

Objective: National Sales Manager with a fast growing firm distributing primarily through Food Chains.

1969— SALES MANAGER
Tucker-Hamilton Corporation
Home Products Division
Morris Plains, New Jersey

Established Food Broker sales force

Obtained 82% all commodity distribution in original markets on new floor care products

Appointed Manufacturer Reps and Master Distributors in the professional floor care field

Supervised packaging graphics and distribution plan

Created promotional and marketing strategy

1966-1969 EASTERN REGIONAL MANAGER
U.S. Home Products Co.
Plastic Products Division
New York, New York

Achieved better than a 30% sales increase by reorganizing region from 6 direct men, 5 brokers, and 2 distributors into a 30 broker, 10 distributor and 4 District sales manager sales force

Improved profits by decreasing small unprofitable orders by 70% and increasing tonage by more than 33%

Secured and directed West Coast warehouse and shipping point

Recruited for this position by well-known executive recruitment firm

1964-1966 EAST CENTRAL REGION MANAGER
Lilac Foods Company
Los Angeles, California

Supervised $12,000,000 in sales through Food Brokers and Grocery outlets

JAMES AUBREY ROBINSON

Responsible for the direction of sales
trainees, office administration, and four
public warehouses with region

Successfully introduced many new Lilac
Items including Liquid Lunch and "Skinnie"
diet drink at both District and Regional
level of responsibility

Promoted from Salesman to Chicago District
Manager to East Coast Region Manager

1958-1964   ASSISTANT TO MANAGER--SUGAR SALES
D and H Foods Company
San Francisco, California

Successfully executed sales program for
introduction of Sweet Touch sugar in major
Northern cities of Columbus, Cleveland, and
other major points in Michigan, Indiana, and
Illinois

Sold powdered and confectioners sugar to
chains and wholesalers in 10 states east of
the Mississippi

Promoted from salesman to confectionary
product specialist to Assistant to Manager of
Sugar Sales

Education   1955-1957 Ohio University, General College
1953-1955 Iowa, College of Education
1969   SMI Field Sales Management Course

Military   Specialist 1st Class U.S. Army Quartermaster
Corp. 1951-1953

Personal   Age 37
Married, 3 Children
Excellent Health

References   Excellent business, personal, and financial
references will be provided upon request.

Robert A. Dawson
1477 Floral Drive
Woodland Hills, CA 91340
(213) 469-2317

EDUCATION

M.B.A. Northwestern Graduate School of Business Administration, 1963.
Emphasis on Planning and Control, Business Information Systems, Management
of Technological Change, Human Relations, Marketing/Sales Management, and
Advertising; top fifth of class. Finance, New Enterprise, Marketing, Retailing
clubs; paid for all education from high school on with scholarships and sav-
ings from personal salaries.
B.S., Tulane College, 1956, Chemistry/Engineering.
First all science majors, third in class, 3.56/4.0 grade point, Officer
All-College Council, junior A.C.S., National Honor Society, Phi Lambda
Upsilon, president Chem Club, student chairman Career Festival, director
Homecoming and other social activities, five scholarships.
Teaching Assistantship, University of Illinois, 1956-57.
Studies toward the doctorate in organic chemistry, steroids. Alpha Chi
Sigma chemical/social fraternity.

EXPERIENCE

General Management Consulting, 2 years, Los Angeles-San Francisco area.
Client studies in corporate policy and planning, new product/market development, sales analysis, EDP systems, sales/distributor incentive programs,
traffic and distribution, customer services, advertising, market research
and planning, pricing.
Universal Datronics, Div. Megobyte Corporation, 1 year, Los Angeles and
national sales. Complete electronic data acquisition hardware and associated industrial information systems from market need to viable products.
Advertising, sales promotion, market research, product specifications and
development; built and trained sales force and distributor groups; technical liaison on computer interfaces and commo links.
Springfield Design, Div. Springfield International, 3½ years, Los Angeles
and national. Planning and estimating, budgets, production control, standards,
capital expenditure and acquisition analyses, sales management, development
of complete MICS. Negotiations and contract administration with national
publishers for production of regional magazines; six new systems and products;
proposals for new business totaling several million dollars annual. Additional experience purchasing, inventory control, product auditing in graphic
arts, coated products, and adhesives with Foster-Harding Div. of Norton, 3M,
and smaller companies; summers, part-time during school, and as independent
consultant.
Organic Division, Petroplastics, 3 years, Chicago/St. Louis, national promotion. New product surveys, plant feasibility and planning, data retrieval
system for computer forecasting, marketing services administration, long-
range strategy concepts and implementation, corporate task force for com-
puter-oriented business systems. Five new products for petroleum additives,
functional fluids, resin materials, and paper chemicals product groups.
Personal selling multi-million dollar territory; sales motivation/monitoring
systems.
Chemicals Div., International Enterprises, 3½ years, Minneapolis and national.
Raw materials to hormone intermediates and clinical end-products for pharma-
ceuticals, new steroid data storage and retrieval system, market and product
development with major drug firms, processed foods marketing, PERD/CPM techniques to shorten product/market development, pilot line implementation,
product life cycle analysis.

RESUME #5

JEROME MC CAULEY
1337 Camino Flores
Oxnard, California 93072

RESUME OF RECENT EXPERIENCE

ASSOCIATE PROFESSOR

September 1972 to July 1974 Trenton Engineering College
                                      Trenton, New Jersey

Taught Architectural Drafting—Second year.
Introduction to architectural drafting, Space design,
Room & House design, Floor plans, Elevations, perspective
& rendering, Roof & House frame structure design, New
Jersey building codes.

Taught Mechanical Drafting—First, Second & Third year.
Basic mechanical drafting, Orthographics, Sketching,
Introduction to descriptive geometry and geometric pro-
jection, Introduction to Technical Illustration &
Industrial design, Solving industrial problems of design.

ASSISTANT PROFESSOR

September 1970 to July 1972 Purdue University
                                      Layfayette, Indiana

Designed two year terminal course and taught various
aspects of vocational drafting for engineering technician
related to design and manufacture of electro-mechanical
products.

Mathematics: trigonometry, vector forces—two and three
dimensional force systems, Quality control: specifications and engineering drawing interpretation for manufacture and quality control, tooling, holding and clasping
devices, Geometric and positional tolerances, Basic and
advanced Mechanical drafting, instrument drawings, A
Study of production problems. Introduced a new seminar,
Concept of Dimensions, which studies spatial perception.

SENIOR ENGINEER

July 1974 to present   Galaxies Industries
                                Trenton, New Jersey

In charge of engineering and production.
Established Management Committee, procedures
manual, inventory and purchasing controls. Set
up quality control program. Established an
engineering committee. Started time study data
collection to establish standards. Increased
production by initiating supervisory training
program in time & motion study.

(1971)

MARTIN SPRINGER
14701 Town Line Road
Cleveland Heights, Ohio
216-932-4808

PERSONAL DATA:

Age: 47, Married, Two children. Am an ardent tennis player.
Active in community affairs. Enjoy hunting and fishing.

MILITARY SERVICE:

In Army for two years during World War II. Attended
Princeton University and Williams College for three months
each for West Point Preparatory Courses. Honorably discharged.

EDUCATION:

Attended Kenyon College for two years. Attended Ohio State
University for one year. Majored in business administration.

EMPLOYMENT HISTORY:

I. 1968 to Present
    AVONDALE REALTY COMPANY, Cleveland, Ohio
    Vice President and Director. Responsible for development
    of sales promotion programs, placement of advertising in
    local newspapers, securing photographs of property listed
    by Avondale, including aerial photography of industrial
    sites. Responsible for liaison between mortgage companies
    and legal firms representing buyer and seller. Negotiate
    with buyers and sellers to determine final sale price.
    Responsible for keeping records of all transactions made
    on weekly and monthly basis, and for administration of
    office personnel. Sold over 4 million dollars in 18
    months to increase company sales versus previous year by
    15 perccent.

II. 1964 to 1968
    AVONDALE REALTY COMPANY, a division of AVONDALE CORPORATION.
    Vice President and General Manager. Director of
    Residential Marketing. Until spin-off in 1968, Avondale
    Realty was part of Avondale Land Development Corporation.
    Was responsible for administration of office in newspapers.
    Developed long and short range plans for corporation
    growth. Sold condominium property. Responsible for
    Avondale Information Center operation. Responsible for
    analyzing results of 25 sales people and training to
    improve performance. Created concept of "Information
    Center," which has been credited with doubling Avondale
    residential property sales, now standard industry practice.

RESUME #7

(1971)

MARTIN SPRINGER
14701 Town Line Road
Cleveland Heights, Ohio
216-932-4808

JOB
OBJECTIVE:

Senior real estate marketing management
position with dynamic company.

REAL ESTATE
MARKETING
EXPERIENCE:

AVONDALE REALTY COMPANY
Cleveland, Ohio

January 1968
- Present

Vice President and Director

Responsible for overall management of
company in owner's absence and creation
of all sales and marketing programs.

Personally sold over four million dollars
in investment real estate in 18 months,
to increase total company sales by 15%
over previous year.

Joined Avondale Realty at request of new
owner, following spin-off from Avondale
Corporation.

June 1964 -
January 1968

AVONDALE REALTY COMPANY
a division of AVONDALE CORPORATION

Vice President and General Manager
- Avondale Realty Company
Director of Residential Marketing
- Avondale Corporation

Responsible for management of realty
company including finance, personnel,
advertising, short and long term planning,
condominium sales. Developed Avondale
Information Center. Responsible for
administering and training staff of 25
people.

Maintained $40-55,000 net profit each
year. Administered full marketing program
for Avondale Corporation. Member of Division
Management Committee.

"Information Center" led to doubling of
corporate residential sales, and is now
standard industry practice.

Industry honors:

Elected President of Pierce County Business
Development Association. 1967-68

Four

The building blocks
of a better resume

At this point, you must be anxiously waiting to start your own resume. You've read one complete chapter on resumes, and undoubtedly what you'd like now is a format for success, one you can "borrow" to write an effective summary of your own career. At the end of this chapter you'll find one which experience has shown to be extremely effective for the thousands of job-seekers who've used it. Obviously, there is a big temptation to turn to the end of the chapter immediately and to start drafting your resume based on this model. But, if you can possibly do so, resist that temptation! Instead, consider three building blocks that are essential to making a resume function at its maximum effectiveness.

You may be saying to yourself: "I don't need any ABC's. I've written resumes before. I'd like to get right on with it and start copying the format that works." That could be a mistake! First, because each job-seeker's goals are different; each one's career is unique. And often this means that the standard resume must be altered to accommodate career differences. Blindly copying a format could prove to be a big error in these cases. For some people the company they worked for is more important than the position they held; for others, the position is far more important than the company. The "standard" format might be misleading without understanding the underlying principles behind it. In addition, the last thing you want your resume to do is to look as if it were turned out by a one-flight-up resume writing outfit. If you just copy a format that fifty thousand people have also used, and don't adapt it to your own needs, it may very well seem as if it had been turned out by a resume mill. When you are familiar with the building blocks, however, you can flex the format to suit your own personal taste and make the resume truly your own creation. Let's look then at the three key elements your resume must have to make you a "standout" candidate.

1. A job objective

A great many resumes in my files have *no* job objective at all. Sure it's easier to leave one out. But a job objective is a good bet for three reasons.

☐ It gives you an oppportunity to go after something better than you now have—to *define* the kind of job you really want. You may be ready, for example, to take on a controller's position after three years as an assistant controller. Without a job objective specifically stating this, your reader might easily assume you "took a flyer" by sending your resume in response to an ad for a controller. With it, the reader would *know* that you felt you were ready to move up, and that's the reason why you are looking.

☐ It gives you an opportunity *in less than one sentence* to summarize some special advantage that you offer any employer—the special "competitive edge" that makes you someone your prospective boss should pay particular attention to.

☐ Perhaps most important, a job objective forces you to *focus* your resume. Everything you include in your resume following your job objective should be designed to help you achieve your goal. So a good job objective forces you to emphasize those aspects of your career that best support your candidacy for the particular position you've chosen, and to downplay experience that is irrelevant to this goal. Why write in depth about some position you've held that does *not* relate to your stated job objective—only to find you haven't sufficient space adequately to cover your experience that does?

At this point you may be wondering how in one short sentence you can both focus your resume and show the reader why you might be a particularly valuable candidate for the job. It can be done! The first thing you have to do is ask yourself three questions:

☐ What *specific* position do you want? (That includes the title you might expect in such a position. Avoid vague terms like "A position in which I can use my skills as . . ." etc.)

☐   Where do you want to do it? (The type and size of company.)

☐   What special reason might the prospective employer have for wanting you to fill this job (in broad-brush terms, and in half a dozen words)?

Here's an example of this type of job objective:

<u>Controller</u> in a medium-size manufacturing company in a situation to which systems plus accounting experience would be valuable.

All three elements are included in this one sentence! The writer tells you precisely what he is going after. He gives you a special reason why he might be of real value to his prospective boss: both systems and accounting experience.

But, you say: "There are several different titles I might go after. All in the same field. What if I'm unsure as to which title to go after?" In a situation like this, put down the most senior title you *know* you can reasonably expect to secure. You can still use your resume to apply for other jobs that are not quite as good. In the case of the controller, for example, he could also have applied for a position as chief auditor, or chief cost accountant with the same resume. He would have been considered a "heavyweight" candidate, but unless he had too many years of experience he wouldn't have been eliminated for trying for the better title.

Why should you use the best realistic title that you can go after? Because you'll *organize* your resume in order to support it, and so have a better chance of getting that title than had you organized your resume for other less senior titles! Don't misunderstand. It's foolish to use a title that is *not* attainable for someone with your experience. That will only disillusion you and lengthen your job search. But if the title is reasonably attainable and the best one you can go after in terms of your career, it's the one that will *help you* write your strongest possible resume.

Another question you might raise is this: "What if I'm not sure which type of company I'd like to work for?" There's nothing that says you can't leave out that element of your job objective. It's easier not to include it. On the other hand, the focus of your job search may be blurred if you don't make this type of decision. It takes self-discipline to decide what it is that you really want to do next, and what job and type of company are most likely to help you in your total career. Certainly, it's hard to narrow the choices down by focusing on specific positions and types of companies. But if you don't do this for yourself, other different jobs will come along. And the temptation is always there to take one even though it could hurt your career and put you back in the job market sooner.

A third question may be on your mind: "What if I'm not sure what makes me specially qualified for the particular job I am going after? Can I leave this off?" There is nothing that says that you *must* include the half-sentence that reveals why you might be a particularly valuable candidate for the specific position you seek. But taking the trouble to go through your career and to boil down the essential plus you have to offer can help you to set the entire tone and direction of your campaign. If you can't summarize your special worth, nobody will know of it unless they figure it out from the balance of your resume. They might not spot it. Why take a chance?

Lots of people ask if they could leave out their job objective because they might be suited to several different positions and would be equally satisfied with any. Why not just leave off the whole thing in this case? Nothing says they can't do this. But they lose two important advantages when they do. First, when a prospective employer looks at a resume and discovers immediately that the candidate's job objective is the same as the position he's seeking to fill, he is bound to feel a rapport with the job-seeker. (He's looking for what I'm offering.") Why give up this advantage when the cost of printing resumes is so cheap! Use one resume to go after one type of job; a second for the alternative. Beyond that, if you try to write one resume to go after two different objectives, you are likely to end up with a resume that is less *targeted* against either of your alternative goals. Remember, one key to a successful resume is to emphasize only that experience that makes you a strong candidate for the one position you want. If you use one resume for two different positions, obviously it has to blur the impression you're trying to create.

2. The SCOPE of your responsibility in each of your jobs

Several resumes in the previous chapter included *detailed* job descriptions—laundry lists of duties and functions the individuals who wrote these resumes performed. Most prospective employers simply won't take the time or trouble to wade through such tedious and petty listings. Still, prospective employers want (and need) to know what your previous job experience was all about. An effective way to avoid boring your prospective boss to death and yet let him or her know what your responsibilities were in each of the jobs you've held is to explain your *role* in each position you've held. Let them know exactly where you fitted in the organization. You can do this in a brief (three- or four-line) paragraph just by providing answers to the following questions:

☐ WHOM DO (OR DID) YOU REPORT TO DRIECTLY? If you report to a vice-president or department manager, that in itself says something about you.

☐ WHOM DO (OR DID) YOU REPORT TO INDIRECTLY? If you report to the department manager routinely but on special projects directly to the senior vice-president who is the department manager's boss, you reveal that you might be department manager timber yourself.

☐ WHO REPORTS TO YOU? The titles of several people reporting to you suggest the scope of your responsibility. If you direct the efforts of the scheduling and inventory control managers, your prospective boss will know you must be knowledgeable in the details of production planning.

☐ HOW MANY PEOPLE REPORT TO YOU? State the specific numbers of people. If a sales staff of ten reports to you, that's one thing. If it's a sales staff of five hundred, that's another. Obviously, with such information the reader immediately has a better feel for you *and* the organizations you have worked for. And, if you have had several jobs with more and more people working for you in each, the short "scope" paragraphs defining your role in each case will quickly reveal your personal growth as your prospective boss scans your resume.

☐ WHO ELSE REPORTS TO YOUR BOSS? In some instances, it pays to ask yourself this question—particularly if your title is not as good as those of other people reporting to your boss.

If, for example, you report to the president along with several vice-presidents—but you aren't a vice-president—you enhance your stature by the fact that you and they both report to the same person.

☐ WHAT'S THE OPERATIONAL BUDGET YOU CONTROL? If you're responsible for a five-million-dollar advertising budget, that's one thing; a ten-thousand-dollar budget, another.

☐ WHAT'S THE PERSONNEL BUDGET YOU CONTROL? If you control the payroll for a large staff, this suggests a great deal about the responsibility that rests on your shoulders.

☐ WHAT, IN BRIEFEST TERMS, DO YOU DO FOR THE ORGANIZATION? Here's your opportunity to reveal in one *sentence* exactly what you do for the outfit. "One sentence!" you exclaim! How can I possibly boil down everything I do for my organization in one sentence?" Not easy, I'll admit, but well worth trying to do, because when you boil down what you do into one sentence, you automatically broad-brush your position and, in so doing, reveal your true *role* in the organization. You can't do anything otherwise!

Together your answers to these questions add up to the scope of your responsibility in the organization. And your scope statement is far more convincing evidence of your level of experience than any list of functions or duties ever could be. Consider this example:

Chief Engineer. Report directly to vice-president, manufacturing, and during his lengthy overseas business trips, directly to president. Direct engineering staff of fifty professionals plus thirty clericals. Responsible for department operational budget of $2,000,000 plus payroll of approximately $1,500,000. Responsible for all engineering functions for this plastics manufacturing company with annual sales in excess of $100,000,000.

Consider your own career this way and you'll be surprised at how much greater clarity you give to each job description. Incidentally, note how much more impressive your role in each organization sounds to you compared to a turgid accounting of your job functions and duties. Chances are your prospective boss will also be more impressed by this bird's-eye view of your experience!

3. Your WORTH in each of the positions you've held

A well-written scope paragraph will go a long way toward convincing most prospective employers that you are *capable* of doing the job that needs to be done. By describing the role you played in your last company, you provide your next boss with a feeling of confidence that you could, perhaps, play a similar role in his company. But your prospective boss surely wants more than to know you are capable. He wants the person finally selected for the position to do an *exceptional* job with it—better than could be done by all the other capable candidates. And that's where your worthpoints come in.

In a resume, obviously, you can't relate your worthpoints with quite the same detail as when you relate your specific contributions during an interview. The reader of your resume just wouldn't sit still long enough for you to do this. So you need to write your worthpoints in a special telegraphic way that gets your basic message across fast, and is at the same time memorable and dramatic. Remarkably enough, you can reduce your worthpoint to only two sentences with a little practice. In the first, you:

☐ State specifically what you did, and
☐ *Why* you did it (in general terms).

Another way ot stating it is this. Your first sentence:

☐ Should reveal the tangible, concrete action you took and
☐ The overall objective of this action.

The second sentence should:

☐ State the specific result of your action, plus
☐ Any secondary results that ensued from the first.

The second sentence is the "payoff," clear and simple. The most effective worthpoints waste no words. The actions you undertook, the results that you achieved should be specific, tangible, understandable, translatable to the needs of the employer, and presented in the minimum number of words possible. As you write each worthpoint, imagine, if you will, that your resume is a telegram. Every word costs you money so only include those that are essential. Here are several examples to guide you. From a marketing executive:

Introduced Vaseline Intensive Care lotion to capitalize on broad acceptance of brand name and to create new sales to compensate for eroding market for Vaseline petroleum jelly. Vaseline Intensive Care lotion is now the #1 hand and body lotion, and a $30,000,000 business.

From an engineer:

Introduced new mass-strapping process to replace costly hand soldering of electronic component parts. New process reduced assembly time-per-unit from forty to twenty minutes, and reduced labor costs by over 50%.

From a senior management person:

Consolidated two smaller subsidiaries, neither of which was able to afford internal product development programs. Within three years research department, organized by combined subsidiary, developed two new patented petroleum products which quadrupled sales of the combined organizations.

From a controller:

Recommended computer processing of customer payments to provide more timely audits of accounts receivable. New system provided a means for instant identification of, and immediate communication with, overdue accounts and reduced average accounts receivable from sixty to forty-five days.

In two brief sentences the worthpoints the above job-seekers use establish them as persons whose areas of responsibility operate more effectively and efficiently than they did before each of the people arrived on board. Combined, the *scope* paragraph plus a *worthpoint* paragraph (following it) are like a one-two punch. To use another analogy, the scope paragraph is like your balance sheet. It gives your prospective boss a picture of where you are at each point in your career. The worthpoint that follows is like your income statement. It shows the changes that have taken place since you assumed your position.

At this point you may have several questions: "What if there are a great many worthpoints I *could* include underneath each of my scope paragraphs. Which should I use? How many should I include?" The right worthpoints to include are the ones that best support your candidacy for the job objective you've stated at the top of your resume. If you can think of ten worthpoints from your current position and only two or three really demonstrate your ability to take on the job you're going after, they're the only ones to include! In a tightly written resume irrelevant worthpoints don't do a thing except distract your prospective employer, interrupting the consistent line of proof you offer of your ability to get done the job you want him to believe you can get done.

As for the number of worthpoints to include, it makes good sense to provide more for recent jobs than for former ones since it creates the impression that you are able to get more done today than you could in the past. There are several exceptions to this rule, however. If you've held one position far longer than another, you may want to include more worthpoints for the longer-duration job than for the shorter one. Similarly, if your current position is less relevant to the job objective you're going after than a former one, it pays to include more worthpoints from the former position. And you can leave off the two-sentence worthpoint paragraph entirely for your earlier positions that are not immediately relevant to the job you presently seek. In this situation, your inclusion of "earlier" positions is just to account for where you have been, not to add proof of your ability to take on the job you are seeking. So your title and, perhaps, an abbreviated scope paragraph is more than enough.

When you have developed your job objective, scope and worthpoint paragraphs for each relevant job, you've completed 90 percent of the work necessary to develop a strong selling document. Let's consider the final 10 percent for just a few moments; then at long last you can start your own. These include:

☐ EDUCATION Your formal education (college and graduate school) offers your prospective employer an opportunity to determine your mental and leadership capacities early in your adult years. Many resumes I come across include only the job-seeker's college and degree. Even if you attended college years ago, it still pays to include your place in the class (top 10 percent, top third, etc.) or your grade-point average (3.5 out of 4). If neither of those is exceptional, include your grade-point average in your major. Even if you are only in the top half of your class, it might pay to include this fact. If you don't, your prospective boss could easily assume you were in the bottom half. If you completed college less than ten or fifteen years ago, include extracurricular activities that suggest you're well-rounded, and a leader among peers (for example: chairman, school newspaper; president, student organization). Unfortunately, some job-seekers get carried away when it comes to education and include far too much detail about their college experience. Temper your enthusiasm for including laundry lists of courses and organizations to which you belong. Include only those that best support your candidacy—those that suggest you were the sort of person the ideal candidate would have been in his early years. It stands to reason that the younger you are, the more important each activity or grade is. The older you are, the less space you need to devote to your education.

☐ CONTINUING EDUCATION   If you have taken courses since college (at your company's expense, perhaps, or independently) to help you in your chosen field, they should be included on your resume. Many company-sponsored courses— such as those given by Xerox, DuPont, General Electric, IBM —are known for their quality. If they are relevant to your job objective, a two-week intensive seminar or thirteen-week course could be more valuable in terms of your next assignment than your B.A. degree.

It could be a mistake to include this type of training in the formal education section of your resume however. Since this type of education occurs subsequent to college, and since each section of your resume is usually written in reverse chronological order, you could end up burying your college or graduate-school experience below an AMA seminar. If you utilize a separate "continuing education" section, however, and incorporate this section after your formal education section, you avoid this problem and put the two types of education into proper perspective.

Keep in mind, too, that several kinds of continuing-education courses could actually hurt you in your job search! The candidate who has completed a course in selling insurance or real estate usually gets himself in trouble when he includes

these on his resume. Doing so suggests that he is an entre-
preneur in his free time and might well be expected by his
prospective employer to moonlight on the job. Few employers
want this sort of person in a *full-time* position. They'd prefer
the person who relaxes when he's not working at his full-time
job, and who comes to work refreshed, not tuckered out from
showing houses. There's another type of course that should be
included in your "continuing education" section *with caution:* and that's "human relations." The excellent Dale Car-
negie course is one such type of program. Several executive
recruiters have pointed out that frequently candidates who
take such courses have a human relations problem to begin
with. If you do include such courses, be sure they are really
very relevant to the job you're after. (The salesman, for example, may take such a course because it is routinely given to
all sales people in his company.)

☐ PROFESSIONAL CERTIFICATIONS, AWARDS, PUBLICATIONS If
you have enough information to relate, you may want to use
a separate section for each of these general areas. If not, it's
a good idea to group awards, certifications, and publications
in this general category. Again, one caveat: make sure they
are relevant. A real estate broker's license is nice to have, but
questionable in a resume if your business career is that of a
financial analyst. If the certification you have is extremely
relevant to the position you're going after, this section be-
longs between your career experience and formal education,
rather than following the latter. The accountant obviously
should want his prospective employer to learn—as soon as
possible after describing his business experience—that he secured his CPA certification. Why bury this fact after his un-
dergraduate education?

☐ INDUSTRY ASSOCIATIONS Many job-seekers include all the
industry associations they belong to even though they have
done nothing more than pay their annual membership dues.
Belonging to the AMA means next to nothing to the prospective employer. Anyone can purchase an annual membership
card. But if you've beeen active in your association, that's another story. If you've conducted seminars on behalf of your
associations, by all means relate this experience. If you've
been a member of any standing committee, an officer in your
association, don't leave this off your resume! All of these ac-

tivities may provide addditional contacts or insights that your prospective employer may be interested in securing. But listing clubs and associations for which you do nothing more than write a dues check is pointless. You could bettter use the space to include another worthpoint.

☐ MILITARY EXPERIENCE If you've spent any time in the armed forces, you need to include this fact on your resume if for no other reason than to account for your whereabouts during these intervening years since college. If you are a younger job-seeker, just out of the service, your military experience can be used to demonstrate your worth relevant to the position you are going after. Consider your military position as you would positions in business and develop worthpoints in each, which demonstrate your administrative capacity, leadership ability, etc. If it has been some time since you were discharged, however, and your military career isn't relevant to your current position and job objective, then just use a line or two to indicate the duration of your stay, your branch and specialty, and your rank at the time of your discharge. One suggestion for older job candidates: If you were in the service *prior* to college, and want to appear a little younger to prospective employers, then consider leaving out your military experience altogether. Just start your resume with your formal education. No one questions the years before college. If you do this, you can subtract a few years from your life.

☐ PERSONAL DATA Some resume manuals suggest you include your marriage status, dependents, health status, and physical characteristics (height and weight) at the very top of your resume. Don't! If you happen to be single, and your prospective employer has his heart set on a stable, married individual, by putting your vital statistics up at the top you are inviting your prospective boss *not* to read the rest of your resume! The same holds true if you happen to be short or divorced. If your prospective employer doesn't care for short or divorced people, he may never bother reading about your outstanding qualities. It just doesn't make sense to include any personal information at the top of page one. If you do include such statistics, the place to do it is at the end of your resume after your prospective employer has formed an opinion of you based on what really counts—your work experience and education.

More important than your vital statistics is the information that you reveal about your personal interests and background. It's worth including something about this "other side" of you if only to prove that you are not just "all business"—that you are a well-rounded and interesting person. But beyond this, including something personal can help in another way. Given a choice between two people, your prospective boss will have to hire the one who appears to be capable of accomplishing most for him. But, given a situation where you and someone else have similar experience and have made nearly identical contributions, then the swing factor may well be something totally unrelated to business. For example, you and your prospective boss may both play tennis. Your prospective boss may need a fourth, and, just that simple, you may get a job.

If you doubt that personal information can sometimes spell the difference between a turndown and an interview, consider this. A manufacturing-staff friend of mine told me about the job interview that led to his current job. It seems he and his interviewer didn't talk business for very long. Somehow or other the conversation turned to a small item at the bottom of his resume, the small town where my friend had grown up. It turned out to be the same hamlet in western Canada that the prospective boss came from. The common geographical background of the prospective boss and the potential employee brought the two together. My manufacturing-staff friend was offered the job and accepted it. Keep in mind, then, that something personal can make a difference. And you can never tell what personal item on your resume is going to be of greatest interest to your prospective boss. Frequently sports are a common denominator. It might be hobbies such as woodworking or photography. It might just be old school ties, or civic associations in which you are active, such as Lions or Elks. It could even be a political group or church organization.

At this point I am often asked whether or not the mention of political groups or church affiliations can hurt. Suppose your prospective boss is a Republican and you are a Democrat. Will that knock you out of the ball game? With a few bigoted people, yes. But you wouldn't want to work for them anyhow. On the other hand, if you present your personal background in a positive fashion, you're likely to touch on a common interest that could be beneficial in your interview. For example, you may be in charge of the speakers' program for Kiwanis; your prospective boss may be in charge of the speakers' program for the junior chamber of commerce. He may want to learn more about the speakers' program in your organization. And . . . your resume may well end up in the stack marked "arrange for interview" instead of that other stack to receive the usual "Dear John" letter.

While your job objective, scope and worthpoint paragraphs are "musts" for your resume, there are some things that your resume can do without. Here are several.

1. *Your Age* "Employment agencies and first-line personnel people recommend that job-seekers include their age." Of course they do! It makes it that much easier to eliminate them from consideration. But unless you're exactly the right age your prospective boss has in mind, including your age has to hurt. And unfortunately, unless an executive recruiter tells you, you have no idea whether your prospective boss wants someone older or younger than you. So why spoon-feed this information to him. Instead, make him realize you are an outstanding candidate based on your scope and worthpoint paragraphs. Then, let him try to figure out your age after that (based on when you completed college). Some job-seekers I counsel are reluctant to accept this suggestion. But of the thousands of candidates who have left their age off their resume, none here told me that this hurt them in their job search, while many who have omitted their age have advised me that they have been interviewed by employers who said to them that they had younger (or older) candidates in mind, but wanted to meet them because they were impressed by their resume. Keep in mind that it is against the law for employers to discriminate against any candidate because of age, or to ask for age on an employment application. Why help employers get around the law instead of trying to get them to meet you and be impressed by you in spite of your age?

2. *Questionable data* Every so often I run into a resume where the candidate includes his birthplace outside of the United States. For persons applying for engineering positions that involve government contracts, this can create problems that don't need to come up until an interview (where they might be resolved). It is illegal to discriminate against candidates on the basis of their national origin. If the prospective employer has to worry about a candidate's security clearance, the time to work that out is at the interview. Don't let a prospective boss assume you might not qualify.

Some prospective employers discriminate against male candidates who are single ("they're too unsettled"), and female candidates who are newly married ("they're likely to start a family just when I've trained them"), and against both male and female candidates who are separated ("they're going through an emotional trauma and wouldn't work out on the job"). Personal prejudices run deep, and even though they are not permitted by law, exist nonetheless! If you are a candidate who falls into any of these categories and who feels compelled to include this type of information, a suggestion: *bury* this information in the personal section of your resume—between your hobbies and your interests. Make your prospective boss search for it, at least! And hope he discovers how competent you are before he comes across it.

3. *The statement "References will be forwarded on request"*   Include this line if you have the space and want to, but it's totally unnecessary to do so. This line was originally recommended a decade ago when many job-seekers actually included names, addresses and phone numbers of references on their resumes. At the time, the experts in the field counseled that giving out reference names hurt job-seekers since it would be in their best interest to force prospective employers to call and request these names in person. (With references stated on the resume, a prospective boss could check out a candidate without the candidate ever knowing he or she was being considered for the job.) Times have changed, however, and hardly any resumes written today spell out the names and addresses of references. So the line "References will be forwarded on request" is actually a relic of the past.

4. *Your office telephone number*   For many prospective employers, your office phone number rings a negative bell because it suggests either that (1) the people you work for *know* you're leaving, or (2) you're foolhardy enough not to care if they find out. (What if your boss answers a call for you from a headhunter?) So, whether or not you are leaving on your own, or at the request of your management, you're better off using only your home phone number.

5. *Your salary objective, nor the salary you are paid on your current job*   If there's one thing I've come to realize in my years in business, it's that "salary ranges" are flexible guidelines at best. If a company really wants you, and you're absolutely the right person for the job, there is invariably a

way for that company to stretch to meet your needs. Similarly, if a person really wants a job and believes it offers the potential for a lifetime career, he's likely to bend just a little bit from his own salary requirements. With these two points in mind, it makes little sense to include your salary objective or current salary in your resume. Even if your financial demands are rigid, it still is less than wise to include them on your resume. Cadillac and Lincoln ads don't mention the price tag. They sell the quality of these automobiles. The ads attempt to persuade you to go down to the showroom, where a salesman will review the car's merits in person. The hope is you'll be sufficiently impressed to put out the fourteen grand. Your resume's primary job is to get you into your prospective boss's office, where you'll have a chance to sell yourself in person.

6. *Your photograph* To men, a girl in a slinky black negligee appears sexier than the same girl in her birthday suit. The slinky negligee leaves something mysterious, unknown, and unstated, for curiosity to dwell on. The same holds true for your resume. If you give away everything, there's nothing left to tantalize. One thing you can and should hold back is your photograph.

By now your patience to turn to the "model" resume at the end of this chapter may be coming to an end! But if you will, consider just two additional caveats. They'll take only a couple of minutes to read but could save you hundreds of hours of frustration later on.

1. *Don't lie—not even a "white" lie* This sounds quite simple. But you'd be surprised at how many people alter the past, particularly if they feel it is detrimental to them. White lies invariably come back to haunt. Why take the chance? One small case history should, I think, prove to you the value of being totally honest. An eager young executive, about thirty, whom I counseled a few years ago related this incident to me.

When he was twenty-three, the young executive secured a job that, shortly after accepting it, he found totally unsatisfactory for many reasons. He hated his boss. The work bored him to tears. And, not surprisingly, his boss didn't think much of him. The executive quit in disgust after only four months. (He decided to resign before he got fired.) Thinking of any reference to his sad four months as awkward, he decided to amend his past on a resume he wrote several years later. This, he left out this unhappy four months of his life and instead stated that his next job had started four months earlier than it actually had. The young executive figured no one would know the difference. In the back of his mind, he felt this little lie would avoid the possibility of someone calling the company where he had toiled sadly for only four months, and where he felt his reputation could be tarnished. As you might expect, in true tales of this sort, it just so happened that the personnel director at the very company the young executive was most interested in decided to check past history. In the search, the first thing the personnel director turned up was that the stated dates of employment did not correspond with the actual dates at the young executive's previous job. Needless to say, it didn't take much digging to find out about the four-month job that didn't work out well. The young executive was subsequently called in by the personnel director and confronted with the lost four months. He was indeed embarrassed by the situation. As it turned out, another candidate was selected by this company. The young executive who related this story to me felt that his white lie was the deciding factor in his not getting the job he wanted.

2. *Don't think your resume couldn't be improved* In ten years of counseling job-seekers, I've yet to see a single resume that couldn't be touched up in one way or another. And that includes my own. Periodically, I return to my resume. Each time I find a word here or a sentence there that could be changed to make a worthpoint stand out more quickly, seem clearer or more cogent. If you'll buy the idea that the first resume you put together may not be the most brilliant ever written:

☐ Let some business friends read over your resume after it's finished but before the final typing. Ask them to look critically at its format, appearance, and content. Take their criticism to heart. They are your friends. Or get your resume to a professional in the field to have it critiqued for you. (Each year hundreds of job-seekers pay me forty dollars an hour to have me raise questions they hadn't considered.)

☐ After you have had three or four interviews, look critically at your resume again. Ask yourself whether or not during the course of your interviews you talk about worthpoints that are not included on your resume. Ask yourself if there are any aspects of your resume that prospective bosses seem to want you to clarify. Revise your resume based on what you learned from these early interviews. Be sure your resume sells you on paper as well as you sell yourself in person.

☐ Have your resume rerun if it isn't perfect the first time. If you're thinking about changing jobs, or perhaps if you're out of work, the twenty dollars it takes to rerun your resume may seem like a lot of money. But twenty dollars is really small potatoes when you compare it to the extra money you'll make if your resume sells you harder than your competition. Don't be penny-wise and pound-foolish. If you think you can improve it, rework your resume. Have it rerun. Don't put twenty dollars between you and a better job.

At last there's nothing between you and the chronological resume format I promised. Copy it to your heart's content if you wish. But note you can change it, adapt it, flex it to suit your personal taste and career needs as long as you consider the building blocks and do's and don'ts discussed above. Following the format are several real-world resumes that utilize the basic format. They don't look the same! But the names of titles and companies pop off the page. Paragraphs are short enough to be read and there's sufficient white space surrounding them to make the resumes inviting. And most important, each reveals the scope of the candidate's background and his worth in each of his jobs. The resumes themselves reflect the personality of the candidate and the particular experience each has enjoyed. As long as you keep the critical points in this chapter in mind, you can modify your resume to suit yourself and it will still go a long way to open doors for you.

CHRONOLOGICAL RESUME GUIDE

Your Full Name
Your Home Address
Your Home Phone Number

JOB OBJECTIVE

State as succinctly as possible the type of position you seek. If you have several objectives, make up several resumes. Don't use "or" in your objective. If your objective and background don't fully match, emphasize the strengths you could bring to this position. (E.G: Senior financial officer in situation where extensive EDP experience would be an asset.)

EXPERIENCE:

Inclusive dates

NAME OF MOST RECENT COMPANY worked for, location. Capitalize company for emphasis. (E.G: TECHNITRON, Plainview, Long Island)

(E.G: 1967-1969

Your title presently, or on leaving. Underline for visability. (E.G: Advertising Director, Small Appliance Division)

Short 'SCOPE' paragraph, describing your responsibilities. A maximum of four sentences. Description should emphasize your relation to total operation, scope of your managerial and budgetary responsibilities. Review primary responsibilities only. Avoid "functions" and non-significant aspects of job.

Two to three short, pithy 'WORTHPOINT' paragraphs (each no longer than two sentences) describing your contributions. Make the result come across fast and dramatically. Don't bury your worth.

Your 'WORTHPOINT' paragraphs should start with a sentence which reviews your input against the corporation's general problem. This sentence should be followed by one which provides specific results stated as dramatically as possible. Be sure results and problems are related.

Inclusive dates for previous position

NAME OF PREVIOUS COMPANY AFFILIATION, location

1962-1967

Your title on leaving—If you are cramped for space, you can begin your 'SCOPE' paragraph right after your job title. Be sure to underline title. As noted above, your 'SCOPE' paragraph is followed by paragraphs which will reveal your 'WORTHPOINTS'

As you would expect, your description of previous job is shorter than description of most recent job. You should include fewer worthpoints to focus on the significance of your most recent experience.

If you have worked at the same company in several, progressively more responsible positions, highlight this by citing titles, scope of responsibility, and worthpoints in each position. If you are tight on space (or were in each position a relatively short time) write a special paragraph on promotions, underlining titles, and giving dates of each job held prior to your latest position.

INDUSTRY
ASSOCIATIONS,
HONORS,
PATENTS,
PUBLICATIONS:

Include memberships in associations that provide special
insight concerning your experience, or in which you were
particularly active. Don't include memberships just for
the sake of membership. Although patents and publications
are important, patent numbers and page numbers are not.
Think SCOPE.

EDUCATION:

NAME OF LAST SCHOOL ATTENDED, location. (Capitalize for
visibility) (E.G: PARSONS SCHOOL OF DESIGN, New York,
New York)

Inclusive
dates
(E.G: 1951-
1955

Degree received (Underline for visibility). Departmental
major. Other significant course taken. Honors received.
Academic and extracurricular awards. Significant associations. Offices held. Scholarships.

Inclusive
dates
(E.G: 1949-
1951)

NAME OF PREVIOUSLY ATTENDED SCHOOL, location

Use separate paragraph for each college level or higher
academic institution you attended. Do not include paragraph on high school or prep school, even if you are
particularly proud of it.

CONTINUING
EDUCATION:

Include industry seminars, and company seminars and courses
if relevant. Certificates of completion. Licenses

MILITARY
SERVICE:

Indicate rank at discharge, or current rank if still active.
Branch. Commendations, if significant, and you are out of
the service less than 5 years. Keep this paragraph short,
unless a major part of your career.

SUMMER
JOBS:

Include in resume only if fairly recent and genuinely relevant. Incorporate in your "Education" paragraphs, where
chronologically appropriate.

PERSONAL
BACKGROUND,
CURRENT HOBBIES,
INTERESTS,
ASSOCIATIONS:

This is your chance to share something in common with your
prospective boss that can make you stand out from the other
candidates with the same qualifications. Use to your advantage. Include your hometown, schools. Your current hobbies
...particularly sports. Include civic associations in which
you are active. State previous as well as current positions
held in organizations. Marital status. Children. Bury
"divorce" or "separation" in this paragraph.

REFERENCES:

Use the following statement: "Will be forwarded on request,"
if you have room to do so. Don't give references. Let them
call you for references. Then, give the right ones for each job.

SALARY
OBJECTIVE:

It is recommended that you do not include any reference to
salary on your resume.

AGE/RELIGION
RACE/SEX
BIRTHPLACE:

Do not include. These items are not required and in many
states are illegal. Your age can be determined from date you
graduated from school.

DEXTER BLAIR
415 Lyndhurst Avenue
Oradell, New Jersey 07161

Job Objective: <u>Administrative Management</u> position in a
situation in which financial background
will be of benefit.

1967-Present: CHIEF ACCOUNTANT, Capitol Press, Inc.,
Ridgewood, New Jersey.

Responsible for all accounting functions of
this $5,000,000 publisher of educational
and business training programs. Responsible
for directing office staff of 32. Joined
company as accountant. Promoted to Chief
Accountant in three years.

Made company's first formal work flow
analysis and system for accounting department to reduce work process time. This
resulted in profit statement delivery ten
days after close of fiscal year vs. two
months lead time prior to instituting
system.

Initiated study of royalty payments to
uncover potential savings in this
significant cost area. Discovered royalties
were being paid on items in error. Initiated
system to avoid errors which saved the
company $50,000 to date.

Responsible for introducing a new payroll
system to reduce duplicate record keeping
for tax and corporate purposes. This has
reduced payroll processing time by two-
thirds and payroll tax preparation time by
80%.

Developed company's first personnel record
cards to simplify salary reviews. This has
saved 200 staff hours annually in clerical
processing.

Organized company's first employee credit
union after recognizing employees needed
both savings and loan assistance and have
served as President for four years. The
credit union has won two Federal awards in
the last two years for increases in employee
participation and dividend returns.

DEXTER BLAIR

1965-1967: ASSISTANT TREASURER, Popular Pastimes
Company, Inc., Pine Valley, New Jersey.

Responsible for all accounting for this
$1,750,000 manufacturer of pool tables
and shuffleboards. Directed six person
office staff. Additionally was responsible
for all telephone sales to existing clients.
Directed operation of business three times
each year when President was on selling
trips. Joined company as bookkeeper.
Promoted to Assistant Treasurer in two
years.

Developed receivable system to avoid shipment
of orders to late-paying customers. This
reduced receivable balances and increased
working capital. As a result bank loans were
reduced by two-thirds.

Investigated discrepancies between actual and
reported sales volume of company-owned retail
outlet. Discovered systematic slippage leading to dismissal of manager. Initiated an
internal control system which prevented similar losses thereafter. Received special management bonus as a result.

Developed company's first promotional telephone
sales campaign to increase repeat business to
existing customers. This campaign resulted in
sales of $250,000.

Education: 1964-1968 <u>William Paterson College</u>, General
College and Accounting
1969-1970 <u>International Accountants' Society</u>,
Advanced Accounting
1972-1973 <u>University of Wisconsin Extension</u>,
Credit Union Management

Personal,
Background,
and Interests: Brought up in Northern New Jersey and attended
schools there. Hobbies and interests include
bowling, photography, music, and the theater.
Am a member of <u>New Jersey Officer's Federal</u>
<u>Credit Union</u>. Married, age 27, three children.
In excellent health.

DAVID H. BOLTON
Pennyville Road
Manhasset, New York 11076
(516) 498-3298

<table>
<tr><td>JOB
OBJECTIVE:</td><td>General Manager of industrial products company needing individual with
sales, production and engineering background.</td></tr>
<tr><td>BUSINESS
EXPERIENCE:</td><td>BOTSFORD-MELDRUM COMPANY, Baxter-Fairbridge Division
Hartford, Connecticut</td></tr>
<tr><td>(1969-
Present)</td><td></td></tr>
</table>

Vice President and General Manager (1975-Present)

Reporting to the Group Executive, responsible for marketing, sales,
production, engineering, purchasing and personnel in 4 plant locations
employing 1200. Division has sales of more than $30,000,000 in 3 lines
of electromechanical products.

Promoted to General Manager to correct a 50% unit volume loss occuring
during prior 8 years. Designed and installed forecasting and production
control system to improve deliveries. This restored on-time customer
service to 93% from 50% and led to a 40% sales increase over 2 years.

Reorganized marketing department and field sales force by related
products to provide greater attention to major accounts. As a result,
division recaptured lost market share and enjoyed 30% productivity
increase in the field.

Undertook program of permanent overhead reductions to offset severe
decline in gross margins. Was able to eliminate $1,100,000 in overhead
annually. Margins rebounded more than 70% above previous level.

Implemented an inventory control system to reduce surplus raw materials
and work in process. Freed floor space, reduced associated manpower and
reduced surplus assets by $2,000,000. As a further result, return on
operating capital was improved.

Accelerated design, tooling and repackaging to introduce first new
products following 4 years of inactivity. Launched a marine line in
18 months adding 7% to sales.

Elected Vice Chairman, Building Equipment Board of Directors, Eastern
States Electric Manufacturers Association.

BAXTER-FAIRBRIDGE, INCORPORATED (merged with Botsford-Meldrum, 1975)
Hartford, Connecticut

Vice President, Operations and Planning (1969-1975)

Reporting to the President, directed the manufacturing, engineering and
physical distribution of Baxter-Fairbridge and Bolton Divisions with
$55,000,000 in sales from 7 plant and 6 warehouse locations employing
2500.

Installed short interval scheduling and capacity planning system in
new plant with low productivity. As a result, raised output more than
70% with no increase in the labor force.

Tightened forecasting, safety stock management and scheduling to reduce
inventories by $3,200,000 raising inventory turn to upper quartile of
the industry.

Structured engineering bills of material and labor for the computer to eliminate inaccuracies and high obsolescence. Identified $1,000,000 of obsolete inventory and provided clerical savings of $250,000 annually.

BOLTON MANUFACTURING CORPORATION
Roslyn, New York

(1966-1969)   <u>Vice President, Manufacturing and Engineering</u>

Reporting to the Executive Vice President, responsible for the manufacturing and engineering in 3 plant locations with sales of $21,000,000 employing 950.

Selected a new plant location to meet needs of additional sales and reduce manufacturing cost. 200,000 sq. ft. was designed, constructed and staffed with 650 in 15 months with annual savings of $1,700,000.

Investigated and established manufacturing source in Japan to provide additional capacity for major product line losing share. Increased capacity by 18% at an annual savings of $750,000.

(1961-1966)   Held a series of progressively more responsible manufacturing positions including <u>Production Manager</u>, Circuit Breakers (1961-1962); <u>Engineering Manager</u> (1962-1964); <u>Manufacturing Manager</u> (1964-1966). In latter position was responsible for all operations at plant producing sales of $13,000,000.

(1958-1961)   <u>Sales Manager, Western Region</u>

Responsible for 8 salesmen and 6 agents in 7 Western States. Increased sales from $300,000 to $2,800,000 during this period.

RAPIDTRON ELECTRONICS CORPORATION
Los Angeles, California

(1956-1958)   As <u>Project Director</u> reporting to the Vice President, Engineering, directed progress of $13,000,000 airborne reconnaissance system.

<u>EDUCATION:</u>

(1954-1956)   WHARTON SCHOOL OF BUSINESS ADMINISTRATION, Cambridge, Massachusetts
M.B.A. Degree, graduated upper third of class.

(1945-1948)   MASSACHUSETTS INSTITUTE OF TECHNOLOGY, Boston, Mass.
M.E. Degree, graduated upper half of class. Delager award for service to the school. Varsity Lacrose. Gear & Triangle Honorary Society.
Chi Phi fraternity.

<u>MILITARY SERVICE:</u>   (1951-1954)--Lt. (jg) U.S. Navy, Bureau of Ships, honorable discharge.

<u>EARLIER EXPERIENCE:</u>   (1948-1951)--worked for the National Security Agency and in family business.

<u>PERSONAL:</u>   Active in sailing, tennis, skiing, riding and photography. Licensed pilot and radio amateur. Member: Brattleboro Yacht Club, Flint Ridge Ski Club

NOEL S. SIMPSON

Old School Lane   Res. (312) 359-4372
Barrington, IL 60067

Corporate Finance and Development

1972-
Present

PETERSEN CORPORATION, Chicago, Ill. Private
business development concern with $80 million in
capital. Invests in equity of developing companies
and provides management services as major or control investor.

Vice President, Group Vice President, Treasurer --
Responsible officer for companies with up to $250
million in total sales and for new investments in
non-technical fields. Manage financial, strategic
and managerial resources to build independent
companies. As Treasurer (1972-74), responsible
for corporate finance, planning, relations and
acquisitions. Member management, executive and
valuation committees.

- Managed reorganization of companies and investments resulting in a $9 million net cash improve-
  ment.

- Improved cash management resulting in a $400,000
  annual gain.

- Structured financial offering resulting in $20
  million of capital availability with investor
  continuity of interest.

1966-72

RANDOLPH COUSINS, Philadelphia, Pa. Major regional
investment banking firm founded in 1800.

Associate -- Responsible for special situations.

- Originated and negotiated acquisition of 70
  year old medical company. Introduced new product
  line program resulting in a 400% profit and sales
  increase.

- Converted an unprofitable investment company into
  an operating concern with acquisitions forming
  two product groups, Spartan Manufacturing to
  sales of $200 million and $10 million in profit
  with NYSE listing.

- Reversed 15 year decline in Ultra Medico resulting
  in a 15% growth rate. Replaced 80% of operations
  and recruited new management.

1963-65	TRYTON CORPORATION, Philadelphia, Pa. Aluminum producer and leading manufacturer of jet engine components.

<u>Assistant to the President</u> -- Responsible for corporate development and planning, cash fore-casting, profit planning and capital budgeting.

Aided the planning and execution of four strategic programs resulting in a profit increase from 2.5 million to $14 million.

1961-63   NORTHSIDE ELECTRIC COMPANY, Phoenix, Arizona

<u>Market Development</u> -- Promoted to intra-company sales, then advanced sales planning, then to new market development where project led to later leadership in new business of time-sharing.

Education: NEW YORK UNIVERSITY GRADUATE SCHOOL OF BUSINESS ADMINISTRATION

1959-61   Master in Business Administration Degree in June, 1961. Concentration in finance, control and marketing. Financed own education.

1954-56   PADDLEFORD UNIVERSITY, Lincoln, Nebraska

Bachelor of Arts Degree in Economics in June, 1956. Ranked in top quarter of class. Distinguished Military Graduate, Law School honor scholarship. Elected officer in student organizations.

1952-54   UNIVERSITY OF GENEVA, Switzerland   ANTHONY COLLEGE:
          Institute of European Studies.   Nebraska
                                                   Honor scholarship
                                                   Sports

Professional Affiliations: Association for Corporate Growth, New York University Business School Club, director, various corporations.

Military Service: 1956-59 U.S. Air Force jet pilot. Senior air defense controller at Belgium headquarters. Honorable discharge as Captain.

Background, Interests: Raised in Lincoln, Nebeaska. Enjoy sports, travel and family activities. Director, Inverness Assoc-iation; member Paddleford Metropolitan, Cove Point, and Woodsend Clubs.

References: Available upon request.

Married, 4 Children

CONRAD D. STAPLETON
77 Pleasantapple Way
Coltsville, NY 10176
(914) 747-1012

JOB OBJECTIVE   Senior Product Manager in a situation requiring
extensive advertising and promotion experience.

PRESENT POSITION   VALUE-PLUS DIVISION, INTERCONTINENTAL CORPORATION

1976-Present   Product Manager, NEW PRODUCTS, LAUNDRYON SOAP
and CARBOLENE CLEANER, reporting to Group
Product Manager.

Recommended and obtained test market authoriza-
tion, then managed all phases of development of
THREE test brands, scheduled for introduction
during Fall/Winter, 1976. Combined first year
national volume projects to $20 million, with
advertising budget of $6 million. Concurrently
developing several new products for 1977 test
marketing.

Also responsible for two established brands;
LAUNDRYON SOAP, a $7 million brand, and
CARBOLENE CLEANER, a $4 million regional brand.
Currently work with three advertising agencies
on test and established brands.

1973-1975   Product Manager, WEEKENDER PAINTS, a $6 million
brand.

Developed and implemented a repositioning of
this brand (including new copy and new package
graphics) to counter a 10-year sales downtrend
averaging 10% a year. Repositioning increased
test market volume 16%, and national volume 8%
the following year.

Later initiated development of new more competitive copy than advertising used during
repositioning. Test area sales increased 35%.
National airing is scheduled for Fall, 1976.

Developed plastic packaging that increased
test market volume 10%.

Also developed and implemented profit improvement projects which increased net profit 33%.

1972	**Product Manager**, SHINEZY CAR WASH, a $4 million brand.

Initiated and test marketed an improved aerosol formula and a liquid refill. Both were subsequently expanded nationally and increased brand volume 26%.

RICHARDS-DONALDS COMPANY

1971-1972   **Assistant Product Manager**, reporting to Product Manager.

Concurrent responsibility on PAR and SHIPSHAPE detergents. Developed locally tailored annual promotion plans. These resulted in 30% sales increase on PAR and stabilization of SHIPSHAPE volume.

1970-1971   **Product Merchandising Assistant**

Developed and implemented SUNSHINE SUDS annual promotion plan.

1969-1970   Academic Leave of Absence to obtain MBA. See EDUCATION.

1967-1968   **Account Manager**, Field Sales.

Account Manager for Shopper's Pal, the most difficult chain in Metropolitan Westchester. Achieved sales increase of 10% and distribution of all Lever products, introduced while I was on territory. Based on this performance was awarded Food'N Things Cooperatives, the second most difficult account, and achieved similar results.

EDUCATION   READING SCHOOL, University of Maryland

MBA in Marketing Management. Average grade 3.5 out of 4.0. Thesis: "The Distribution of Pet Supplies through Supermarkets," graded 4.0 out of 4.0. Courses included quantitative methods, finance, accounting and international business.

ELTON COLLEGE, Kansas City, Missouri

BA in Liberal Arts. Was one of 33, out of freshman class of 110, who completed four years of this academically rigorous program. Thesis required each year. Judge in Student Court during senior year.

PERSONAL   Single, U.S. Citizen.

Five

A special resume for use in special cases

In one particular set of career circumstances, the chronological resume described on the preceding pages could actually hurt your chances of landing another job! If you have held several very different, nonrelated positions in the course of your career, and in your current search are hoping to backtrack to a previous career path, the chronological resume may be a disastrous document on which to build your campaign.

If you're not quite sure whether your own career is one that should or should not use a chronological resume, why not compare it to the following example. When Jim, a client of mine, first got out of school he went into sales and worked his way up to the position of district sales manager. After that he became dissatisfied with sales management for some reason or other, and so he secured a position with a research firm, which he has held for five years. Even though Jim did reasonably well with the research outfit—he was promoted to a department head—he still wants out! He has made up his mind that field sales is more his cup of tea, and now he wants to get back to it.

The example above is fairly straightforward. Over the years I've counselled job-seekers who have meandered back and forth between two, three and even four different careers every few years! People in situations like this are not that rare. If you are one of them, trying to sell yourself with a chronological resume has to be a mistake.

Why? Because the last job you held has nothing to do with what you want to do now. Still, according to the chronological resume rulebook, you're supposed to head up your resume with your *present* job. Obviously you run the risk of turning off your prospective boss when you "feature" your nonrelated experience at the top of your resume while other candidates offer current experience that is directly in tune with the job you and they are competing for.

Confronted by circumstances like this, many job-seekers have turned to a "functional" resume as a way out. A functional resume is one in which you describe your accumulated *capabilities,* rather than providing a *timetable* of your career as in the chronological resume. You can include any and every major capability you wish. Jim, the sales-manager-turned-researcher, for example, might use such capability categories as *Direct selling, Territory management, Personnel management, Training, Audit tabulation, Project planning, Field surveys,* etc. Usually, in such resumes, you discuss each of your key capabilities in a separate paragraph or two. The nice thing is that you can organize them any way you see fit. Since there are no dates attached to "capabilities," you can describe something you learned to do ten years ago at the head of page one, if you think that particular capability will be more saleable in terms of the job you are now going after. Similarly, you can describe a capability you obtained on the job you held during the last five years at the bottom of page one or on page two, or if you were so disposed, you could leave it off your resume entirely.

Another thing—in the functional resume, the actual "chronology" of your career can be placed anywhere you like. Most people using a functional resume list their jobs and the dates they held them on page two of their resume, where they are likely to do the least harm. The idea obviously is to turn on your prospective boss, when he first picks up your resume, by *featuring* the capabilities he's probably looking for, and to take your lumps on page two when he discovers in reviewing your brief chronology that the capabilities you feature probably were not learned in your most recent positions. What does a functional resume actually look like? Let's consider our salesman-turned-researcher once again. After stating his job objective—which can be written as for a chronological resume—the balance of Jim's resume might look something like this:

EXPERIENCE AREAS

Personnel Management—Managed 12 salesmen in district. Responsible for hiring, evaluation of their performance. Had lowest personnel turnover of all districts in region.

Training—Regularly conducted training sessions for 12 salesmen and for 50 field auditors involved in various research projects.

Following introduction of a new training program developed by me, my district's sales performance went from #7 in region to #1.

Developed training manual for an audit requested by a foods manufacturer. This eventually became the standard training for all future audits by the firm.

Audit Analysis, etc., etc.

Other Capability Areas, etc., etc.

CHRONOLOGY (usually on page 2)

1975 to present	American Research Corp. New York	Audit Manager
1972 to 1975	American Research Corp.	Auditor
1968 to 1972	U.S. Sales Corp., New York	District Sales Manager
1962 to 1968	U.S. Sales Corp., New York	Salesman

EDUCATION
PERSONAL INTERESTS, etc.

There's only one problem with the funcional resume described above: any prospective employer worth his salt knows from the moment he sets eyes on it that you are trying to hide something in your career. The "functional" resume format is, in a word, a warning signal to many prospective bosses that there's a problem in a candidate's background. As such, there's a very good chance that if you use a functional resume, you'll defeat the very objective that caused you to develop it in the first place. Because the functional resume looks so unlike a chronological resume, and because today it is infrequently used, it usually stands out like a sore thumb.

At this point you're probably wondering what sort of resume you *can* write if your career hasn't been on a consistent path. Is there any document that will help rather than hurt your current search? Unfortunately I know of no foolproof answer. Anything other than the standard chronological format will, in some instances, work against you. What I recommend to people in this situation is a resume that combines the *look* of a chronological resume with the *flexibility* of the functional format. This hybrid resume of mine follows the standard chronological format described in the previous chapter except for one thing: *you leave* DATES *off the left hand column and substitute careers in their place.*

Let's consider what Jim, our salesman-turned-researcher, might do with his resume, as an example. After he finished writing a standard chronological resume including company names, titles, scope and worthpoint paragraphs, he would simply grab a pair of scissors and piece together his resume with his sales career up front. In abbreviated form, it might look something like this:

JOB OBJECTIVE   *Executive sales position* with firm seeking individual with knowledge of sales management and research functions.

EXPERIENCE

SALES
MANAGEMENT   U.S. SALES CORPORATION, New York, N.Y.
District Manager—Reporting to Regional Manager, and in some instances directly to National Sales Manager. Responsible for directing 12-man sales team with annual volume in excess of $10,000,000 for 4 years.

Developed comprehensive training program for my district which improved its sales performance from #7 in region to #1.

Developed new hiring procedure designed to reduce high manpower turnover. Reduced turnover from 30% to 12% in one year.

[Other relevant sales management worthpoint paragraphs would follow the two shown above.]

DIRECT SALES   *Salesman*—Responsible for U.S. Sales Corporation territory with volume in excess of $1,000,000. Reporting to district manager. Sold full line of U.S. products for 6 years.

Rose from #9 position out of 12 salesmen in district to #1. Held leadership position for 3 years.

Developed new sales presentation to introduce new product line in my territory. Achieved distribution in 80% of outlets in 7 weeks. My presentation became standard for company.

[Other relevant sales worthpoints.]

RESEARCH MANAGEMENT

AMERICAN RESEARCH COMPANY, New York, N.Y.

Audit Manager—Reporting to Vice President Operations. Direct 15 person auditing department. Responsible for tabulations on all American Research Corp. field projects—approximately 60 studies each year valued at $6,000,000.

Developed training manual for an audit requested by a foods manufacturer. This became the standard audit training format for all audits by the firm.

FIELD AUDITING

Auditor—Joined American Research as a temporary auditor on a health-aids project. Was offered full-time auditor's job as a result. Was promoted to Audit Manager after 18 months.

After describing his experience in his sales and research careers, the rest of Jim's resume should follow the standard chronological format with one exception. Somewhere on page two, in addition to Education, Personal, Military, Honors, etc., Jim will need to include a Chronology similar to the one shown in the functional resume described earlier. If he's smart, Jim will make it as inconspicuous as possible, using single spacing for the section, and leaving off capitalized words and underlines. If possible, Jim should try to "bury" this section in between the Military and Education sections of his resume, hoping that his awkward career path goes unnoticed until after his prospective boss has become turned on by his background in selling.

Quite frankly, the hybrid resume described above won't work all the time. Some prospective boss somewhere is going to get his hackles up when he realizes that the company and position you describe at the top of your resume isn't your most recent one. But if you'll take the word of the hundreds of job-seekers who have tried both, the hybrid resume works in many cases a lot better than the functional resume and can help you make the best of a difficult-to-sell career path. Most job-seekers who have used the hybrid resume report that prospective bosses are totally *unaware* of the chronological paste-up job until the job-seeker gets to the interview and then points out that the order of jobs in the resume itself doesn't quite agree with the chronology shown on page two. It's safe to say that the hybrid format works to get you in the door. Beyond that no claims are made. Certainly your prospective employer will be disappointed—or in some cases a little angry—to learn that the job you highlight at the top isn't your most recent one. But if you handle yourself well in your interview, and are frank and forthright about your career situation, you at least have a fighting chance against other candidates whose career paths are more appropriate to the opening.

Six

Girding yourself for
the lion's den

When I was in college, the night before any major exam a group of us used to have a bull session—our objective being to "psych out" the questions that the instructor was going to ask. If we knew the questions, we figured we could work out the answers beforehand and so be one step ahead of the game. We didn't always luck out. But we hit on the central topics covered in the test the next day often enough to make it worth holding that pre-exam session again and again. Obviously psyching out an exam is a lot easier than determining in advance how your first interview with a company will develop, since you've never met the "instructor" or seen the "classroom." Even so, advance preparation for job interviews has paid off handsomely for thousands of job-seekers and could pay off for you.

In suggesting you try to improve your interview performance before you ever meet your prospective boss, don't think I'm recommending you make an effort to "psych out" your interviewer. Not at all. What I do propose is that you try to learn as much as you can beforehand about how to handle the situations that will make your interviews successful or not. This type of advance planning offers several advantages. If nothing else, your interviewer should sense that you are better informed than the next person, and that is likely to suggest to him that you're more interested in the job than your competition. More than that, however, advance preparation can help you guide your interviewer toward a more *positive* interview. Many executives are not used to meeting prospective employees on a regular basis. They don't know what questions to ask; what directions to pursue. If you are "buttoned up," beforehand you may be able to help your prospective boss use your thirty or sixty minutes together to maximize its value to him as well as you. You can't help your interviewer unless you have certain information under your belt relevant to the interview *before* you walk in the door.

Gathering this data may seem a difficult assignment at first. But keep in mind that interview preparation gets easier and easier each time you do it, since that hardest part is locating the sources and learning how to use them. After you've prepared for a couple of interview sessions, it will take less time to prepare for those that follow. Remember, too, that you don't need to prepare for meetings with every company you contact initially by letter, or with every company you learn has an opening through an executive recruiter or employment agency. Reserve your preparation time for those companies where an interview is actually scheduled.

What types of preparation should you pursue? Here are some things I suggest you consider. You may think of others.

1. Learn about the company, its present and its future

If you are meeting with someone at a publicly owned company, there are a great many sources of information about the firm available to you. The *annual report*—and particularly the president's message in it—will tell you where the company has been, and more important, where it thinks it's going. You may be interviewing for a job just because the company *is* pursuing new businesses or trying to shore up weaker ones. You'll find the *profit-and-loss* section useful, too, since it may clue you in on what the company's past problems have been and suggest the types of strategies that the company may be thinking about for the future. Where can you get an annual report? Call the *corporate* secretary of the company you're going to interview and ask for one. Or even the secretary of the person you are planning to see. So what if your prospective boss learns you've called for an annual report? Doing so shows your interest and professionalism. You can find annual reports on file in many business libraries, too. If there are not many days between setting up your interview and taking it, the library may be your best bet. Some larger brokerage firms also maintain annual reports of the more actively traded companies as well. If not, they will at least have a one-page writeup of the company's performance from *Standard & Poor's Register of Corporations, Directors, and Executives,* or from another source. These writeups are not as good as annual reports, though, since the flavor of an annual report can often provide a better clue as to why you're being interviewed.

There are plenty of other sources of worthwhile information about companies—even privately owned companies—that you might consider. Often corporations are written up in business magazines like *Forbes, Fortune, Business Week,* etc., and newspapers like the *Wall Street Journal.* Articles are most likely to appear if the company is pursuing new directions, which could involve the position you're applying for. Often the articles are "placed" by the companies themselves through their P.R. firms and reflect the company line. Many libraries have the F&S Index and other indexes to business articles that list "mentions" of companies. They're much like the *Reader's Guide to Periodical Literature,* and just as easy to use.

Another way to gain additional insight into a company is to familiarize yourself with its primary products or services. If the company makes consumer products, a trip to the supermarket or drugstore to look at its brands (as well as its competition) could prove very worthwhile. If the company makes industrial products, perhaps a phone call to a distributor could net you some catalog sheets that are worth a few minutes of your time. Of course, if you go through a good executive recruiter, he may be able to provide you with a *package* of such material. The point is that one way or another it is worth doing a little legwork to get some grounding concerning the company you might work for.

2. Learn about the people you'll be working with if you get the job

There are several good reasons for doing so. First, you might share something in common with a prospective boss or his associates. That could make the difference if you and your competition are otherwise on a par. Obviously, if you do discover a common bond, plan to refer to it during your interview so that your interviewer is made aware of it. Second, in investigating the people you might meet, you may discover a clue as to their approach to the job you are applying for. Did the president of the company come up through manufacturing, finance or marketing, for example? Obviously, the prior disciplines of the people at the top could affect the company's modus operandi and your satisfaction with the company itself.

How can you determine something about your boss? Check at your library to see if it has a copy of *Who's Who in Business* or similar biographical directory. Usually listings include schools and prior business associations as well as a summary of the executive's progress at this present affiliation. Other references to consider: Standard & Poor's and Dun & Bradstreet writeups of the companies you're interviewing. If the person you're meeting with hasn't made it into a biographical reference book, consider calling a local newspaper or trade magazine. From time to time these publications carry biographical material when an executive gets a promotion. If you run into a dead end, you might ask yourself if you know anyone who currently or formerly worked for the company. Such an acquaintance may give you valuable background not only concerning the person's former associations and education, but about his personality and prejudices as well.

Again, don't forget the executive recruiter if you've learned of the job through one. Chances are he has met personally with your prospective boss and you should probe him for any insight he has. Don't count on an employment agent for much background on personalities, however. Chances are his contacts are through personnel and not directly with the line managers who are going to meet you and make the hiring decision.

3. Learn as much as you can about the job you're competing for

If you learned of the job through a newspaper ad, go back and reread it *line for line*—and between the lines as well! Most executive-wanted display ads provided some sort of a description of the ideal candidate. Match yourself to the ad requirements objectively; know where you will shine and what your weaknesses will be before you enter the door. Be prepared to discuss *in depth* the specific experience you have that matches the needs outlined in the ad.

If you secured your interview through a recruiter, there's a good chance he has a formal job description that he wrote up with your prospective boss. Ask for a copy of it and study it as though your next job depended on it—because it just might. And keep in mind that both the newspaper ad and recruiter's job specs probably list desired qualities in order of importance, since that's the natural way the person developing the ad or specs would state them. Keep that priority list in mind as you allocate your time to various topics during your interview.

4. Develop a list of intelligent questions you'd like to ask the interviewer

One of the favorite interviewer questions is "Do you have any questions about us?" Have in mind a half-dozen well-thought-out ones that reflect your knowledge of the company, the job to be done, and people involved. Otherwise you're likely to respond during your interview with the typical "Gee, I don't really have any questions" answer. Worse still, you might be guilty of making up questions on the spot that are superficial, irrelevant, or even embarrassing.

5. Develop a list of questions you think the interviewer is likely to ask you

After learning as much as you can about the company, the job, and the person filling it, what things about you will the interviewer want to probe? Be critical of your weaknesses as you develop your list. Think of the reasonable objections you'd raise about your own qualifications, were you in your prospective boss's shoes and trying to decide whether to hire you in spite of your weaknesses.

6. Develop to-the-point answers to the questions that will probably be asked of you

Think of reasonable answers. Write them out. Boil them down. Say them over and over until they're second nature to you. If you have a tape recorder, listen to them to make sure they are clear, succinct, and convincing. It's amazing how long-winded some job-seekers can be in an interview when they grope for an answer on the spot, and how professional others appear when they answer directly and cut through to the heart of the matter.

7. Learn the route to the company and the time it takes to get there

A small point, perhaps, but a most important one. The worst way to begin any interview is late. It's inconsiderate of the interviewer's time; who needs a thoughtless person working for him? The following story explains why it pays to ask your interviewer's secretary the exact route to where your interview will take place. A job-seeker told me he had a date with someone at the Shulton company—the people who make Old Spice. Their plant is in Clifton, New Jersey. The job-seeker didn't call for instructions because he had seen the plant many times. It fronts the Garden State Parkway, one of the major arteries in the area. Unfortunately for the job-seeker, there's no access to Shulton from the Garden State and the plant has to be approached through a maze of back roads that he did not know. It ended up taking him more than twenty minutes to arrive at Shulton after he had passed the building on the Parkway! Those twenty minutes were among the most frustrating of his lifetime, he advised me, and the perspiration on him by the time he walked into his interview fifteen minutes late was incredible.

There's an eighth point you must include as part of your advance preparation and that's learning about—and then doing something about—your interview idiosyncrasies and style. In fact, I consider this item so important that I've devoted a separate section to it at the end of this chapter.

But first let's consider the *day* of your interview. What can you do then to maximize the value of any advance preparation? Here are some suggestions:

☐ DRESS AS THOUGH YOU ALREADY HAD THE JOB The great majority of people reading these pages don't need any advice on dress; they naturally dress right for any occasion. But if, perchance, you haven't given much thought to dress and its impact on your success in interviews, this suggestion: Don't look as if you're going to a wedding or a baseball game. Dress in the clothes you think your boss will wear. It's as simple as that. If your prospective boss interviews you in shirtsleeves, take your jacket off. One job candidate I coached told me that taking off his jacket was actually the key factor in getting his job. The man who interviewed him considered himself to be a real "shirtsleeves" worker and had on only a shirt and tie. The candidate asked if he could take off his jacket. That was it. The interviewer smiled and told him he was "his kind of man."

During seventeen years of talking with job-seekers, I've suggested to several candidates that they shave off their beards. This suggestion may make you think I'm a fuddy-duddy. I'm not. I don't care if you have a beard or hair down to your shoulders but I do hate to see a person put any obstacle in front of himself when it comes to getting a new job. If you suspect your prospective boss has a short haircut, you might as well get used to the fact that if you don't have one too, he might downgrade you—consciously or subconsciously. If you work for an advertising agency at which long hair may be in style, then your hair ought to be long. The point is this: Don't give yourself a black mark by wearing your hair long or sporting a beard if you suspect in the slightest it may be held against you. Get the job first. Then let your beard and your hair grow any which way. This suggestion may sound like an infringement on your personal freedom. But remember, you're looking for a better job. Give in a little with your ego—at least for the duration of your search.

This same principle holds true for women executives. Flashy hairstyles and gaudy attire can be equally devastating to a woman as to a man *if* it's out of place. Dowdy, unpressed clothing, even if it's in style, can be just as bad. It suggests you didn't care enough about the job to do anything about looking your best. The simple secret of interview attire is to wear the same style of clothes as your prospective boss is wearing and to make sure they are clean, pressed and not worn. Enough said.

☐ PLAN TO ARRIVE EARLY If you lose your way and you plan to arrive fifteen minutes early, at least you'll have a cushion so that you can be prompt for your appointment.

☐ USE THE WAITING TIME BEFORE YOUR INTERVIEW TO PREPARE YOURSELF FOR YOUR MEETING Read over the information you have collected on the company, people, job. Read over your list of questions for the interviewer, and the ones he is likely to ask you.

☐ WHEN YOU'VE COMPLETED YOUR REVIEW, LOOK AROUND THE WAITING ROOM You may discover additional data that can aid you in your interview. Frequently in the reception area you'll find the company magazine. It may well have articles on new developments in the company's growth that are germane to the position you are applying for. It also might include a writeup of the person you are going to see. If he has been promoted and you are applying for the position he vacated, there's a good likelihood his promotion may be announced in the corporate newsletter. If there are any display cases of company products, or awards hanging on the walls, or pictures of the various company locations, check them out, too. Any extra insight you have might come in handy.

☐ RELAX Look over your materials as much to keep occupied as to benefit from your review. Don't sit empty-handed, growing more tense by the minute. Having well-thought-out materials to review puts you ahead of 99 percent of the people you compete with. Keep that in mind. It will make you feel more confident, and your attitude will reflect itself in the interview when you enter the lion's den a few moments later.

☐ LOOK AROUND THE OFFICE If you are ushered into your prospective boss's office by his secretary and are told that your interviewer will be back in just a few moments' time, look around. You may see pictures on the wall, or other clues (a golf putter in the corner, perhaps) that suggests a mutual interest between yourself and your prospective boss. Keep in mind, however, that while looking around at the obvious is a good idea, looking at materials on the desk and reading them upside down is in poor taste! If your prospective boss had wanted you to see such materials, he would have faced them in your direction! When you've made your "quick inspection," take a few deep breaths and calm down.

HOW TO BE YOUR BEST SELF

A number of years ago I was asked to help an executive, then in his thirties, in his quest for a better job. In those days my help was limited strictly to resume counseling. After a couple of sessions, this executive developed what we both felt was a fine resume. Three months after our last session he called me. He was in trouble. His resume was apparently working, because he was getting in the doors of the companies he wrote to. But he hadn't had a single nibble. Not one offer in all this time. I suggested he drop by to discuss his problem. Without warning him in advance, I used our session to simulate a job-interview situation. At the end of our simulated interview, I stunned him by saying, "Based on the last forty-five minutes, I wouldn't hire you on a bet." I went on to explain that he struck me as unnecessarily antagonistic. He challenged virtually everything I said. I admired his perceptive mind. I admired his questioning stance. But he made such a negative impression on me that I found myself continually on the defensive. And if that's the kind of impression this executive made on others, he would have a difficult time ever getting a job.

The key question of the day was what could be done for this executive to help him overcome his problem. My suggestion was this: "For five minutes before you go into your next interview, program yourself to be your best self. Say to yourself, 'I'll give the interviewer the benefit of the doubt. I'll be more positive than I usually am. I'll question things just a little bit less than I normally do.'"

My suggested course of action was not designed to make over this executive. Not at all. It was intended to help him compensate for an obvious weakness, and in so doing reveal to his prospective boss his best self. I was sure that just thinking for five minutes about how negatively he came across would make him a little less abrasive during his interviews. Just being conscious of how he projected would make him just a tiny bit more sensitive to the effect of his questioning mind on the person who might become his boss.

Three days after our mock interview session, I received an ecstatic phone call from him. He told me that he had had two interviews with the same company in the two days after our meeting. During the second interview he was offered a job. He was unabashedly grateful, although when you think about it, all I did was act as a sounding board to help him know how he came across to his interviewers.

Now you might say that programming yourself to be a better interviewee is a hypocritical approach to take. You might well feel that if your prospective boss doesn't want you just the way you are, you really don't want to work for him anyhow. This alternative view is, I suppose, legitimate, but I don't subscribe to it. When you read an ad for a new product or service, it sells the good things this new item or service brings. It doesn't dwell on the things that are not so good. You'll find out the not-so-good things when you investigate further. It's a sure bet, though, that you won't investigate at all if the good points of the product don't intrigue you first. Programming yourself prior to an interview has a single purpose. It helps you show your best self to your prospective boss. It gets him intrigued enough to check your references. He'll learn your bad points then. Don't worry. But he won't check your references at all if the only things he remembers about you are your weaknesses.

Had the suggestion I made to this executive not resulted in success for him, I never would have made it again. The fact that he managed to land a job only two days after our discussion, following so many unsuccessful interviews, however, led me to investigate interview techniques further. I asked friends who had interviewed job candidates what mistakes were most commonly made by them. Then I began to simulate interviews with all the job-seekers who sought my counsel. I was anxious to see whether they too were making mistakes that could be corrected. This investigation led to three conclusions. A lot of good people were missing getting good jobs simply because they didn't present themselves in the most favorable light during their interviews. Most of them were unaware of the problems inherent in their interview style. Most, if not all, of the problems were correctable once they surfaced.

To help you sell your best self, try the following two-step program.

First, have someone help you identify your interview weaknesses. A friend of a friend whom you haven't previously met is the best person to help you do this. If the friend-of-a-friend is someone in your field so much the better. This objective third party is likely to provide the best appraisal of your personal selling techniques.

If you don't have an objective friend, there's another alternative. Frequently in your job-seeking campaign you'll receive letters from companies or executive recruiters who state:

> We don't have a job opening suited to your experience at this time. However, we would like to meet you so that we may know more of your background in the event an opportunity for which you are suited does become available.

If you have the opportunity to meet someone who doesn't have a job opening for you, you have a perfect chance to review with him what he really thinks of you. After the formal interview is over, say to him, "Since we're not talking about a specific opening at this time, may I ask a small favor of you? Would you give me a critique of my interview style? Let me know of any personal idiosyncrasies I might not be aware of. It could help me in future interviews."

This is a flattering opportunity to be helpful. Most executives will be more than willing to do this much to help you in your job search.

After you have identified any interview weaknesses you may have, you're ready for step two. I call it your "personal compensation plan." Five minutes before your next interview, think about what you can do to minimize your weaknesses. That's all. Just being conscious of the problem is enough to help you avoid it without changing the real you. Listed below are the more common negative impressions many interviewees make, and how you can minimize them.

1. You don't appear enthusiastic

Once when I was taking an interview I realized that I had done a strange thing. As the executive I was talking to described his company's plans for marketing a new product, I said, "Well, the first thing we might do, is . . ." The strange thing was that I was so wrapped up in my prospective boss's business problems that I suggested what *we* might do even though I was not a member of the firm. Afterward it struck me how enthusiastic I must have sounded. I resolved, from that point forth, to use the word "we" when referring to a prospective boss's problems that might become my own.

Given a choice between a person who is exceptionally bright but not particularly enthusiastic over the job I have to offer, and an individual almost as bright but tremendously excited about my company and the job opportunity, I'd be inclined to take the second person. Why? Because I know he'd give the job his utmost, while I'm less sure about the first candidate. If you are inherently enthusiastic, you've got a lot going for you. However, if enthusiasm is not your middle name, then you ought to do something about it. Not to change yourself, mind you, but to make your lack of physical enthusiasm less obvious. And, as I said before, it's simple. For five minutes, promise yourself to look bright-eyed and bushy-tailed, to reflect enthusiasm, to comment positively on what your prospective boss may be talking about. To use the word "we" when you have a chance. To be encouraged about the potential opportunity. Even if you're not sold on every last element of your prospective boss's plans, try not to sound skeptical. When you get the job, you will have a chance to change the elements that concern you. But if you make a big deal about the things that you don't enthusiastically endorse, you may never get an opportunity on the job to make the changes you'd like to make.

2. You overwhelm your prospective boss

A number of years ago when I was in brand management with a large firm, I interviewed a young man for a job in my department. He literally bounded into my office. He could barely restrain himself while I described the job to him. When he was given the chance to talk, he took off like a Boeing 747. His exploits were perilous. His solutions were a match for those of Jack Armstrong, all-American boy. He reminded me more of a high-school cheerleader than a businessman. I wondered how well he would fit into our group. How well he'd listen at meetings. How much of a team person he would be. All in all, he struck me so much as a junior superstar that I was afraid to hire him in case he overwhelmed the people with whom he'd be working. If you tend to overwhelm, five minutes before your next interview promise yourself that you will be a little more diffident, sell yourself a little less aggressively, listen a little more, and promote your cause with just a little less bravado.

3. You appear anxious, nervous

Anybody who isn't nervous at a job interview probably hasn't any brains at all. After all, you don't know the person you are about to meet. You only know that in the balance lies your opporutnity to get a better job. The problem is that if you *appear* overly nervous, your prospective employer may look on a calmer candidate as fitting in better with his organization. If you appear ill at ease, smoke cigarette after cigarette, tap your fingers on the desk or chair, play with a key chain, or show any other nervous sign, tell yourself to hide it in the next interview. Rest your hands on the arms of the chair firmly. Resolve to do without a cigarette until after the interview. Tell yourself: "You are ahead of the eighteen other people competing for this job because you know how to go after a better job in a professional way. You should be confident because you can and will get the job you want." In a word, five minutes before your next interview, tell yourself you know more about job-seeking than any of the candidates you compete with. And give 'em hell.

4. You appear over-relaxed, flip, or nonchalant

If you have a couple of job offers in the bag, you may tend to be pretty relaxed about interviews. You may come across so relaxed that you blow the one opportunity you want most. Whatever the reason, if you project as being too relaxed (to the point that you seem not to care), tell yourself five minutes before your next interview that your other job offers fell through and you've lost your current job to boot. With that to shock you, chances are you'll appear genuinely interested. And your prospective employer is more likely to be interested in you.

5. You talk too much, too little, too loudly, or too softly

Back in school I had to take a course in public speaking in which each of us gave a recorded speech. Afterward we listened to ourselves. One thing was obvious to me during that playback session. I spoke too fast. Even today, if I am not thinking about it, I speak too fast. Most of us don't notice our speech patterns unless we hear ourselves on a tape recorder. But a friend or business associate might. So ask one how you come across when you speak. Once you know if you have a speech weakness. remind yourself of it before your next interview. It should largely correct itself. While you're considering your speaking habit, you might also want to consider your propensity to dominate the conversation. Some people talk too much, others not enough. Once you know which side you err on, plan to do the opposite. You'll probably end up talking just the right amount.

This list of weaknesses is not meant to be all-encompassing, just to bring to mind the most common personality faults that I've bumped into. You may learn that yours are unusual as you run through practice interviews with friends and business associates. The important thing to remember is that, once you know your weaknesses, they can be corrected to a large degree by simply thinking about them. If you have several weaknesses, you might want to jot down a key word or two for each. There is no doubt that you could put all your weaknesses on a very small scrap of paper. Look at it in the reception room. Whatever you do, don't go to any lengths to change yourself. If you just note your weaknesses, they will change themselves for the better. And you'll be yourself—your best self.

Seven

Selling yourself in person— making initial interviews work harder for you

At the start of my classes in interview techniques, I always ask: "What's the key objective in any interview?" Invariably someone says: "To find out whether you're really interested in the job." Another: "To sell your background to the prospective employer." A third: "To give your interviewer a chance to see whether you'd fit in his organization." And then, at last, someone says: "To get a job offer." The critical objective of every interview is just this! And if you can't get the offer, you should at least try to secure the next best thing—another interview so you can try for the offer again, perhaps with someone else who is in a better position to say: "The job is yours." Don't misunderstand. These other objectives are worthwhile. But the *key* objective of any interview has to be to get yourself as close to the job offer as possible—*even one you can turn down!*

What strategy is most likely to get you an offer? From my experience, only one will do it—and that's to convince the interviewer that of all the candidates he's considering, *you're the most likely person to get done what he needs to get done.* Now it may well be that you're *not* the most "qualified" candidate; that someone with better skills is applying for the job. But if you do a better job *convincing* your prospective boss that you'll secure the results he's looking for, he has no choice but to pick you.

How you go about convincing an interviewer that you can do the job better when you may be only equal to other candidates (or even not quite as good) is what this chapter's all about. Over the years I've developed a plan that has helped thousands of job-seekers do just this. To make it work for you, however, you should consider future interviews in a way that you may not have thought of them in the past. Don't look at interviews as an hour spent with a prospective employer. Rather, think of them as an opportunity to achieve *four specific objectives*. And be aware, throughout your meeting, that your task is to achieve them one by one—knowing full well that you must concentrate on the first before you go on to the second, and so on. This objective-by-objective approach to interviews may seem strange to you at first. Once you've tried it, however, I think you'll see why it has been effective for so many successful candidates in the past.

Objective 1. Uncovering the real needs of your interviewer

The typical job-seeker tries to talk as much as possible about himself in the hour (or half-hour) allotted to him by an interviewer. A reasonable point of view, perhaps, since it could be his one and only opportunity to promote his cause in person. Unfortunately, this approach has left countless job-seekers frustrated and without offers saying: "What did I do wrong? I thought I'd really done so well in that interview." What these interviewees did wrong was very simple—they talked about themselves in ways that were *irrelevant* to the *needs* of the interviewers; they described experience and worthpoints that were meaningless in terms of the particular job they were applying for.

The secret of Objective 1 in your interview is to discover the real things your prospective boss is looking for—the things he feels must be done by the person he gives the job to; and also to discover the type of person he feels is necessary to get these things done. And it is imperative for you to uncover the needs of your prospective employer at the very start of your interview—before he gets you talking at length about yourself. "Great theory," you exclaim, "but will it work in practice?" *It can—only if you make it*. This is not easy, but if you keep Objective 1 clearly in mind as you approach the interview—and if you plan in advance to *control* the situation—you can do it.

Let's say, for example, that after the usual "good mornings," your interviewer comes right out and *asks you* to fill him in on the details of your background. What then? Aren't you forced to begin with: "Well, I graduated from college in 1955, and then I joined such and such company," and so on? Not really! You can just as easily summarize your experience in thirty seconds or so—even if you've been in business twenty years—and then redirect your interviewer back to your first objective. Suppose for a moment that you are in marketing; you could say, "Well, I've had twelve years of marketing management experience, ranging from assistant product manager to director of product marketing, which is what I've done the past two years." Then, *without stopping,* you could go on to say: "I can give you a whole lot of specifics in my background, but I'm sure that they'd be more relevant if I were more familiar with the job that needs to be done and the kind of person you'd like to have do it. Then I could zero in on the things you'd like to hear more about." After that, without a moment's pause, you could ask your interviewer to provide you with more details by saying something like: "Could you fill me in more about the job? The only things I know about it are what I saw in your ad" (or heard from the recruiter or employment agency, or whatever is the case).

Of course, not every interview you take will start off with your employer asking you to talk about your background. He could start by asking you any kind of question. The principle remains the same. Spend the least possible time giving him an answer, and get him back on the track of telling you about his needs—the kind of job to be done, and the kind of person needed to do it. Say, for example, he asks one of the toughest questions going—why you want to leave the company you are now with. You don't *have* to provide him with chapter and verse about what is the matter with your current situation. (Unfortunately most interviewees out of a pure heart, or a lack of understanding of strategy in interviewing, do just this.) What can you do instead of spelling out in detail the reasons you want to leave where you are now? Tell your interviewer first that you're really not sure you want to leave. Then tell him that a friend or executive recruiter (or whoever it was) called you and told you briefly about the job, and it sounded too good not to learn more about. Finally, *without a pause,* add: "So I'm here because I want to know more about the job. Could you tell me what needs to be done, and the kind of person you're looking to do it?"

No matter how your prospective boss starts the interview,

get him to talk about his needs *before* you reveal your experience in depth. If you don't discover the benchmark by which he's judging candidates at the beginning of your meeting, you may never develop the opportunity of finding out later on. And unless you know his needs well, your description of your experience may be far afield—may emphasize things of little interest to him and gloss over the things he's hoping he might hear. Don't think for a moment that controlling your interview toward achievement of your first objective will be easy. It takes practice to answer naturally and briefly and then to move directly into the critical question about the prospective employer's job opening.

To improve your ability to control future interviews, review your previous ones. Determine if there is any one question that seems to come up at the start fairly often. Then practice your answer on a tape recorder. Listen to yourself to see if your answer is short and to the point, and don't delay for a second in asking your interviewer to tell you more about the position he wants filled.

Once you've got your interviewer talking, the next challenge is to keep him talking. *Open-ended* questions like "Can you tell me more about that?" or "Why is that particular need so important to you?" are your best bet. As a rule of thumb, keep probing until you draw out *three* key needs or qualities your prospective boss is seeking to fill in hiring someone.

Why three? Because most people have a tendency after they get the interviewer talking to want to chime in as soon as they've uncovered one of the things the interviewer is looking for in his ideal candidate. Resist this temptation! The first need an interviewer reveals may not be the most important one. If you fall prey to temptation and start talking about your background as it relates to the first need the interviewer mentions, you may not get the opportunity later on to uncover other important ones. However, if you can get your prospective boss to talk about three types of experience he seeks, or about three qualities he is looking for in the person he hires, chances are he's zeroed in on the one that's uppermost in mind.

How do you get him to go from one need to the next? Or to move from one personal quality to another? Simple! *Summarize each and urge him to carry on.* It doesn't take a whole lot of words to do this, but it can keep your prospective boss going until you uncover the real needs that he wants to fill. For example, an office-manager candidate might say to his prospective boss: "So the ability to manage a lot of diverse people is important. Is there any other personal quality that's also a must?"

How long should you let the interviewer keep talking? When should you take over and start telling him about yourself? As long as your interviewer is carrying on an animated description of problems and needs, don't stop him! In fact, encourage him! Keep up your open-ended questions until you feel you fully understand the needs area your interviewer is concerned about. Then move on. A candidate I know spoke with a potential employer from eight one Saturday morning until two in the afternoon. During that entire time the employer dominated the conversation, describing the manufacturing problems his company faced. Finally, the candidate asked to take over because he only had an hour left before his plane was to take off. When he took over he knew *precisely* what to talk about. He summarized his experiences and discussed worthpoints that showed his prospective boss he could handle similar manufacturing problems. Obviously, if any interviewer is willing to discuss his problems *in depth*, he must consider you a serious candidate for the position. It wouldn't make sense for him to go on at length with someone he wasn't interested in. In the instance described above the job-seeker was hired as vice-president of manufacturing.

And what if your prospective boss identifies three needs and you can only fill two of them? Probe until you discover a fourth one. When you run into this situation, *don't summarize a need you can't fill* prior to asking for another. No need to reinforce something that you are weak in for your interviewer!

Objective 2. Relate yourself to your prospective boss's needs

When you've uncovered three needs your interviewer feels are critical to successfully tackling the job you're applying for—three needs you are confident you can meet—you're ready to try to achieve the second major objective of your interview. Objective 2, very simply, is to convince the person you are meeting with that you are the candidate who can resolve the problems he wants resolved because your background and experience are appropriate to such problems, and because in point of fact, you've solved problems in the past very much like the ones your interviewer is facing now.

How do you go about relating your experience to the needs you've uncovered? Again, it's a matter of control. When your interviewer has finished telling you about the third need he has, chime in. Summarize all three needs for him. Then, without a fraction of a second's pause, *ask* for the chance to talk about yourself. It shouldn't take a whole lot of effort to convince your prospective boss to let you take over. Say you've played back three key problems to him; you could easily add: "With the thorough grounding you've given me, maybe this would be a good time to start telling you a little more about me." If your interviewer feels he's covered the key facts about the job he wants done, why shouldn't he let you take over?

The moment you do, you're on the way to achieving Objective 2. If possible, categorize your jobs, your assignments, your experiences—and talk about them in the context of one of the problems your prospective boss has presented to you. Then talk about those jobs and assignments you've had that are relevant to the second problem your prospective boss has raised. And so on.

Unfortunately, it's not often possible to organize your experience by needs areas. That's particularly the case when your interviewer specifically asks you to talk about yourself in the more formal, traditional chronological format. (He says to you, for example: "Start at the beginning and bring me up to date.") How, then, can you talk about your background and still prove that you can meet your prospective boss's needs? By emphasizing the jobs and assignments you've had that are *relevant*. No one says you must spend the same amount of time discussing each job in your career. So spend the bulk of the time allotted to Objective 2 discussing in depth only those positions in which you have faced problems similar to the ones your possible future employer has identified as important to him. And in each case, offer specific examples that demonstrate you have both the experience and ability your prospective boss is seeking in the ideal candidate. As a corollary, when you are reviewing a portion of your career that is not particularly relevant to your interviewer's needs, summarize it in a sentence or two. As long as you don't leave out a part of your life, you're responding to his request.

What's the best way to get across to your prospective boss that a particular experience you've had is, indeed, relevant to the needs you have uncovered in the position you are applying for? Over the years, I've concluded that the most effective format for getting your worthpoints across in an interview is to start off by saying: "One of the problem areas you've indicated is important to you is similar to a problem I once faced." Then:

□ STATE THE PROBLEM   Relate the situation you faced that parallels one your prospective boss now faces—simply, briefly and concretely. Include the company, location, date, and how the problem occurred, if necessary. This description adds authenticity to your presentation right at the start. And it makes the worthpoint you are describing sound like a *relevant third-person story*, rather than a boastful statement of how good you are.

□ INTRODUCE YOUR SPECIFIC SOLUTION TO THE PROBLEM MATTER-OF-FACTLY   Don't sound as if you are proud of yourself. Simply state the facts. Tell what you did and, if it's pertinent, how you did it. Describe your contribution as though you were a third party telling the story. And don't explain how you analyzed the problem. Only what conclusion you came to and the action you took. Don't say that some others in your company were dummies because they wanted to do something else. No need to knock your management or your peers. Stating positively what you did is enough.

□ REVEAL THE RESULT (OR RESULTS) OF YOUR ACTION CONCRETELY   Make the good news the climax of your true story. The more specific you are, the more believable and memorable your worthpoint will be. Avoid nebulous conclusions like: "I was a great success." State the precise dollars you saved, or the percentage of growth you achieved, etc.

While I suggest you be as specific as possible in telling your prospective boss about those experiences you've had that parallel his current needs, one word of caution: be sure you are direct and clear in your presentation; that you don't make your worthpoint more complex or detailed than it needs to be. Or you'll definitely tune out your interviewer.

How can you find out if the way you present your worthpoints is clear, concise and to the point? *Practice describing the best of your worthpoints in advance.* You can be certain that the ones you think are most important to you will probably be important to your prospective boss as well. And the best way to be sure you describe them right is to rehearse them out loud. As with your probing questions, tape them if possible. Listen to them a day or so later to see if you understand your own worthpoint. And time yourself. See if you could say the same thing in less time, and still make it cogent to your listener. Be critical. Ask yourself if you came to the point of your story soon enough.

If you get a chance, describe your worthpoints to a friend or a member of your family. Get their reaction. Are you coming across *clearly* and *quickly* enough to keep the conversation going? Make sure you don't sound as if you're bragging. Tell what happened without glowing adjectives about yourself. Let your interviewer draw conclusions as to your worth rather than you summarizing a worthpoint for him with something as self-serving as: "So you see I really have a lot of valuable experience in this area." If your experience is clearly outlined, your interviewer will feel you've solved problems like his before, and that you can solve them again for him!

One final thought on achieving Objective 2. Categorize all your worthpoints *before* your very first interview. One of your experiences may demonstrate a variety of personal qualities or capabilities if you emphasize a certain aspect of it. (The same worthpoint, for example, may show your profit orientation, ability to work under pressure, ability to come up with creative solutions, ability to recognize problems, etc.) Know *in advance* the full potential of each worthpoint in your arsenal, and know how to adapt it to your present situation.

Objective 3. Holding your own under cross-examination

For many job-seekers this is the toughest to achieve. It's that part of your interview in which your prospective boss challenges the relevance of your experience, asks potentially threatening questions, and pursues your weak points—the very things you were trying to avoid bringing up at all. No one will say that achieving Objective 3 isn't tough, but you can make it a whole lot easier if you follow these suggestions:

☐ DON'T FREEZE UP WHEN THE CHALLENGES COME   It's a totally natural thing for your prospective boss to probe your experience for potential problems. Let's face it, when you buy a new car or a new home, you'll want to ask questions to make sure that your investment is a good one. Like it or not, you are a "big ticket" item that your prospective boss will have to make a major investment in. So it's not at all unreasonable if your interviewer wants to reassure himself that the picture you've painted about yourself is accurate; that you haven't left off anything about yourself that would alter his assessment of you. Keep in mind that when your prospective boss agreed to an interview with you, he must have been impressed with your background. Either your resume or cover letter sold him on you, or the employment agent or executive recruiter recommended you highly. Whatever the reason, your prospective boss must have thought well of you before you met, or he wouldn't have wasted his time getting together with you in the first place. So don't feel that the tough questions are to discredit you. Not at all. They're simply to help your prospective boss reassure himself that he's making the right decision.

☐ AVOID A CROSS-EXAMINATION AT THE BEGINNING OF YOUR INTERVIEW   Challenging questions at the start of your hour with your prospective boss can be disastrous. The cross-examination is the part of any interview in which you are obviously under the greatest stress. And for this reason, you just might not come across as your best self. It's far better therefore, to establish a rapport with your interviewer before the third degree comes. Fortunately, if you consider your interviews as a series of objectives and make it your business to overcome Objectives 1 and 2 first, you and your prospective boss can develop a positive ground before you have to tackle any tough questions. If you can get your interviewer talking about his problems at the start, there's no reason for challenges to your experience at this point in the interview. Similarly, when you review your experience in the context of its relevance to the problems your prospective employer faces, he should be totally receptive to what it can do for him! So by tackling Objectives 1 and 2 when the challenges come you can talk about your potential weaknesses from the position of strength established earlier in your interview.

☐ STAY CALM, KEEP POSITIVE—EVEN IF IT HURTS Some interviews could raise the hackles of a Nobel Peace Prize winner. They ask their challenging questions in such a way as to bring you to a boil. Don't fall prey to this tactic. Stay cool. Remember that the cross-examination is the one portion of your interview that is most similar to what a meeting would be like between you and your prospective boss should you join his company. If you become defensive—even if it would be reasonable to do so—it could keep you from getting the job. If you tense up because someone questions your credibility on some point, your prospective boss is likely to think that you'd tense up under similar conditions if you got the job. On the other hand, if you take tough questions in stride—see them simply as an opportunity for your prospective employer to confirm that you are as "buttoned up" as you have appeared to be earlier in your interview—and handle challenges matter-of-factly, your interviewer has to say to himself: "This person would be easy to work with even if the going gets rough."

☐ KEEP THE CROSS-EXAMINATION THE SHORTEST PART OF YOUR INTERVIEW The longer you dwell on your interviewer's doubts, the more he'll remember them. If you spend ten minutes of a one-hour meeting validating your interviewer's concerns about you, that's one-sixth of the total time. But if you let the challenges drag on for thirty minutes, you've spent half your time with your prospective boss defending yourself. At this point, you're probably saying to yourself that keeping the time spent on cross-examination short is not easily done. You're right. But it can be done.

As in handling Objectives 1 and 2, the secret is in control. If you answer an interviewer's probing question and then sit back, you give him a chance to keep on digging. Why should he switch to other, potentially less dangerous topics when he's latched on to one that obviously concerns him? If, on the other hand, when you've finished answering your interviewer's tough questions, you *immediately* ask him a question or take up a topic concerned with his already expressed needs, you have a chance to redirect the conversation naturally to a more positive area. Let's say, for example, that your prospective boss challenges your background because the job he has to fill requires someone who can manage three hundred people, and in your present job you've only managed fifty. You could say that for you, the key to managing fifty people is delegation of responsibility and that if you managed three hundred people, you'd probably add one more layer of delegation. Then you could sit back thinking to yourself that you've answered his question well. On the other hand, you could offer the identical answer, and then, without a moment's hesitation, redirect the interviewer's thinking to a needs area alluded to earlier, by asking him to discuss it in depth, or by relating a worthpoint that is appropriate to it. Keep in mind that in conversation, one question naturally leads to another. You're entitled to ask yours once you've answered your interviewer's. One caution: be sure that the question or topic you raise leads to a discussion that is on safer ground. Don't ask questions that could keep the challenge going.

At this point you might ask: What if your interviewer answers your redirect question and then returns to the discussion of your weakness? That, unfortunately, is his prerogative! But it's also yours to try to move him away to a safer topic with another question after answering his. Never deny your interviewer a short, nondefensive, honest answer to his question. But don't wait like a sitting duck for him to probe further into an area when you've given him your best answer. That's tempting fate!

☐ NEVER CHALLENGE YOUR PROSPECTIVE BOSS'S CHALLENGE   After an interviewer has raised a question about your background, the worst thing you can do is to tell him point-blank that his concern isn't justified. You're in effect telling him he's stupid for having brought up his question. And there's no need to do this even if the prospective boss's concern isn't the least bit legitimate. Instead, why not tell your interviewer that you can understand why he might have asked the question that he raised. Show him that you appreciate his intelligence by letting him know his question is reasonable, even if it's not a legitimate question in your case. How easy it is to say, "I can see why you might have raised this question," just before you offer your answer to it. When you do, your prospective boss must think to himself that you are a reasonable person, if nothing else.

☐ AVOID "BUTS" AND "HOWEVERS" WHENEVER POSSIBLE In the thousands of practice interviews I've conducted with clients, I usually throw in a challenging question just to see what kind of response I get. Ninety-five times out a hundred my clients answer by saying something like: "I know I've only had three years experience and you said you required a minimum of five. *But* that's not a problem. You see, etc. etc. etc." The moment you use the word "but," you're automatically picking a fight. It's a word that says "what you just said is wrong." How can you avoid "buts" in your answers (or "howevers," which are almost as bad)? Listening back to a tape of a practice interview a number of years ago I discovered an answer. Say nothing. *Pause in place of "but"* and go right on to answering the challenge your interviewer raises. For example, your prospective boss might say he's a little disappointed that you haven't got an MBA. Why not respond to him like this. "True" *(Pause)* "Right now I manage five people who do have MBA's. That hasn't been a problem." In pausing, you eliminate the need for a "but." And you avoid calling your interviewer's attention to the fact that you've just disagreed with him.

☐ KEEP YOUR RESPONSES TO INDIVIDUAL QUESTIONS SHORT, PLAUSIBLE, AND POSITIVE For some reason or other, when job-seekers find their backgrounds or abilities challenged, they feel that the best response is to offer every possible explanation of why the challenge isn't important. I've heard answers that include five and six explanations of why a particular weakness is in fact no weakness at all. The result is a five- or ten-minute answer when a thirty-second answer would have done just as well, if not better. When you bring out all the cannons to shoot down a question your prospective boss has raised about your background, you are declaring the challenge is all-out war. Had you given a simple, direct answer you'd have kept the challenge a simple skirmish, and have been done with it. Keep in mind that your goal in Objective 3 is to provide reassurance that the challenge raised isn't so important that it could offset what you've proved in 1 and 2—that you have the experience to answer the needs your prospective boss has in filling the position he's now hiring for. As a rule of thumb, try to keep your responses to difficult questions to one, two, or three sentences. If you go on beyond that, chances are you're going into more detail than was called for, and you're probably raising more questions in your interviewer's mind than you need to. What if you have three or four explanations for a particular weakness in your background? Shouldn't you give all the reasons, if you have them? Why bother? If your potential boss is seeking to reassure himself about you, why not just offer the single, strongest, most plausible explanation and leave it at that. As long as you set your prospective employer's mind at ease, you've overcome the hurdle. As a case in point, the answer that the non-MBA candidate gave earlier—"Right now I manage five people who do have MBA's. That hasn't been a problem"—is short, to the point, plausible. Even if he had five other answers to the challenge, he couldn't have done better than use the one-sentence response shown above. But don't take my word for it. Try a short, direct, plausible response the next time your experience is challenged. I think you'll be delighted because it works!

Objective 4. Going after what you came for

At the start of this chapter, I suggested that your real goal in any interview is to get yourself as close to a job offer as is possible. Your final objective, therefore, in every interview you take is to get your prospective boss to take action that will do just this. Obviously, if you are meeting with a possible employer for the first time, you can't really expect him to make you a formal job offer. But there's no reason on earth why you can't expect an invitation back for a second interview with one of your interviewer's associates if you've done well with objectives 1 through 3. Similarly, if you've had several interviews and you've handled the situations well in each, there's no reason not to anticipate a job offer. Your final objective in "early" interviews, then, is to walk away with an appointment to see the next person up the line. Your final objective after a number of interviews is only slightly different: to get your prospective boss to decide on you, and ask you aboard.

It wouldn't surprise me in the least if this is the point where you want to bow out. You may think the first three objectives are totally reasonable, and you're planning to think of your next interview in terms of them, but you may be getting cold feet as you think of persuading your prospective boss to grant you another interview. A story about Henry

Ford comes to mind whenever a client of mine winces at the thought of directing his interviewer to invite him back. It seems that Ford was paired up with an insurance company executive at his local golf club tourney. During their play around the links, the insurance executive blurted out: "Henry, we've been members of this same club for years and have played together on many occasions. We're good friends, in fact. Why is it you don't buy your insurance from me?" Henry Ford replied: "You never asked for my business." The fact is ninety-five out of one hundred job-seekers wouldn't think to try to set up an appointment for a further interview—feel it would be presumptuous to do so. But if you handle it correctly, it's the logical conclusion to any interview. So why not try?

How do you bridge the gap from Objective 3 to 4? Again, control is the answer. If your prospective boss has asked you a couple of questions to reassure himself, as you respond to the third or fourth such challenge, you might immediately ask him a question that leads directly into a discussion of your next interview. That question is *"Whom* will I be meeting next if I'm one of the finalists for this job?" Your first step is to find out the name of the next person up the line. Fortunately, you don't have to ask this question out of the blue. You can use any bridge to it that you feel comfortable with, like "Mr. Interviewer, from my point of view this position is just what I've been looking for, and if I've judged our meeting right thus far, I think you feel I have the sort of background you're looking for. If this is the case, *whom* would I be meeting next if I'm considered further for the job?" Try creating an approach to the "who" question that you are comfortable with, and memorize it word for word. This is a critical question and you have to ask it right. One other thought about the "who" question: you don't have to leave it for the cross-examination. If you think things have gone extremely well in reaching Objectives 1 and 2, there's nothing to stop you from asking it at the end of Objective 2. Usually a prospective employer will have questions unresolved in his mind and will want to take you into the cross fire, but if you feel the timing is right, you can proceed to your "who" question earlier in some cases.

What kind of reaction can you expect when you ask your "who" question? Probably your interviewer will be surprised, since he probably wasn't expecting it. But undoubtedly he has the name of some executive in mind whom you would meet during the interviewing process, and it shouldn't be all that difficult for him to come up with a name. Will your interviewer be put off because you asked for a name? Those who've tried the "who" approach are pleasantly surprised to find that most interviewers think it's a reasonable question, which doesn't faze them at all—even if they hadn't really planned to tell you the individual's name at your meeting! Certainly asking the "who" question won't eliminate you from consideration if you've done well with Objectives 1, 2, and 3. So it's worth taking your interviewer this far in achieving Objective 4.

The "who" question by itself isn't likely to get an appointment for a next interview. Your next goal is to get the answer to the "when" question. At this point you want to know what's the most likely date to meet the person whose name you've just discovered. The best way to ask this question is by making an assumption—that in fact you will be meeting with this person—and by saying something like this: *"Will* I be meeting with Mr. X during the next week or ten days?" No doubt you'll have to gird your loins to ask this because the question is based on a presumption—that you have *sold* yourself to your current interviewer and you are indeed one of the candidates who will be invited back. Some of the people I've coached shudder at this question and ask instead: *"Would* I be meeting with Mr. X during the next week if I'm considered further?" Asking the question this way may get them off the hook, but it's not quite as effective as assuming you are already among the finalists. That's because if your interviewer answers your *"Will* I be meeting Mr. X in the next few days?" question, he is actually committing himself (perhaps unconsciously) to arranging an appointment for you to meet with the next person up the line. You need no longer worry whether you're going to be considered for additional interviews. You're ready for the third step in getting your next interview. Now your goal is to pin down the precise time it will take place.

To get yourself in Mr. X's appointment book, you've got to ask a "what" question at this point. The best way to ask your "what" question is to ask it, and without stopping, offer several reasonable alternative answers, any one of which works to get you what you came for. Consider this example: "What's the best way to set up an interview with Mr. X?

Could your secretary do it today so we can pin it down? Or do you think it's better if I call Mr. X's secretary directly?" Either way, you're going to get your next interview. If you've taken assertiveness training, chances are you'll see this line of questioning as most reasonable. But if you haven't, let me ask you to consider two facts that might persuade you how logical it is to ask the "who," "when," and "what" questions.

First, when you do this, you do what any professional sales person would do. You make it easy for your "customer" to buy. Instead of asking your interviewer *if* he wants someone else in your company to meet with you to discuss the position further, you ask much easier questions. Asking the interviewer to tell you whom you might be meeting with, and the time frame in which the meeting will take place, is a lot less difficult for your interviewer to answer than if you ask him point-blank if he wants such a meeting to take place at all! Ask any salesman and he'll tell that asking a customer *if* he wants to buy what he's selling is a lot tougher than asking the customer when he'd like it shipped, or how he'd like delivery made.

Second, you've achieved what you came for. You've got your next interview written down in your appointment book. You've put yourself closer to the job you seek. Keep in mind that your interviewer will probably meet a dozen candidates who are qualified enough to get in the door. It stands to reason that he won't be setting up additional interviews for all of them. You have put yourself closer to a job offer than the vast majority of your competition. And that's what it's all about.

When you've had three or four interviews with a company, setting up another interview is no longer enough—it's time your prospective employer made you a job offer. How can you direct your interviewer to do this? Again, control is the answer. Usually, by the time you've had two or three interviews, the cross-fire part of your meeting is pretty casual. The tough questions are behind you, or you wouldn't have been invited back again and again. Still, whoever interviews you may have some questions on his mind and you may feel yourself drawn into cross-examination in this interview, as well. If you are, control is again the answer. After you've finished answering any Objective-3 question, simply, directly, and in the fewest words possible, be prepared to ask a leading question of your own that will persuade your prospective boss to make you a job offer.

If you are in an enviable position of having another job offer in your pocket, a variation of the "when" question is in order. You might ask your interviewer, for example, when he thinks his firm will be able to make a decision concerning you since you do have a concrete offer from another firm and find yourself on the horns of a dilemma. There's nothing wrong with assuming control and saying, "I've got a problem," Mr. X. You see, I have an offer from the ABC company, and they're pressing for an answer from me. In all candor, I'm much more keen on the job with your company. That's why I was wondering if you might be able to reach your decision concerning me within the next two or three days. What do you think?" When you do this, you are putting pressure on your prospective boss, no doubt. But the competition should work in your favor. The fact that you are in demand should make you that much more desirable. If it turns out that you are not as well regarded by your interviewer as you thought, and if he lets you know that a decision won't be made for weeks or months, knowing this could help you make the right decision concerning the other company. On the other hand, you may just find that asking this when question speeds up the selection process and gets you the job you want sooner.

If you aren't lucky enough to have another job offer in your pocket, there's still a question that you might ask, during your third or fourth interview, which could result in a job offer. After you've answered some question, without hesitation, ask this one: "When can I start?"

On the surface this may seem extraordinarily presumptuous. And yet, if you ask the question with an enthusiasm that shows your genuine interest in the job, your prospective boss should not react negatively. If you say, for example: "Mr. X., I'm excited about this job opportunity! When can I start!" your interviewer should see by that question that you are caught up in the excitement, the opportunity, the challenge that the job has to offer, and he should be flattered by it. Even if your prospective employer isn't quite ready to ask you to join his firm, the question shouldn't create a difficult confrontation. It's easy for your possible new boss to answer your question without feeling put upon. He might say, for example: "Well, we haven't really thought about who our finalist will be. We're still interviewing several good people. So I can't tell you when you could start just at this time . . . if you're the one whom we finally select." On the other hand, if your prospective boss is genuinely interested in you, and you ask a question like "When can I start!" there's a good likelihood he'll say to you, "When could you join us?" In a word, you can help him to bypass the question of whether it's you he wants, and go on the easier question of the date you'll be ready to begin work.

Often, in third and fourth interviews, the person meeting with you has been sold on you by those who interviewed you earlier on. This interviewer will make the final decision—but unless you do very badly during Objectives 1 and 2 of this interview, you're probably going to get the offer you seek. In situations like this, when it comes time for Objective 3, it's not there. Instead, your interviewer asks you if you have any questions you'd like to ask him. If this happens, you're home free. If you say: "Just one, when can I start!!", your prospective boss might be nonplussed for a moment. But he's likely to think that not only do others in his own organization have high regard for you, but you have a high regard for his organization. He's likely to answer: "As soon as you can!!"

As with the case of directing your prospective employer to grant you a second interview, some of you will have great hesitation about directing your prospective employer to make you a job offer. If you are truly concerned about the "When-can-I-start?" question, keep in mind the telling parallel that I alluded to before. The smart salesman never asks for the order point-blank. He asks easy questions that assume the order has already been made. And asking when you can start is just such a question.

If the "when" question is just not your style, there is a "what" question that you might also want to consider in your third or fourth interview. If reaching Objective 3 is a breeze—as it should be by this time—seize an opportunity to say something like this: "Mr. X, I'm convinced this is the company I want to go to work for. What more can I do to convince you and your associates that I'm the person for the job?" This question could lead your prospective boss to give you a special written assignment to "convince him" in one or more areas where he's not convinced you're the right person. But after three or four interviews he probably knows enough about you not to do this. It's more likely your prospective boss will say to himself, "I really need no further convincing. This person is the right one for the job." In which case you're likely to get a job offer.

Will the techniques I've described work for you? If the experience of other job seekers is any indication, there's no doubt that they will. Of all the tools offered in this book, none yields more favorable comments than uncovering prospects' needs before revealing your experience, matching your experience to these needs, avoiding confrontations over interviewer doubts, and using the last part of your interview specifically to secure additional interviews. But in all fairness, I should point out that exercising control in an interview is not easy for most job seekers. At each of my classes on interviewing, I invite some of the participants to take practice interviews with me. Despite the fact that they have just finished listening to a discussion of the same ideas this chapter takes up, invariably one (or even two) of the participants blows it. They allow me, the interviewer, to convince them to talk about themselves before they know what it is that I'm looking for, and so they go on at length about things I'm not interested in! On the other hand, the participants who are interviewed later in the class catch on to the earlier interviewee's errors and uncover and match needs brilliantly! The biggest failing of most practice interviewees is in *not* going after a follow-up interview. Why don't they do so? Some, because they get cold feet about asking who and when. But more often than not, it's because they forget to ask! How about you? You can learn to apply these techniques, of course. But to make them work, you have to practice them until they are second nature to you. When they are, you'll find you'll never go back to ordinary nondirected interviewing again.

Eight

Good answers for good questions

Some interviews are more difficult than others. In large measure, the degree of difficulty depends on the questions your prospective boss asks you. Some questions are genuinely tough. Tough enough to upset you and develop a sense of strain between yourself and your interviewer. This chapter deals with ten of these questions that seem to come up fairly frequently. The answers given here aren't necessarily the only ones. But they work. They've been tried. They can make what could be a difficult moment during an interview a whole lot easier on you. A word of caution in providing these answers. Put them in your own words. Understand the basic idea behind each, but don't memorize the answers. Let them be yours.

1. Why do you want to leave your current affiliation?

There are several good answers to this question. The first and most obvious is "I want to earn more money." No one ever knocked this answer. For most people, leaving their current affiliation will net them more than they could make in their next raise. Typically, the company that hires you away will pay 20 percent more than you are making to obtain your talents. In contrast, at your own company you can count on an annual raise of between 6 and 8 percent. Of course, some executives use outside job offers as leverage to get more money from their present employers, but most of us will earn 6 to 8 percent more each year where we work.

The second, and equally good, answer to the question of

why you want to leave is: "Because I've ceased to learn. I'm looking for a job where I can grow as well as contribute." This answer is in no way intended to knock your current employer. You're *strongly* advised never to do so. It simply means this: you're the kind of person who wants to learn while he works, and you've mastered the job at your present company to the point that it's too easy for you. You're seeking a greater challenge than is available in your current job.

A third answer to the "why-do-you-want-to-leave" question is: "My present company's growth hasn't been as fast as my personal growth. So there are fewer chances for promotion within than are required to fulfill my personal ambitions." This answer has two virtues. It suggests that you are personally ambitious. It suggests too that, were the company you are now with to grow faster, you would succeed and you would be promoted. It becomes a question of the timing being wrong.

The simplest of the three above answers is "I want to earn more money." If you can use this answer, it's probably your best bet. The other two will get you by, however. Whatever you say, don't tell your prospective boss that you want to leave because your current company is no damned good. Why? If you feel your present company is no damned good, what will you feel like after a few years with the company you are now interviewing? Your prospective boss may well get the idea that you are not satisfied for very long, and that his company will be next on your blacklist.

2. What are your growth prospects at your present company?

If you answer this question quickly, without giving it enough thought, you may come out with an answer that could hurt your chances of landing a job. If, for example, you answer, "Not too good. I'm boxed in; that's why I'm looking for a new job at this time," you'd be falling into a trap. An answer like this must make your interviewer think that you're not the best at your company. Otherwise you'd know how to get out of the box! What you want to do is convince your prospective boss that you're leaving in spite of the fact that you are the best person at your present company. There are several things you might say to put the situation to your advantage. For example:

In the long run I think my chances are excellent. It largely depends on how soon my boss is promoted. His boss has been with the company twenty years and has another seven to go before he retires. So I'd have to wait quite a long time for my boss to move up. I don't know if I'm quite ready to wait it out. I know I have the opportunity to move up. It's a question of timing.

Or, you might say:

The fact is I'm in line for a promotion. The real problem lies in our company's growth. When I joined, it was growing much faster than it is today. The way it now looks, all of us will have to wait some time for the company to grow enough to justify any new senior positions. So my chances look good if we can get the company going again. But I don't know if I'm willing to wait. It's just a matter of timing.

In these examples, the candidates described themselves as people ready to be promoted, or capable of being promoted, but unable to get a promotion when they wanted because of circumstances beyond their control. If your prospective boss thinks your chances are good at your present company, he will be more inclined to think your chances are good at your next company. And he'll be more inclined to hire you.

3. What are your greatest strengths?

For some people this is an easy question. They know precisely their strengths and have examples at their fingertips to support each. But for many interviewees the question comes as a bit of a shock. And they seem flustered for a few moments while they collect their thoughts. It would be presumptuous of anyone to tell you your own greatest strengths. Only you know them. But there are a few strengths that, if they are yours, are worth mentioning. Why? Because they are the most wanted strengths in the business world.

☐ INTELLIGENCE   Some people call it intellect. Some say they're smart enough to handle the situation. Others prefer, "I have enough brains." Businesses need intelligent people— intelligent enough to know they have brains—and brains enough to let prospective bosses know this fact when they are asked.

☐ COMMON SENSE   While there's no doubt you have to be

smart to succeed in business, not every intelligent person does succeed. Why? Because some people don't use their brains well. Common sense is the ability to nose out the core problem and to tackle it, to avoid the peripheral aspects of the business, to go right to the heart of the matter. If you have this ability, your prospective boss should know about it.

☐ DRIVE Or the ability to work long and hard, not only when the chips are down, but as a general rule. Some people become so involved with their professions that they think about them twenty-four hours a day. If you're the sort of person who can't leave the office at the office, let your prospective boss know. You are worth two people who quit thinking at five.

☐ MATURITY Two things stand out as examples of maturity: first, the ability to establish work priorities, to know where to place your effort when all of a sudden many things must be done at once; second, the ability to assess not only business problems but the relationship of people to these business problems. It's an asset to recognize how those with whom you work react to their problems and to one another.

☐ AN ABILITY TO DEAL WITH PEOPLE The smartest people are not necessarily the most successful people. The ability to relate to people, to encourage people, and to need people can sometimes overcome brains and common sense. If you have a natural talent in this area, let your prospective boss know.

☐ KNOWLEDGEABILTY Obviously, prospective bosses look for people with industry experience similar to that of their own business. At the very least, they expect to hire someone with functional experience that reasonably matches the demands of the job to be filled. They know it is easier to train a person who already knows their business. If you and your competition have almost equal knowledge, however, then your other strengths—brains, maturity, etc.—will be much more important than your knowledge.

In highlighting the most wanted strengths, again a caution: Flaunt them only if you have them. Do not mention them just because they're listed here. And be prepared to back up all your strengths with worthpoints that support the assessment of your strong points.

4. What do you consider to be your greatest weaknesses?

This is one of the toughest questions faced by job interviewees, and particularly if you're unprepared for it. Yet it is a question that does come up, and you should have an answer that helps to sell you. Typically, unprepared job candidates answer this question in a way that hurts their chances. For example, a job-seeker might say, "I'm not good with figures." Or, "I sometimes have difficulty with people." Or, "Sometimes I tense up under pressure." Each of these answers makes you look less desirable in the eyes of your prospective boss. So the secret of answering this question is to find negative traits your boss would like you to have. Here are some "positive weaknesses" that you can talk about—if you have them. They cannot be faked.

☐ IMPATIENCE   Impatience with other people. Impatience with yourself. Impatience to get the job done. There's no question that impatience is a weakness. But it's a great one to have. You're impatient with other people because they don't get their part of the job done in time. Putting it another way, you want to see the whole job done when it's due. You're impatient with yourself because you're not growing fast enough. Putting it another way, you are ambitious. You want to grow in knowledgeability and in maturity. What boss could be disappointed with a person who is striving to improve himself? You're impatient to see the job done. Loosely translated, you have a sense of urgency about your job, a sense of concern about moving the corporation ahead. A fault your prospective boss by all rights should admire.

☐ OVERDRIVE   This weakness is closely related to impatience. Perhaps one leads to the other. You drive yourself hard, perhaps overly hard. Your spouse tells you you don't know when to stop. Sometimes you drive others the way you drive yourself. You push yourself to the extent of your own capacity, and sometimes even more. While overdrive is a fault, particularly when your own overdrive leads to pushing others, it is certainly an admirable fault. Why? Because it can only lead to moving the business ahead. What boss wouldn't like a person working for him who does the work of two, because he drives himself so hard?

☐ TENDENCY TO OVERVIEW   Given a choice, you prefer to try to put all the pieces together, rather than to look at any particular piece. You prefer an assignment involving a broad analysis of a problem, rather than detailed administrative duties. This is a most acceptable weakness, since it makes you a prime candidate for a leadership position with your prospective company. Most top-echelon executives do seek out the big picture and leave minutiae to smaller minds. Even if overviewing is a fault of yours, don't say you can't handle details, because even when you get to the top, you have to handle some details—just different ones. Rather, tell your boss you prefer to consider big concepts rather than minute specifics.

☐ YOU'RE HARD TO PLEASE The status quo doesn't necessarily satisfy you. You sometimes question the world about you. You don't satisfy as easily as the next person. While no one likes a totally negative employee, you'll probably agree that the person who challenges what is going on about him is better than the person who accepts everything blindly and without question. Because the executive who sees what's wrong has the opportunity to correct and amend it. The person who doesn't consider the alternatives can make no changes at all. Don't be afraid to say that you are hard to please. Most top executives are. Probably your prospective boss is, too.

☐ STUBBORNNESS WHEN YOU'RE RIGHT There are no two ways about it. When you have the facts, you stick to your guns. You don't give in. This doesn't make you the most popular person on campus, but you don't mind running the risk of upsetting a few people. It's a lot easier to say "Yes." People like it better, and life is simpler. But you prefer to make your life a little more difficult when you are convinced you have the facts on your side. You will give in. But you don't like to let go until you're absolutely sure that the alternative is more correct than your own idea. Stubbornness is a genuinely undesirable trait, since others may resent it. But if you have to have a weakness, stubbornness isn't a bad one to have, since the opposite of stubbornness is a lack of conviction. The person who sticks to his guns has to have guts. He is never wishy-washy on the job.

Before leaving the question of your greatest weaknesses, there are several points that should be made. First, you don't necessarily have to discuss them all. If you get asked about your weaknesses, cite one or two. Second, if you don't fall heir to the weaknesses described above, by all means, don't mention them. But if some of these faults are really you, don't be ashamed of them. There's good in each. Third, keep in mind a positive illustration of each weakness. For example, the executive who is stubborn might have saved his company one hundred thousand dollars by refusing to buy a piece of equipment when alternative equipment would have been superior. He may have fought with middle-level management—even with top management—because of this conviction. The proof of the pudding is the result of his stubbornness. His machine outperforms the other machine by a wide margin and saves a hundred thousand dollars. A strong worthpoint related to your greatest weakness can turn a minus into a plus for you.

5. What do you want to be five years hence?

If you answer that you'd like to be president, you're terribly unrealistic—unless, of course, you happen to be an executive vice-president now. Very few prospective bosses are looking for ninety-day wonders, men and women in middle management who can assume the presidency in less than five years. So you look naive if you answer that way. You are being hired for your expertise at your present level. To suggest that you will rise through the ranks like a rocket, passing others by, is presumptuous to say the least. On the other hand, few prospective bosses are looking for people who expect to sit still for five years, contented doing what they're doing now. In order to avoid extremes when you answer this question, you might say, "In five years I would like to be in my boss's job, with prospects of being in his boss's job in the not too distant future." There is a good reason for answering the question this way. You should expect to be in your boss's job within five years. If you can't make it in that time, you are hardly the person your prospective boss should hire. At the same time, if you think you should be close to securing his boss's job in that period of time, you are exhibiting a reasonable amount of personal ambition.

6. Do you mind taking a personality test prior to joining our company?

The answer to this question should be obvious: "No, not at all."

Why should the answer to this question be so obvious? If it's asked at all, you can be absolutely sure that there's a policy stating that every new employee will take a battery of psychological tests. There's no point in saying "No" if you're at all interested in the job.

Some people rebel against personality tests. If you do, you might consider two things. First, the fact that they are given should not necessarily condemn the company you are interviewing. Frequently these are the tools used by personnel departments as a matter of record to determine for future use what kind of employees stay with a company longest and do the best. They are generally not relevant to the decision to hire you or another person. Second, if you are concerned about taking such psychological exams, you might spend a few minutes reading the appendix to William H. Whyte, Jr.'s *The Organization Man*, published by Simon and Schuster. It provides a brief (five-page), interesting commentary on personality testing. You'll feel better prepared and more confident when you take yours.

7. What do you want to make on your next job?

In standard phraseology, "What are your salary requirements?" Your answer to this question depends on when it's asked. If it's too soon, perhaps on the first or second interview, you're better begging off the question. If this company has "the" job you're looking for, why state a salary requirement that might knock you out of the ball game? It makes you an unknown yet premium-priced player. If you are asked your salary requirements early in the game, why not say, "I'm pretty flexible on that score. I'd rather talk about finances after we've decided together whether I'm the right person for this job." Let them be convinced you are the only person they want. Your bargaining position will be that much stronger. Don't let your prospective boss use your salary requirement as a factor in determining whether he wants you. Let him use your salary requirement as a personal challenge after deciding he must have you.

If you're asked your salary requirement on your third or fourth interview, or after your prospective boss has expressed very keen and specific interest in you, give the answer he seeks. Forthrightly. Positively. Not apologetically. Not as a question. You should expect a 20 percent increase when you leave your current concern to join another company in a similar capacity. This figure, of course, depends on the economic situation. But remember this: As I suggested earlier, a company expects to pay a premium for going on the outside. They expect to pay for training by some other firm. So ask for at least 20 percent more than you're currently making. If you feel confident of their interest in you, ask for 25 percent. The important thing is this: When your prospective boss has been sold on you as his first choice, he'll pay a little bit more to make sure he gets you. Your first job is to make sure he wants you.

8. What are you currently making?

To most people this is not a difficult question. They are pleased to state their current salary, recognizing that it will be considered in their prospective boss's own salary offer. For two groups of people, however, the question concerning current salary is a tough one.

The first group of people includes those who are currently underpaid. Chances are they are considering leaving their present jobs simply because they *are* underpaid. These people are concerned that if they reveal their lower-than-fair current salary it will lead to a low-ball offer from their prospective boss. These people are also concerned that their current low salary suggests they have less responsibility than really is the case.

The second group of people who are concerned about the "what-is-your-current-salary" question are those executives who have a financial package of which salary is only one part. Those people may be paid a bonus and may have stock options on top of their salary. Obviously, if a company you are interviewing offers only salary, you have to take this into consideration, since you will lose out on the cash value you received from a bonus and/or stocks.

For those who are currently underpaid: Tell your prospective boss your current salary without hesitation. And then add, audibly, "That's precisely the reason I am here today." Let your prospective boss know you know you are underpaid by industry standards; that you're leaving your present employer because you want to make a wage comparable to that of others in similar jobs in your industry. Your prospective boss should get the idea quickly.

For those of you who are currently receiving a comprehensive financial package: Tell your prospective boss what your current salary is and then add, "The total value of my current financial package is $——. This is made up of the following: my stock is worth $——. My guaranteed bonus is $——. My incentive bonus is worth $——." It is not a reality to consider your current earnings based on salary alone, since no matter how or when you are paid, it's the total value that counts, not the bits and pieces.

9. What do you think of your present boss?

Sometimes an interviewer will ask you point-blank what you think of your present boss, or perhaps the president of your company. When this occurs, you can pretty much count on your prospective boss knowing your present boss, or the president—personally through a trade organization, or by reputation. In this case, your prospective boss in undoubtedly trying to find out, among other things, whether your opinion of the person in question is similar to his own. I personally think it's an unfair question. But it is asked, nonetheless. If you are confronted by this question, be positive even if it hurts. If you think the president is a tyrant, say instead, "Our president is an extremely strong leader. He's firm in his handling of people and a demanding executive." Whatever you do, don't give an emotional response, even if you think the president is a son-of-a-bitch. The reason is simple. Your prospective boss is not only trying to find out if your judgment agrees with his, but also whether or not you're a loyal employee. Be honest in your appraisal of the person in question, and couch your thoughts in words that should come from a loyal employee.

10. What actions would you take if you came on board?

Your initial response might be to describe the changes you would make if you were hired to fill the position you're interviewing for. Suppress that inclination. Instead, say that the chances are likely that you wouldn't do very much at all for a while. Not at least until you had a chance to really evaluate the situation from the inside. After all, it's most difficult to determine a course of action without having been totally immersed in the problems involved. The adage, "Fools rush in where angels fear to tread," certainly fits here. If you wish, there is nothing to stop you from adding: "If the situation turns out to be what I think it might be, I might take the following type of action . . ." Whatever you do, don't look like a whirling dervish who has come in to change an organization before he has had a chance to see what's good about it.

There will undoubtedly be other difficult questions that you will face on job interviews. While we obviously can't discuss the answers to these specific questions without knowing them, two last thoughts:

First, whatever the question, try to answer it in the most positive manner, particularly if it is in regard to your present affiliation. Whatever the question, try to turn weaknesses into strengths. Whatever the question, be as honest in your answer as you possibly can. If nothing else, you'll be admired for that.

Second, if you come across a tough question, one that throws you, make a note of it right after the interview. Think about it for as long as it takes you to come up with a reasonable answer. Say it over to yourself until your answer becomes second nature to you. And tuck it in the back of your mind. It probably won't come up again, but if it should, it makes life a whole lot easier to have a well-thought-out answer—and one in which you have confidence—rather than to have to think out your answer on the spot, under pressure, all over again.

A SUGGESTION: Reread this chapter in a couple of days. Fix in your mind the questions and answers suggested here that are appropriate to you. Consider this chapter much as you would a practice college entrance exam in your junior year. It's intended to help prepare you today for what interviews may be like tomorrow. It should give you confidence that you won't be coming up against tough questions cold turkey. Even if you can't subscribe to all of the answers given here, at least you'll start thinking of your own responses before the question is asked.

Nine

Tough interview situations and how to take them in stride

It happened ten years ago. But it's so vivid in my mind you'd think it took place yesterday. It was undoubtedly the worst interview I ever had. My interviewer was an executive recruiter. After glancing over my resume, he spent a half-hour trying to convince me I should not leave my current company. Since I thought the choice of whether to switch jobs was mine, I literally battled with him. His insistence annoyed me. I countered his arguments with every logical reason I could think of. Within ten minutes there was an acrid atmosphere in the room. We never did discuss the job opening he called me about. I went away feeling he was either damned stupid or a bastard.

Throughout the day I thought over what had happened that morning. By the end of the day I had convinced myself that the executive recruiter was retained by my current company and, among other things, was obligated to persuade all people considering leaving not to do so. The following morning I phoned him and confronted him with my theory. He assured me that he was not retained by my current company and, in fact, knew no one there: he had taken his perverse tack at our interview to see what I was like when I was angry. He said that as an interview technique he always adopted a belligerent stance and frequently argued with job-seekers about why they wanted to leave their current firms. Then I realized what had taken place. I had allowed myself to get suckered into an interviewer's trap.

In subsequent years I thought a lot about this disastrous interview. I concluded that had I realized what the interviewer was trying to do, I not only could have avoided the confrontation, but actually could have turned that interview into a positive personal sale.

The objective of this chapter is to help you avoid some of the typical mistakes interviewees make simply because they don't assess the interview situation correctly, and thus are unable to respond to it in a way that promotes their cause.

Here are ten tough interview situations that might well face you in your job search, and some suggestions on handling them.

PROBLEM 1.   Your interviewer won't open his mouth. He simply won't keep up a conversation. You've tried every possible way to get him to talk about the type of job that needs to be done and the kind of person he's looking for to fill the position that is open. Nothing seems to work. The silence is deafening.

ANALYSIS/ACTION.   If you run into a situation like this, it's for one of two reasons. First, your interviewer *wants* to keep you dangling. He has no intention of making your meeting easier by letting you in on his needs. He wants to see how you do on your own without guidance. He is giving you sufficient rope to hang yourself. It's a not uncommon interview technique. Second, and a more probable reason for the silence, is that your interviewer is simply not equipped personally to handle meetings with candidates. While he could be a great conversationalist when he knows you well, he simply lacks a talent for talking with strangers. He's just not comfortable in the situation. Whatever the reason for the silence, it's in your best interest *not* to let it go on for too long. Both you and your interviewer are bound to feel self-conscious about it. Chances are your prospective boss will find an excuse to end your interview earlier than anticipated, rather than sit there and squirm.

Your best course of action under the circumstances is to keep talking. But don't make the mistake of talking about *your* background. Your life story may be the first thing that comes to mind, but it's probably not the topic that will do you the most good. Instead, talk about the needs and challenges you feel your prospective boss has, and as you discuss each, try to relate your experience to them. But how on earth would you *know* these needs if your prospective boss won't open his mouth? Here's where your advanced preparation comes in handy! Refer back to the newspaper ads, or the needs that the executive recruiter outlined for you. Refer back to the annual report, or other articles you may have read about the company. There's nothing wrong with saying: "Mr. Jones, that *Business Week* article on the dramatic change in the competitive situation in your business fascinated me. At our own company we faced a very similar situation. The problem was . . ." etc. The important thing is that you keep the interview going and keep your interviewer interested. Talking about his problems and those specific worthpoints that suggest you could help him solve these problems does *both* these things. If the interviewer left the talking to you to see if you would "hang yourself," he is likely to be very impressed with your ability to talk about your experience as it concerns his business. If, on the other hand, the silence you experience reflects a lack of interview skills on the part of your prospective boss, he will genuinely appreciate your carrying the ball for him, and making your interview more valuable to him—as well as a more pleasant experience for both of you.

PROBLEM 2. Your prospective boss won't stop talking. Once you invite him to tell you more about his company, the job, and the kind of person he is looking for, he literally takes over. He carries on at length about the problems and challenges facing his company. The more he keeps talking, the more anxious you become that you'll never have an opportunity to sell yourself during the thirty or sixty minutes allotted to you. You are afraid that your interview will close without your prospective boss having discovered you are the best candidate for the position he is seeking to fill.

ANALYSIS/ACTION. If after uncovering the three primary needs or challenges facing your prospective boss, you have made several attempts to take over and he has shown no interest in discussing your background, there's still a way you can demonstrate your interest in the job and your ability to handle it. And that's to interject thoughtful questions as your prospective boss goes on with his monologue—thoughtful questions that focus on the challenges his organization faces or the opportunities for the future. Obviously your interview preparation can pay off well for you in this instance. Good, solid questions prove your understanding of the interviewer's problems. Meaty, specific questions suggest you know the subject, that you have faced similar situations to those your prospective employer now faces. Good questions are not a one-for-one substitute for good worthpoints, however. So you should still try, from time to time, to inject them, if at all possible, into the conversation. And, consider asking your prospective boss this question: "How do you see my skills and experience as best fitting in with your organization?" He may well end up talking himself into hiring you!

PROBLEM 3. The person who interviews you seems to have taken a personal dislike to you. Nothing you say pleases him. He asks you where you went to school. When you tell him, he makes a snide remark about your alma mater. He asks your experience with a particular kind of machine. When you tell him, he lets you know that several other candidates have more experience than you. You get no positive vibrations from this person. You feel miserable. You are certain you failed with him.

ANALYSIS/ACTION. No matter how much your interviewer taunts you, keep your cool. Chances are he wants you to lose it. He wants to see how you are in a stress situation. This kind of interview is not common today. Nonetheless, some interviewers still enjoy seeing people squirm. It's up to you. You can be the one person who doesn't squirm, if you try.

How do you go about this? Simple: every time he knocks your contributions or responds negatively to your answers, agree with him. At the same time, suggest that you have made other contributions you would like to tell him about. For example, when he told you your experience on a particular machine wasn't as good as that of other candidates he's interviewed, you might have said, "You're probably right. But the sixty-four thousand dollar question is: Will I make contributions for your company? Now when I was working on the machine, we faced a real rough problem. What I suggested was . . . And the problem was solved." In a nutshell, your strategy is to keep him on your track, the worthpoint track. Don't let him drag you onto his. No matter how hard he puts the screws to you, don't argue with him. Agree with him. Perhaps he's right. Then direct him back to what you've done to help the companies you've worked for. It may not be easy.

But two things are certain. First, you won't get anywhere arguing with this sort of individual. No candidate ever won an argument before he was hired. Who needs that kind of person on the payroll? Second, if you can hold out in spite of the structured stress, your prospective boss will at least think of you as the one applicant who remained calm and level-headed while pressures were exerted on him. And that's not a bad way to be remembered.

At this point I'm frequently asked: "Why not argue with this interviewer? You wouldn't want to work for him anyhow. What difference does it make if you give it back to him as hard as he gives it to you?"

The answer is this: One interviewer does not a company make. It may well be that this style of interview is the particular favorite of someone you must meet during the interviewing process, someone with whom you'd work very infrequently. Unless structured stress is the operational device of the person whom you would work for directly, it would be unfair to assume that you wouldn't enjoy working for this company. However, you might well want to check with friends or associates who could give you a better insight into the working life at this organization.

PROBLEM 4. During the latter part of your meeting, the interviewer proceeds to ask you an endless series of questions, many of which are difficult and some of which can be found in the previous chapter on tough questions. You can almost feel your adrenal glands at work. Your palms begin to get sweaty. You weren't quite prepared for the rapidity with which these questions are asked, nor for the difficulty of providing clear, concise answers to them.

ANALYSIS/ACTION. While the rapid-fire questioning technique is tough on you, it undoubtedly provides a benefit to your interviewer. It lets him know which of the candidates he sees are able to think on their feet and to think calmly under pressure. Your knowledge of the company that your interview preparation netted you, as well as your familiarity with some of the more difficult questions asked by interviewers, will make it easier for you to think on your feet than it is for the person who hasn't been exposed to these questions before. It's sort of like taking the sample driving test prior to the real thing. There will, of course, be questions thrown at you that you don't have the answers for. When this happens, keep the following thoughts in mind:

☐   Answer questions by referring to specific worthpoints, if you can.

☐   If you don't know the answer to a particular question, say you don't know. You will at least be thought of as honest. That may be better than the next candidate.

☐   Don't get flustered. If the rapid-fire questions start to unnerve you, remember they'll unnerve the other candidates as well.

If you keep your cool when others can't, you'll be the standout candidate by default. It is a well-known fact that at the Harvard Business School ninety-five out of one hundred first year students used to fail that first mid-course examination. They failed because the test was designed so that 95 percent *couldn't* pass, no matter how hard they studied! Why did the faculty use such an unfair test? Probably to see how well students functioned after this kind of trauma. Your prospective boss may be trying to do something similar. No matter how frustrated you feel, don't panic. Remain honest and calm. Keep in mind the most important thing you have to sell: your contributions to sales and profits. No one can take them away from you. Remember that the interviewer who tries to pick a fight is probably looking for someone who knows how to avoid one.

PROBLEM 5.   You arrive at your prospective boss's office in plenty of time for your interview. At the time your appointment is supposed to begin, his secretary comes to the lobby to let you know that he is in a meeting and it is running behind schedule. She leads you to your prospective boss's office where you sit for twenty minutes. Since you are expected back at your office within the hour, with each passing minute you grow more nervous. At the end of a half-hour, the secretary reappears and lets you know your prospective boss will be back in just a couple of minutes. Fifteen minutes later he does come in, extremely apologetic. He asks your forgiveness for the delay and wants to start the meeting rolling.

ANALYSIS/ACTION. If you can delay your return to the office without feeling uncomfortable about it, go ahead with the interview as though nothing had happened. Your prospective boss "owes you one" and he should be sympathetic and well disposed toward you before you begin. On the other hand, if getting back to the office—or to another appointment—is of critical importance, it's a different story. You have, at this point, only fifteen minutes left of the hour you were supposed to have with your interviewer. What should you do with it? Two things: first, level with your interviewer about the time bind; second, try to set up another interview date. Your prospective employer undoubtedly feels a sense of guilt about the situation, and he's likely to grant you another full-length interview if you ask for it. If you can, suggest several specific time periods and let him take his pick. For example: "Which would be best for you, Mr. Jones, next Tuesday morning early, or next Thursday at five?" While you may be tempted to try to squeeze in an interview as long as you are there, don't! You're far better off starting from scratch at another time than trying to conduct a meeting knowing you are going to be late someplace else. You'll be too distracted to do your level best. And even if you think you can hide your concern, it's a good bet that you'll abbreviate your interview in some way. Perhaps you'll fail to probe deeply enough as to your prospective boss's needs. Maybe you'll forget to relate a worthpoint that is cogent to a need he has outlined. In a word, take advantage of the fact that your prospective boss is the cause of the delay, and use this advantage to try for an interview when neither he nor you are under any pressures.

PROBLEM 6. Your prospective boss likes you. He tells you so. He's impressed with your contributions. He's impressed with you. But, and it's a very big but, your background isn't *specifically* what he's looking for. In all probability he has met other candidates with experience slightly more in tune with his immediate needs than your own.

ANALYSIS/ACTION. When you face a situation like this, consider taking two steps. First, agree with your prospective boss that your experience isn't as directly applicable as that of some other people who are probably applying for the job. Unless you have forgotten to include some relevant experience on your resume that you are now ready to reveal, there is no point in trying to convince him that your experience is precisely what he wants. He has already decided for himself that it is not. So why antagonize him during the balance of your interview?

Instead, lay out the alternatives for him in a way that perhaps he has not considered. This is not easily done. But you've nothing to lose by trying, so why not attempt it as your second step? Perhaps like this:

> As I see it, Mr. Jones, you are confronted by three alternatives: First, you could take on a person like myself whose contributions seem to impress you but who hasn't had the particular experience you'd like him to have. Second, you could select a person with fewer contributions to his record but with 'just the right' experience. Third, you could wait a couple of months or perhaps even a year and see if you can't locate an individual with the exact experience and the record of contributions you want. If I've summed it up fairly, Mr. Jones, could I comment about the situation?

If your prospective boss accepts your definition of the problem, you have a fighting chance to talking him into hiring you. You have convinced him that there are drawbacks to each alternative. In your case, not quite the experience he seeks. In the case of the person with the exact experience, not quite your list of worthpoints. In the case of the person with both, an indefinite delay until he's been found. After defining the problem, the time has come to try to persuade your prospective boss that your alternative is the best one. Your strategy is to talk the future—specifically, what the situation might be in a year's time:

> Mr. Jones, while I have a little less experience than my competition, in a year's time I think you'll be happier having hired me than the candidates I'm competing against. As my record indicates, you know whatever I've tackled I've done well. In a year's time I believe I will have caught up on the experience, and perhaps even contributed more to your business than my competition, who now has more experience but not more contributions. If you elect to wait for "the" person with a record of contributions as well as the exact experience you seek, you might end up waiting a year to find him. So perhaps hiring me now would be a pretty good alternative. I won't lack for trying!

Obviously this approach won't work every time. But if you are up against a strong bias of "not quite the right experience," you at least have a logical way to attack it. You have found the Achilles heel in the argument that an experienced person would necessarily be better. It's worth a try.

The following interview situations differ from those above. This next group deals with three delaying situations: when you're trying *not* to get a job, or trying to delay either a job offer or your acceptance. While these situations are not as critical as the former, nonetheless, knowing a reasonable solution to each before you find yourself in the situation may make you sweat a little less.

PROBLEM 7. You've been called to an interview. Things have gone amazingly well. You learned a good deal about the company's needs and challenges as a result of your probing. And you became excited about what you might be able to do for the outfit if you were hired. And then it happened. Your prospective boss described the *specific* job he has open. You know it is not for you. You know it is not suited to your professional experience or your career objectives or your salary requirements. And this despite the fact that your resume clearly stated your job objective. You don't know whether the personnel director chose to ignore it, or if the recruiter who told you of this opening failed to send your resume along. It doesn't much matter. The point is that while you like the company very much, the job you find yourself applying for is absolutely, positively not for you. Your problem is to close the interview but keep a strong relationship with this company for the future.

ANALYSIS/ACTION. In this situation there are three things you ought to consider doing. First, no matter how mad you feel inside, don't show it! It will spoil your opportunity to take steps two and three, which are worth hanging on for. Second, make sure your interviewer understands you are not at all interested in the job he's considering you for. Let him know you are sorry about any misunderstanding, but that, as your resume states, you are seeking a different kind of job from the one that he just described. The third step is to try to convince your interviewer that, although he didn't plan to fill the position you want, you are such a good person that he ought to reconsider his company's needs and create a position for you suited to your objectives. This won't be easy. But it's worth a try as long as you've taken the time and the effort to get the interview. Here's how you might approach it:

> Mr. Jones, thanks for describing the current opportunity you have open. I'm very enthusiastic about your company and the prospects you have outlined to me. But, in all candor, I must tell you there's been a misunderstanding between us. The position you're seeking to fill is not what I had in mind. It's really what I was looking for three or four years ago. I hope you won't hold this against me, since I seem to have had a different understanding as to what the job was all about.
>
> While it looks as if you don't have an opening suited to my objectives at this time, maybe in the future your organization may need someone with my background. Let me review with you some of my experience and contributions so you can get an idea of my level of expertise and perhaps see where I might best fit in your organization."

Then sell your worthpoints, particularly at the organizational level you are trying to get the interviewer to hire you at. You may be surprised at the results. A month from now, if you're still looking for a job, you might well receive a call—as a client of mine once did three weeks after such an interview—inviting you to talk about a new position at your level that "has just opened up."

It may well be that the new position is a genuine one. On the other hand, I know of many instances where positions were created around the person the company wanted. The companies were so anxious to obtain the talents of these executives that they reshuffled their existing organizations to make room for the individuals. While you can't count on such good fortune, don't disregard the possibility. Be prepared for an interview situation in which the job is not for you. Don't pack up. Lay your cards on the table frankly and unemotionally. Then, in the context of the position you thought you were applying for, go ahead and sell your worth. You have nothing to lose and a potential job to gain.

PROBLEM 8.   You are on your third interview. Things are going well. You sense that the company is interested in you and that a job offer may well be forthcoming. You like the company. You might well work for it. But—and again, it's a big but—this company is your second choice. You are also interviewing another company, and you would prefer to work for it. Unfortunately, negotiations with the second company aren't as far along as those with the first. The first company calls you to a fourth interview and offers you the job. You are in a quandary. Should you accept the job at hand or hold out for the job you'd really like to have? What should you do?

ANALYSIS/ACTION.   What you really want from company #1 is some time to let you find out whether or not you will get a job offer from company #2. How do you get the time you need? By asking for it in an honest way. Point out that when you relocate, you hope to stay a good many years, and you want to be sure you make the right decision. Let company #1 know of your negotiations with company #2 (without revealing its name), and the point these negotiations have reached. Let company #1 know that you could not accept a job with it in good conscience unless you have a chance to complete negotiations now in progress with both companies. It wouldn't be fair to you, nor would it be fair to company #1 if you hadn't thought out the problem in its entirety. You can ask for up to two weeks to make a final decision. That may seem like a long delay to the first company. When you consider, however, that it has been searching for some time, and that it has committed itself to you, I think you'll be granted ten working days in which to arrive at a decision. Or at least a week. The important thing is this: If you let company #1 in on your problem, it is likely to keep open its job offer for a reasonable period of time while you wind things up with company #2.

You should then approach company #2 with the same honesty with which you approached company #1. Try and arrange a special interview. Explain the pressure being put on you. Ask company #2 if it can move up its decision date or let you know whether you are a prime candidate. If your prospective boss can't see you, give him a call, or write, telling him your problem. *Ask for his counsel and aid.*

If you are a highly thought-of candidate at company #2, there's a very good likelihood it will move faster. If its interest in you is only moderate, it probably won't. In which case you have your answer. The chances of your being offered a job at company #2 are slim. You're better off to accept the original offer at company #1. After all, while it is your second choice, it wants you. That's worth a lot in the long run.

PROBLEM 9.   You arrive at your interview in good spirits. Your prospective boss is enthusiastic about his company. The information he provides you, plus your own research, suggests it is a company you'd like to work for. Your prospective boss tells you that while he has no opening similar to the one you seek, he does have an opening at a lower level, that he'd like you to take temporarily. He tells you that after an unspecified period of time he will try to make a job opening suited to your background. In short, he promises you a fabulous future and asks you take a flyer at a job you really don't want until such time as he can make an opening suited to your needs and objectives. You like the company. You are perplexed over the proposition.

ANALYSIS/ACTION.   You may well be leery of opportunities such as this one, for several reasons. In the first place, you must somehow question an employer who is incapable of seeing how tough taking a step back is for you. Obviously you don't want a job at a lower level than the one you now have. If he is unable to see this problem, you may well ask if he would understand other problems, once you went to work there.

A second reason you may be leery of such a job is the nebulous way future plans are presented. Without assurances as to when and how you will be promoted, it's a risky proposition at best. Supposing you don't like the company after you join it? Certainly you don't want to leave for a position that's lower on the organization chart than the one you now have.

In view of the uncertainties of accepting a position you don't want for an indefinite period of time, you might try to persuade your prospective boss to offer you a job at least equivalent to the one you now have. Your chances of convincing him are obviously remote. But not impossible. Your best leverage is another job offer. If you have one, you might say to your prospective boss:

Thank you for your offer, Mr. Jones. As you know, the future of your company intrigues me. I will mull it over very seriously although right now my answer would have to be no, since I have a job offer suited to my experience level with the ABC Corporation, which is also a fine company. In all sincerity, were I to come to work for your company, I would be putting my career back a year or perhaps more. It's a less exciting opportunity for me since I have the ABC offer.

While I'm mulling over your proposition, is there any possibility that you might be able to dream up some change in your organizational structure that would make your proposition more enticing?

If you don't have a job offer, the chances of convincing your prospective boss to create a position for you at the level you seek are more remote. If you are close to securing another job, you may be able to phrase your comments in such a way that your prospective boss gets the idea that you have a better offer.

If you can't persuade him to give you assurances of the specific time in which you will be promoted, or, better still, a position equal to the one you now have, then my advice would be to keep looking.

PROBLEM 10. This interview is a novel one. Your prospective boss tells you what a great company he works for. He tells you about its tremendous prospects. He waxes eloquently about the wonderful working conditions and the people. He tells you what you would be paid if you got the job—and it's an outstanding financial package. At the end of the interview, your prospective boss asks you when you could begin to work. You pinch yourself. Is this a dream? You didn't open your mouth and you got yourself a job offer, a seemingly great job offer?

ANALYSIS/ACTION. Perhaps I'm a born skeptic, but I'd be afraid of such an offer. If you are offered a job without being asked to discuss your experience and contributions, you might smell a rat. It could be the job. The company may have serious financial or organizational problems ahead of it. If you find yourself in a situation in which you are asked to join the company on your first interview with no effort on your part, relax. Ask for time to think it over and investigate it thoroughly. Don't get caught in a job that turns out to be a bust.

Ten

An answer to answering ads

If you were to gather a group of friends who had completed job searches and ask them where they felt their campaigns were weakest, chances are most would tell you it was in answering ads. Over the years job-seeker after job-seeker has told me just that. Answering ads—particularly blind ones that must be answered via a box number—is for many job-seekers a wasted effort. Many have reported they secured only one interview out of forty or fifty ads they responded to. Some job-seekers have actually received not a single reply to their answers to ads during the course of their job-search campaigns! Yet in recent years I have worked with other job-seekers who have secured one interview for every two responses they sent out. For this latter group, responding to ads is obviously not a wasted effort. The key question to ask yourself, then, before you start answering ads, is why so many job-seekers have such little luck in their attempts to secure interviews through ads. Here or four good reasons:

1. A great many job-seekers answer ads for which they are not at all qualified because they respond only to the job title shown at the top of the ad and not to the content of the ad itself

If these persons had carefully analyzed the specific qualifications stated in the ad, they would surely have realized they had no business responding in the first place. Just because you have been an "Operations Manager," for example, does *not* mean you are a legitimate candidate for every operations manager job you see advertised. If the small print in the ads states you must have ten years of data processing experience and you've had twenty years of cosmetic manufacturing experience, you really can't hope to succeed, even though, on the basis of job title, you'd expect to be in the ball game. This is not to say it's a mistake to respond to any ad when you're not fully qualified. But certainly you can't hold high expectations when you lack the *critical* experience sought by an employer. Likewise, if a company spells out a dozen requirements in its ad, and you meet only two of them, you really can't expect a reply. Other candidates are bound to come closer. Yet, a great many job-seekers respond to ads without reading them thoroughly, and are then terribly frustrated when they're not invited in for an interview! In short, don't bother to respond when you are not a legitimate candidate.

2. Many job-seekers create a poor impression of themselves with the documents they submit in response to the advertiser's request

My files contain "cover letters" scribbled in an almost illegible script. What legitimate business person would present himself in this amateurish fashion? These same files contain letters with misspellings—including the name of the person the ad requested the job-seeker write to: poor grammar; sloppy typing; even notes on yellow-ruled paper. Sadder still are the well-typed letters in my file which say nothing more in three or four paragraphs than "Here is my resume." Stilted phrases like "attached for your consideration" and buzzwords like "in-depth experience" abound in such letters but there's no meat to them. The advertiser receiving such letters has to conclude that the applicant has no idea of how to go about writing a cogent, forceful, direct document in support of his cause. Check the letters you send out. Ask yourself only one question: If you received your own letter, would you say it came from a professional or an amateur? Keep in mind that in cases where resumes have provided proof that the candidate is "adequate" for the advertised position, many a cover letter has downgraded the advertiser's opinion of him. First impressions are that important. A well-thought-out cover letter, professionally typed, enhances your prospective employer's opinion of you regardless of whether your background is or is not the most suitable of those responding to the ad.

3. Many job-seekers rely on their resumes to sell them although this document can hurt their chances of securing an interview

How so? Well, for one thing, chances are your resume describes your career chronologically, with what you do at present right up front. But the advertiser might not be at all interested in the things you now do. If what you did five years ago, however, *is* relevant to the advertiser's needs, you might well be qualified for the position. But in sending your resume, you are asking your reader to unearth for himself that part of your experience he is seeking. He may just not have the time or inclination to sift through your resume to uncover what he is looking for! If another candidate applying for the same job has *recent* experience sought by the advertiser and it's up front in his resume, naturally he'll have the advantage.

Your resume can hurt you in another way, too, by needlessly revealing *negative* aspects of your career that would be better discussed in person once you met with the advertiser. Let's say you are interested in a position that calls for someone with eight to ten years of line manufacturing experience, and you've had fifteen. Your resume in response to such an advertisement says immediately that you are overqualified. If many other candidates have had precisely eight to ten years of experience, you may never be invited in for an interview. This is unfair to you, of course. You have the required experience. In fact you have had *more* than what is called for! But the fault is yours nonetheless for sending a resume in this instance. Had you written to the advertiser about your last ten years of manufacturing experience and saved the other five for an interview, you might have made it in the door. Only if your resume supports you as the ideal candidate—one with almost all requirements sought by the company placing the ad—does it serve you in good stead. Otherwise, you might be better off *not* sending your resume at all!

4. The great majority of job-seekers fail to respond to advertisers' clearly identified needs

Most help-wanted display ads have a wealth of information in them. Often these ads are two and three columns wide; two to five inches deep. Advertisers spend a lot of money for this space in order to define as precisely as possible what they seek in the "ideal" candidate. Often ads like these—which you see regularly in Tuesday's *Wall Street Journal*, for example—list ten or twelve specific requirements that are presumably the basis of the advertiser's selection process. Unfortunately, almost no job-seekers bother to write covering letters explaining how they can specifically fill these needs. But suppose for a moment that the advertiser doesn't see the key words he's hoping to find in your resume because you use different phrases to describe the same experience? Or suppose that you fail, for some reason or other, to specifically mention in your resume a qualification you have that the advertiser insists on? In circumstances like these, the advertiser would never realize that you were the best person for the job. And it's undoubtedly one reason why you could fail to obtain interviews when you sincerely believe you are the "perfect candidate" the advertiser is searching for.

Recognizing that so many job-seekers use cover letters just to ask the advertiser to look at their resumes (which he's undoubtedly going to do anyhow), in 1972 I suggested to a number of my clients that they experiment with a new approach. Results since then have been amazingly good. Some job-seekers reported that advertisers phoned them the same day their letters were received; others reported receiving telegrams advising that advertisers had called and found the candidate not at home. The balance of this chapter is devoted to this approach.

THE "DIRECT RESPONSE" LETTER

Assume for a minute that you are at an important job interview. During the course of the conversation, your prospective boss asks you a very specific question, such as: "Tell me about your managerial experience." Would you hand him a copy of your resume and say: "Why don't you look this document over and see if there is anything in it that answers your question." Of course not! You'd answer him as directly as you could. You'd define the extent of your managerial experience. You'd tell him when it occurred. And hopefully, you'd offer specific worthpoints to prove how your managerial experience actually helped the companies you worked for. While a direct response to your prospective employer's question seems so natural in an interview, only a handful of job-seekers make a similar effort when they respond to ads! It's easy to understand why. It takes only a few minutes to type up a standard cover letter and to slip it into an envelope along with a resume. It takes a great deal longer to compose a special letter that speaks clearly and directly to each of the advertiser's needs! But avoiding the extra effort might be a mistake if your resume isn't sufficient, by itself, to get you in the door. Good opportunities aren't advertised that often. Few job-seekers can afford to let one slip by for lack of trying.

If you accept in principle that responding directly to the specific needs stated in a job-wanted display ad makes sense, and agree that writing a special letter might be worth the extra time on your part, you may still be hesitant to take this approach. You may wonder about those instances where an advertiser asks for specific experience or qualifications that you cannot provide. What should you do then? If you analyze a particular ad and discover there are ten specific requirements sought by the advertiser and that you can fill only three of them, perhaps your best bet is just to send your resume with no cover letter and not worry if you never hear back. In those situations where you can respond to seven or eight out of ten needs, however, why not write a cogent, compelling letter proving that you are the best person the advertiser will find to fill these seven or eight needs, and don't mention the other two or three requirements. Rarely do the mails bring advertisers replies from an ideal candidate who possesses *every* qualification. So the person placing the ad is most likely to hire the candidate who appears to meet *most* of his needs.

Let's assume for the moment that you and one other person do answer an ad that spells out ten specific qualifications. Let's assume, too, that you and your competition both match up to eight of the ten needs. In this instance neither of you is an "ideal" candidate, although you both come close. Now, let's say your competition responds to the ad in a typical

358 Rock Ridge Drive
Old Hyde Park, New York 11472

February 17, 1979

Box E-811B
The Wall Street Journal
22 Cortlandt Street
New York, New York 10007

Dear Sir:

This letter responds to your advertisement in the
Wall Street Journal of February 15, 1979 in which you
outline your requirements for an Assistant Treasurer.
Your advertisement is particularly appealing to me since
the needs that you define seem to be well matched to my
background. Specifically:

- _Project Financing_ - As a First Vice President
  of Dawson-Rumrill & Co. Inc., responsible for
  the firm's tax shelter programs, I developed
  a number of financing projects with a total
  value of over $88,000,000.

  One project, in particular, may be of interest to you. For General Star Corporation,
  (a natural resource company) I arranged long
  term debt financing of $18,000,000 for the
  purchase of a tanker. I was able to secure
  a private placement of this debt at 7 3/8% -
  a point lower than market.

- _Capital Structure_ - As part of Dawson-Rumrill's
  public and private financing assignments
  (valued at over $300,000,000), my responsi-
  bilities included developing appropriate
  capital structures for 23 medium and large
  companies.

  One of the more complicated capital structure
  assignments was for Property Mortgage Investments, Inc. I developed a four part program
  including a modification of debt agreements,
  an exchange of convertible subordinated debentures for senior notes and warrants and

simultaneous public offerings of convertible
subordinated debentures and senior debentures.
This package resulted in a more flexible debt
structure and an increase in the company's
equity base.

- **Private Placements** - Again at Dawson-Rumrill I
  participated in nine private placements (valued
  at $64,000,000) for such diverse firms as
  Eastern Department Stores, Baimbridge Oil
  Corporation, and Property Mortgage Investments
  (which led to the program above).

  The Baimbridge Oil Corporation program may be
  particularly interesting to you since it is a
  natural resource company and had very low earnings at the time of the placement. By design-
  ing a program including senior notes with warrants, plus a mortgage on the oil properties,
  I was able to secure $5,000,000 from Quadrangle
  Life Insurance Company of New York at very
  favorable terms.

In total, I have had 15 years with Dawson-Rumrill in
three successively more important positions plus two
years with Goodbody Properties, Inc. as Vice President.
I am a graduate of the Northwestern Business School (top
half of class) and Purdue University (top 10% of my
engineering class). I would be delighted to review my
full salary history with you on a more personal basis
when we get together.

In closing, let me reaffirm my interest in your position - based on our apparent match - and suggest that we
meet soon to discuss your specific needs in greater detail.

                    Sincerely,

                    Robert S. Thompson

fashion with a resume and a cover letter. But you respond with a letter in which you express your interest in the opportunity based on your belief that the advertiser's needs are matched by your background. Then, let's say you go on to review *point by point* each of the advertiser's specific needs and your qualifications that relate to them. And for good measure, you offer worthpoints describing how you succeeded in dealing with similar needs for the companies you have worked for. Who do you think the advertiser might call first? It's a good bet he'll call you. First, because you've shown genuine interest in his ad and have addressed yourself directly to it. And, secondly, because your ability to fill each of his stated needs is obvious. This is probably not true of your competitor's resume, which, after all, was not written specifically to respond to this one ad.

This actual direct-response letter was sent by Bob Thompson, a client of mine. Only the names have been changed.

Let's consider for a moment the specific techniques that Bob Thompson used:

☐ At the very beginning he expresses a genuine interest in the opportunity and gives a specific reason for his interest.

☐ Bob responds to each of the advertised needs, one by one, underscoring it at the start of the paragraph so that the advertiser knows which specific qualifications he is replying to.

☐ As Thompson deals with a particular qualification he starts with a paragraph in which he provides sufficient *specific* information concerning his background (title, company, etc.) to assure the advertiser that he is, in fact, qualified to respond to the ad.

☐ In a separate paragraph, Bob describes a relevant worthpoint as proof that he is not just qualified by virtue of title or experience but has contributed in the particular needs area.

☐ The elements of the format taken together add up to this thought: "Mr. Advertiser, I understand the problem. I am qualified to deal with this sort of problem. And, perhaps more important, I've had luck in solving problems like it before."

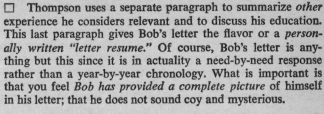

☐ Thompson uses a separate paragraph to summarize *other* experience he considers relevant and to discuss his education. This last paragraph gives Bob's letter the flavor or a *personally written "letter resume."* Of course, Bob's letter is anything but this since it is in actuality a need-by-need response rather than a year-by-year chronology. What is important is that you feel *Bob has provided a complete picture* of himself in his letter; that he does not sound coy and mysterious.

☐ In the final paragraph Bob repeats his interest in the position and his reason for interest *and asks to learn more about the advertiser's needs.* It's a refreshing change from the many cover letters you may have seen, which end with the candidate asking for an interview in order "to review *my* background in greater detail."

Several facts surrounding this letter might interest you. First, Bob Thompson received a phone call from an executive recruiter within twenty-four hours of mailing his letter. Second, Bob was invited to go two thousand miles for an interview at the company's expense and was offered the job. Third, in his letter Bob discussed only three of the five stated needs. He was unable to meet two other qualifications so he left them out of his letter altogether. Fourth, the specific experiences Thompson alludes to in his letter actually occurred three years (or more) prior to his writing this letter. For two of the previous three years Bob had been vice-president at a different firm from the one he talks about in the beginning of his letter. For the past year, Bob had been both employed by a small real estate firm, and then unemployed when things did not work out. As you looked over the letter, chances are you didn't realize the experiences Thompson reported were, in fact, quite dated.

Maybe you are bothered by this. Was Thompson less than honest in sending this letter and not submitting a resume? Should he have advised the advertiser in his letter that his experience was not current? If these questions concern you, it's because you are conditioned to responding to ads with a resume plus cover letter. *Bob Thompson responded specifically to the advertiser's request that candidates provide background information on how they could fill the advertiser's particular needs.* Had Thompson sent his resume, his chances of getting an interview would undoubtedly have been jeopardized. The direct-response letter may not be the traditional approach, then, but it was extremely effective in getting Bob Thompson what he wanted—an interview. Obviously when Bob got to his interview the weaknesses in his experience were exposed as he reviewed his background (and resumes) with his prospective employer. And he still was offered the job.

This experience is not unique. It has occurred again and again with this type of direct-response letter. In Bob's case, he did not send a resume as it would have hurt his cause. In other instances it's worked *with* resumes when the resume has contained nothing in it that runs counter to the qualifications sought by the advertiser. The direct-response letter can work to get you in the door for an in-person hearing of your worth. It won't take away weaknesses once you meet your prospective boss, however. So be sure you match most if not all requirements before you answer an ad this way. Otherwise you are likely to be disappointed when your interview turns sour. The key to job search is still an offer. The direct-response letter is a door-opener, nothing more.

Developing a letter format that has the potential of opening doors is really only half the battle in making "help wanted" advertising pay off in your job-search campaign. The other half is uncovering more help-wanted ads! Most job-seekers are content with looking in this week's local paper, and as a result they are exposed to only the tip of the iceberg. If you really want to do an effective job in securing help-wanted ads that might just hold out an opportunity for you, you've got to multiply the number of sources that you see regularly. How do you do this? Here are several ways you should consider:

☐ Get hold of *back issues* of the classified section—eight to ten weeks' worth. Many jobs aren't filled in this period of time! It may be that you are the candidate a company has been waiting for. I know of an executive who was the ninety-seven applicant the company interviewed. It had been looking for nine months before he came along. (This executive laughingly claims he got the job because the company was too tired to look further.)

☐ Subscribe to the *Wall Street Journal* or plan to pick up Tuesday's edition on a regular basis. The Mart (executive help wanted) section of the *Journal* is undoubtedly the best single source of leads for executive positions I know of. If you don't live on the East Coast, you might ask an East Coast friend to send you copies of this section of the Eastern edition. It usually lists more opportunities than the other editions, and if you are willing to move to further your career, you ought to get hold of the Eastern Edition regularly. Similarly, if you are now on the East Coast and are thinking about moving, you can subscribe to the Pacific Coast, Southwestern, or Midwestern editions as well as the Eastern Edition. There are many opportunities that are *not* advertised nationally.

☐ Subscribe to *The New York Times* Sunday edition. It costs $28.95 per quarter if you live fifty miles outside of the New York area, and, as such, is a very inexpensive investment in good job leads. When the *Times* is shipped out of New York, it may not have the classified section. (If you check with the local *New York Times* representative, you may be able to arrange to get it.) The business and finance section is always included, however, and this section contains eight to ten pages of executive help-wanted display ads each week.

☐ Subscribe to *The National Reporter of New Job Openings*, published by a subsidiary of *Performance Dynamics*, 400 Lanidex Plaza, Parsippany, New Jersey 07054. NRNJO culls two-hundred newspapers and reprints help-wanted display ads in bookstyle type. The *National Reporter*, however, is expensive. You can buy about 6 weeks' worth of digests for $70 ($11 per issue) or as many as 17 weeks for about $130 (including 4 back issues that predate your order, and 13 weeks of upcoming ones).

If you have the spare cash, and an inclination to move, this is the best alternative. But if you do go to NRNJO, several cautions. A number of my clients have reported that after buying the digests they have received solicitations for other Performance Dynamics services, such as career consulting. And the price for such consulting was steep: $4,000 and more!

One other consideration: a number of my clients wrote to box-numbered ads that appeared in NRNJO, only to discover that the newspapers had closed these boxes out and that their letters were never received by the advertiser. It would appear that in some cases the delay in receiving the newspapers, culling them for executive ads, categorizing them, and then reprinting them had taken such a long time that the jobs were no longer available. Obviously, if you use such services, write immediately after you have looked over the ads that appeal to you. In short, the service could be of some real benefit if you can afford it. But be leery of other services offered to you by the parent organization that automatically secured your name.

☐ Read the business pages of your local daily paper. Look for announcements of promotions and appointments. If you spot an announcement of a promotion for someone in your field for whom you might like to work, write to him. Don't be concerned that you don't know him. Congratulate him on his promotion. Let him know you'd like to work with him if he's thinking about new blood to increase the effectiveness of his operation. Send him your resume. He may get back to you with an offer for an interview. The worst he can do is turn you down. Why not give it a chance? Don't stall until the executive gets settled in his new job. For some reason or other, newspapers always seem to publish promotions long after they take place. The executive you congratulate may well have been in his current assignment long enough to have evaluated his staff's performance. He may have already decided he needs someone from the outside. And, you may be Johnny on the spot.

☐ While you're looking at the business pages, note any companies moving into or out of your area. It's a safe bet that companies moving into your area will want mid-management and even senior management people. A quick note to the person you might work for—expressing your interest in the company and detailing your contributions—couldn't hurt. When companies move out of an area, often people who have been with them for years decide not to move along. If you are willing to move to the new locale, you may well be a prime candidate for a job.

☐ Look at back copies and current issues of trade periodicals in your field. Most have job opportunities or classified sections in the back. Some ads will be duplicates of those you'll see in the *Wall Street Journal*. Others will be new to you. Before you subscribe, check your local library. Most have the leading business periodicals on file. And they are the ones likely to have ads that interest you.

One final thought: no matter where you see an ad, send your letter and/or resume five to seven days after it first appears. A survey by a leading executive recruiting firm revealed that 75 percent of the total answers to ads were received within four days after the ad's appearance. If you send your letter out on the sixth day, you're a lot more likely to get it seen and noticed. And if your prospective boss has been inundated with letters during the first four days, he's probably going to be in a better mood when your letter comes in with a smaller stack of mail.

Eleven

How to uncover hidden job opportunities with a "cold turkey" letter

When you first think about it, writing cold turkey to people you don't know at companies you don't know about positions that you don't know exist probably seems a little ridiculous! Yet, about one in ten* job-seekers gets his job this way. So unless you're willing to forgo the potential jobs available only through this source you can't afford to neglect this avenue in your search.

The concept of writing directly to companies about a possible yet unknown position has been promoted extensively since the late 1950s by Carl Boll, a well-known search consultant, and at the time it worked extremely well for executives with something to sell. The Boll approach (as I call it) has several elements:

☐ A FIRST PARAGRAPH DESIGNED TO "SNOW" THE READER WITH YOUR ACCOMPLISHMENTS   The idea is to bowl the reader over with your ability to do something that the person reading the letter is presumably interested in getting done.

☐ CURIOSITY   In a Boll's letter, you reveal your accomplishments (three or four of them) without telling specifically who they were for. The idea is to entice the reader to learn more about you—or, to put it another way, an attempt to get yourself an invitation to the prospective employer's office.

---

* According to an ongoing survey of where persons attending my lectures secured their "last" jobs.

☐ CREDITABILITY You try to achieve this by mentioning that you graduated from Harvard Business School (or whatever school is your alma mater).

☐ ADDRESSEES ARE COMPANY CHIEF EXECUTIVES Presidents are the target of your Boll's letter on the grounds that the president knows all the executive positions within his organization that require filling; others under him might not know of openings since they might be on the verge of getting fired.

According to Tom Bartlett (a close associate of Carl Boll whom I got to know in recent years), if you wrote a Boll's style letter you probably could secure an average of three top-level interviews for every hundred letters sent out, provided that your mailing list was a good one for your particular background. While this number of interviews may not seem large, Carl and Tom quickly point out that as with every job-seeker, you only need *one* job! A typical "cold-turkey" letter written in Boll's style is on page 160.

During the 1960s I recommended this style of letter to every job-seeker I counseled, and most reported excellent results. I would recommend this approach to you without hesitation, except for one thing. For some candidates today, it doesn't seem to work as well as other letters. Of the hundreds I personally know who've tried it in the 1970s about seven out of ten tell me they're getting no more than one interview out of one hundred letters, and often it is not the type of interview that can lead to a job offer. It's worth spending a couple of minutes trying to figure out why the Boll's letter doesn't seem to work as well for many job-seekers today, since this unique letter might still be the route for you to take if you can overcome the problems inherent in it. Why then, is the Boll's cold-turkey letter less effective for some candidates today than it was in the 1960s? Some probable reasons.

☐ ITS NOVELTY MAY HAVE WORN OFF So many presidents have received this letter that it may have ceased to have the shock value it did in the early years. In this regard the director of manpower planning at the nation's largest food manufacturing company advised me that when a Boll's style letter is received by the president of his firm, his secretary immediately forwards it to the personnel department for a perfunc-

Mr. R. L. Hanson
President
Provident Assurance Society
400 Memorial Tower
East Hanover, New Jersey 07936

Dear Mr. Hanson:

As a financial officer in the group pension department
of a leading insurance firm, I developed new pension
investment strategies which are planned to improve pro-
fitability by 50%. I did this by developing the firm's
first product-by-product planning and financial monitor-
ing system to better determine how to maximize growth
within capital limits.

If your firm is planning to add to its senior group
pension staff, you may be interested in some of the
other contributions I have made during my career with
this firm:

* Developed new procedures which saved $100,000
by freeing up marketing staff personnel from a purely
service function, permitting them to concentrate on sales.

* Earlier, as manager of the subsidiary operations
financial staff, was responsible for a study which led my
company to add life insurance to the product line, then
limited to product-liability products. This is anticipated to increase overall company sales by more than 60%.

* Located and secured a $10,000,000 independent
health insurance firm. Following acquisition, was responsible for merging the subsidiary into my company's total
operations.

Prior to joining the insurance company, I worked for a
major Wall Street investment banking firm. While at this
firm I created a limited venture capital partnership and
secured $5,000,000 to support 5 high risk businesses. The
original investments are now estimated to be worth
$35,000,000.

In total I have 17 years experience in pension and investments. I am a graduate of Columbia University School of
Business, and William and Mary College.

At your convenience, I would enjoy meeting with you to
discuss a possible career with your company, and to explore
my background and your needs further.

                              Sincerely,

                              Stanley P. Harcourt.

tory reply. All that effort down the drain! The president doesn't even see your letter.

☐ MANY PEOPLE WHO EMULATE BOLL'S STYLE MAY NOT HAVE A STRONG ENOUGH FIRST PARAGRAPH They simply haven't achieved anything in their current or previous jobs that is startling enough to make a company president sit up and take notice. Or, if the writer has achieved dramatic results, he may not be able to relate them forcefully enough to get much attention. Not every job-seeker has this flair, as Tom Bartlett and Carl Boll would tell you.

☐ A LOT OF CHIEF EXECUTIVES TODAY ARE CYNICAL ABOUT COYNESS A letter with no company names may arouse curiosity but it may also arouse resentment. (What's this clown trying to do? Pull the wool over my eyes? Why doesn't he present the facts?) Many who have used a Boll's letter advise me that the company president has written back, saying "Please send me a resume with further details." Curiosity isn't enough to get some executives into the "Oval Office." It might not be enough in your case.

If the Boll's letter doesn't appear to be as effective as it once was, and you're just about to reject it for yourself, keep in mind that for some job-seekers it still works extremely well! If you have an outstanding background, and can describe your contributions dramatically, you have an excellent chance of selling yourself by this technique. If you write to a company president who has not previously been inundated with the Boll's-style letter—a smaller company, perhaps—you have a good chance, too. If you have the knack for writing things in such a way as to arouse curiosity without arousing resentment, it could work well for you. If you can answer yes to all the "if's" above, try it!

But don't start writing just yet. Wait until you've seen another alternative I developed a few years back, when job-seekers started telling me they weren't doing all that well with their Boll's-style letter.

As you look at this second approach, keep in mind that trying to come up with a letter that could outpull Boll's wasn't easy! It had to have a dramatic opening statement impressive enough to get past secretaries who were protecting their bosses, and to open the eyes of those same bosses to the potential value of meeting the person who wrote it. Any alternative to the Boll's letter you use has to have an opening paragraph with that kind of impact!

After testing a number of alternatives with scores of job-seekers, a new first paragraph was discovered that led to more interviews per hundred letters sent out, for a majority of those who tried it, and it is leading to at least three and as many as seven interviews per hundred letters sent out—results consistent with what the Boll letter did in its heyday! What are the elements of the first new paragraph?

☐ *First*, it immediately touches a *sensitive nerve* with the reader. It takes up a topic of genuine importance to him. How do you discover in advance what will turn your reader on? *Put yourself in your reader's shoes*: identify a particular problem the reader might have that he needs help with, one that he would be willing to discuss with you—or anyone, for that matter—as long as he felt you had some valuable experience in this area. After all, it costs your reader nothing to pick your brain at a meeting. He's not obligating himself any further than that.

☐ *Second*, the first paragraph of the new letter suggests why you might be an appropriate person to talk to concerning the problem. You've got the *credentials* to discuss it intelligently. Maybe you do have some ideas your reader hasn't thought of.

☐ *Third*, it is sincere, down to earth. You don't try to impress your reader with some superman-like accomplishment in your past. You want to deal with him as one professional to another from the start.

After pinpointing a real need your reader has, and establishing that you are a logical person to talk to about that need, the balance of your cold-turkey letter should try to create the impression that you might be able to *solve* his problem for him. In that respect, it's similar to the Boll's letter except that wherever the companies you have worked for add credibility to your story, you mention them. This letter is not designed to get you in the door by arousing curiosity. Rather, it's designed to get you a hearing because you may

216 Ferryboat Lane
Port Chester, New York
10747

October 9, 1979

Dear

If it takes too long for new ideas to become saleable
products at your company...and your developmental work
is not meeting your reasonable expectations...I'd like
to meet you. I believe that I might have something to
offer you in this regard.

* As <u>Product Development Manager</u> at <u>Cameron
  Industries</u> I developed a dry process
  "perfect binding" system for office use,
  which retails at 20% of the cost of competitive systems on the market. I was able to
  take the concept from drawing board to
  marketplace within 4 months by adapting,
  modifying and personally constructing the
  machinery necessary to establish the pilot
  manufacturing operation.

* Later as <u>Director of Manufacturing</u> & <u>Plant
  Operations</u> I directed and supervised the
  planning of production, material handling
  and construction of the processing equipment for the binding systems, then started
  up production that resulted in annual volume
  at the $500,000 level. I also trained and
  monitored the staff which resulted in a
  tripling of binding unit assembly and a quad-
  rupling of cover processing within 6 months
  of start up.

* This operation became sufficiently attractive to lead its sale to a conglomerate
  within two years, representing a 5:1 return
  on the initial investment.

  I am presently responsible for developing
  plans/programs for possible entry into the
  manufacturing of specialized office products.

My background also includes experience with Inventory Control, EDP Methods and Marketing Research. My formal education includes a B.A. in 1971 from Syracuse University
as well as study at Stevens College of Technology in the
areas of Electrical Engineering and Business Management.

I am 30 years old and in excellent health. I am fluent
in French and Swedish.

At your convenience I would like to learn more about your
product development program, and the challenges now facing
your firm.

Sincerely,

(914) 461-7436   Scott Summers

have special insight concerning a legitimate business problem your reader is wrestling with.

At the *end* of this new letter is where you suggest that your interview might lead to a position with your reader's company rather than a consulting job—which he may have thought was your objective until then. A number of job-seekers who have used the new approach have reported to me that some executives they sent it to thought they were looking for consulting positions when they agreed to meet with them. This misunderstanding is okay. The important thing is that the letter gets you an interview. When you meet with someone to discuss his problem, you have ample opportunity to suggest that he invite you to come aboard on a full-time basis to solve it. A typical example of a letter aimed at the reader's "sensitive nerve" is on the opposite page.

Which letter is for you? The Boll's-style letter or the newer alternative? Most job-seekers should try them both! Send out fifty letters of each before making your decision as to which pulls best for you. Then use the letter which works best with a hundred more companies on your "prospecting" list. You might even consider sending out the "winning" letter to the fifty companies you sent the "losing" letter to earlier—leaving off those companies that responded to your first letter, of course. Why? Because the secretary may have thrown out your first letter. You have nothing to lose but another fifteen-cent stamp, and your second approach might well make it through to the prospective employer you were trying to reach. And you've created one additional opportunity to sell yourself in person into a position with your interviewer's company—a position that he may not have realized was necessary to fill before you met!

Don't count on getting your next job by writing cold-turkey. But *not* trying this technique is a mistake once you have contacted professional recruiting firms and started them working on your behalf, and have done all you can to secure interviews by answering ads for those "here and now" openings.

Quite frankly, I'm amazed that not every job-seeker tries this approach, and distressed that even those who have found few ads to answer procrastinate in starting on a "cold-turkey" campaign. I suspect that it's because they assume beforehand that developing a list of potential employers will be a mammoth undertaking. Those who have developed a cold-turkey prospect list know otherwise. Don't get me wrong. Discovering the names of companies and people whom you could write to is a time-consuming proposition, but it's not really that difficult. Your reference librarian can help you find a number of directories of companies and officers. If you want to try it on your own, there are six source books that I recommend, since they can give you the names of most major U.S. companies in your field:

□ *Standard Directory of Advertisers*
□ *Standard and Poor's Register of Corporations, Directors and Executives*
□ *Thomas Register of American Manufacturers*
□ *Dun & Bradstreet's Million Dollar Directory*
□ *Dun & Bradstreet's Middle Market Directory*
□ *Moody's Manuals* (Public Utilities/Industrial/etc.)

You'll find at least one of these undated volumes at most public libraries, and larger libraries (at colleges particularly) should have all. Of these, the *Standard Directory of Advertisers* is worthy of special note. One edition is divided by product category or service. If, for example, you are in the appliance business now, and are interested in staying in this field, you'll find the category listing simplifies your legwork. Another edition is by city and state, and if you are interested only in one specific area, it can lead you to companies involved in all fields.

If you are in a specialized field, you're likely to find a compendium of firms in your specialty by asking the reference librarian. For example, the *Investment Banker/Broker Directory* (published by *Finance Magazine*) is a useful source book for executives in the securities field. Similar annuals exist in the publishing and advertising agency fields, and in all probability, in your specialty, if it is not covered by the more general corporation directories noted above.

The real problem is deciding which companies to write to. There's no right way to go about it. You'll have to decide on the criteria for yourself: location, size, primary product, etc. Then you'll have to leaf through one or more of the enormous directories, jotting down names and addresses of those firms that interest you, names of people you might report to. It's a time-consuming job, and there's no valid shortcut that I know of. (The *Standard Directory of Advertisers* does have an alphabetical index in the front, which could help you if you rely on company name only. That could be an undesirable shortcut, however.)

If you exhaust the possibilities in the company directories noted above, you might try writing to industry associations. Large municipal and college libraries should have the *Encyclopedia of Associations* on hand. Your experience in writing to associations should be very favorable. Your letter to the United States Brewers Foundation, for example, is likely to yield a list of all members, the executive officers of each company in the association, and their addresses. Unfortunately, not all industries have active associations, and not all companies belong to the active ones. But if you can't seem to locate the companies you want to reach by thumbing through the corporation directories noted above, writing to an industry association is worth a try.

If your job search is local rather than national, there are several alternative sources for you in addition to those cited above. The chamber of commerce in most major cities maintain lists of local industries. Frequently these are available free. Some are sold at a nominal price. A call to your local chamber of commerce, or even a long distance call to the chamber of commerce where you'd like to relocate, should provide you with a good source of potential employers. A frequently overlooked source of company names and addresses is the local newspaper in the area in which you wish to work. Newspapers often publish annual industry reviews. If your local paper publishes such an issue, you'll find "Compliments of" ads placed by virtually all major firms in your area. Generally, extra copies of this special issue are available from the publisher for a dollar or two.

There's another overlooked source you should consider—the yellow pages. It may not sound like a very sophisticated list, but it's probably one of the most comprehensive in any locality. Since you're beating the bushes, there's no reason to pass it up if your search is local. Still another source of local company names that is often overlooked is a trusted friendly supplier who calls on you in your current position. If you have close ties with a supplier, and can speak to him in confidence, do so. He may have a sales-prospect list of companies in industries related to your own. If you compile a local list of companies you'd like to work for, call each. Ask the switchboard operator the name of the person who holds the title you would report to. Address your letters directly to the executive you want to work for. Don't address them to "Office of the President" or "Personnel Director." If you really want to work at a company, you'll take the trouble to find out the name of the person who might hire you. He's the only one you want to meet.

As you can see from the variety of sources, if you're willing to make the effort, you can develop a lengthy list of companies you might well work for, companies to write directly to. It isn't easy. You may feel it isn't worth the effort. You may decide to tackle this particular phase of your job search only after you've exhausted the opportunities you develop through executive recruiters and ads. That prerogative is yours. But don't lose momentum. If the number of interviews you have each week starts to dwindle, it's time to spend nights in the library securing names of companies that you can write to directly. While writing to companies cold-turkey seems to be a long shot, it has worked for so many people it would be a mistake not to consider seriously this way to a better job.

Twelve

Three other job-seeking letters you should write... and one you shouldn't

The cold-turkey letters talked about in the previous chapters are basic to your job campaign. There are three other letters you should also consider writing, if you are going to maximize your search opportunities through correspondence.

1. Interview follow-up letters

The least-used and potentially most effective job-seeking letter is the one you send out following your interviews. Why most job-seekers fail to send a letter following every interview is a mystery. Perhaps the pressures of time are such that job-seekers give it a low priority. When you think about it, however, the interview follow-up letter can do a number of things for you.

☐ It will help you to be remembered. Chances are you'll be one of the few persons interviewed thoughtful enough to send a follow-up note. Your prospective boss will remember you when others are forgotten.

☐ It's an opportunity to reiterate that you understand your prospective boss's problems.

☐ It gives you a second chance to refer your prospective boss to your past contributions that relate to his current problems.

Mr. A. J. Simson
President
Simson Bearings, Inc.

Dear Mr. Simson:

Thanks for meeting with me yesterday to discuss
a career with Simson Bearings. In talking of
the many aspects of your company's phenomenal
growth, I was most impressed with your corporate
acquisition philosophy.

In this regard, I appreciated your positive reaction to the role I played in my own company's
purchase of Thunderbolt Enterprises, (now a
subsidiary of our firm). As we discussed,
Thunderbolt added more than 25% to our sales
volume. Naturally I was proud of my part in working out final details of the purchase agreement,
particularly since Thunderbolt had been close to
being purchased by our chief competitor, and had
decided against the deal during negotiations.

Again, many thanks for the hour we spent together.
As you undoubtedly realize, the challenge presented
by the specific job opportunity you described at
Simson Bearings sounds extremely rewarding. I look
forward to meeting with you and your associates soon
to discuss your needs further.

                        Sincerely,

☐   It gives you an opportunity to show your genuine interest in the job opportunity. The following letter is from a candidate to his prospective boss. It arrived in the mail two days after their interview. Consider what the prospective boss must have thought about the person who wrote it.

This letter has a lot going for it. It shows appreciation for the recent interview. It reviews a subject close to the prospective boss's heart—acquisitions. It briefly recalls a contribution of the candidate in the very area the prospective boss is interested in. It reveals the genuine interest the candidate has in the specific job opportunity. It confirms the candidate's interest in pursuing the opportunity. When you develop your own interview follow-up letters, keep in mind those major needs that your prospective boss revealed to you during your interview. Play any (or all) back in your letter as long as your own experience is relevant to them. If your prospective boss seemed interested in a particular worthpoint you discussed, refresh his memory by referring to it in some natural way. If on the other hand you failed to discuss a particular worthpoint during your interview—because you forgot to do so, or had no time for it—use your follow-up letter to let your prospective boss know about this relevant experience. When you contrast the letter shown above with no letter (and most job-seekers don't send follow-up letters), you realize the significant advantage you have over competition with a polite, enthusiastic, responsive letter written directly after your interview.

One further point about follow-up letters. Even if you have been able to secure a specific date for an additional interview a week or so after your first, you ought to send one. A simple "thank you" note shows you are a polite candidate, and a businesslike one, as well. Adding a confirming date to your thank you note can be done easily and naturally. Instead of telling your prospective boss that you look forward to meeting him and his associates "in the future," just let him know the day and the time you are looking forward to getting together. Remember, other candidates may meet with your prospective boss between your first and second interviews. A note can keep him thinking of you during this period.

2. Letters to executive recruiter

The next chapter in this book takes up the sources, both good and bad, that a job-seeker can turn to for assistance. One of the best is the legitimate, professional recruiter. I would pay almost any job-seeker making thirty thousand dollars or more annually to try and make contact *by letter* with executive recruiters in his area. To get the most from this important source of assistance, your letter has to help the recruiter determine whether your job objective meshes with any of the searches he is conducting, and to get him interested in you versus the other candidates with similar backgrounds he is considering. In this regard your letter should:

☐ TRANSMIT YOUR RESUME   No good search firm today can work without a resume. Even if they ask you to fill out their own unique application form, most will still send out your resume to their clients.

☐ REVIEW YOUR KEY WORTHPOINTS   When a professional recruiting firm introduces you to one of its clients it will need several relevant contributions that can be used to convince its clients you are a superior candidate. If you list several worthpoints on page one of your letter to recruiters, they can be seen and used on your behalf. Equally important, your worthpoints may be what's necessary to get the recruiting firm to promote *you* instead of the other candidates it has located for the position.

☐ STATE YOUR CURRENT SALARY, OR SALARY REQUIREMENT Inclusion of your salary requirement seems to contradict what was suggested when you answer blind ads or deal direct with companies. True, but there's a reason. Professional search firms want to know how well your salary requirements mesh with the openings their clients have. They feel there's no point introducing you to a company that wants a person earning half of what you do. Thus search firms insist on knowing your salary requirement or past salary. Tell them in your initial letter. It saves a return letter asking for this information.

☐ STATE YOUR JOB OBJECTIVE   In precise, definitive terms. What titles would you consider? What size company? Where would you be willing to locate? Without this knowledge, search firms are in the dark as to how best to help you. Don't delay their efforts. Include this information.

See page 173 for an example of a businesslike letter to a professional firm involved in job search.

As you read this complete and thorough letter, two anxious thoughts may well cross your mind: "If you give away all the information, will the professional recruiter still want to meet you? And don't you need to sell him *in person*?"

If your worthpoints and job objective mesh with the professional recruiter's client's needs, he'll want to meet you in order to recommend you personally. At that time you can talk to him in person about your contributions. It doesn't pay to meet every professional recruiter you write, however. They can't hire you. They can only place you. And they can't do that until they know of a spot for you. Then the recruiter will call you in because you are necessary for him to earn his fee, equal to 30 percent or more of your salary. In a word, he'll be more than anxious to meet you when he can help you, and himself.

3. Response to classified ads

The previous chapter on answering ads was focused on executive "display" ads—those large enough to contain significant detail concerning the openings you are interested in. But what about the "classified"—those two- and three-line ads that include hardly more than a job title and a box number to write to? What then? Should you resort to the typical cover letter that does nothing more than say: "Read my resume. It's attached." You might, but there's another approach that experience has shown works better. And that's to *assume* the advertiser's needs based on the job title and to write a cover letter that highlights the most significant worthpoints from your resume that you think the advertiser might be interested in. Consider the following example on page 174.

While your letter written in response to a job title can't hope to be as effective as one written in response to the advertiser's specific needs, it has a lot more going for it than the typical cover letter. What do *you* stand to gain by this format?

Gentlemen:

For the past five years I've managed the production at a major factory of one of America's blue-chip companies. The results of the people I've directed speak for themselves:

> Production up 250 per cent on two products; up 175 per cent on two others.

> Return on Investment in new capital equipment recommended by me is under three years.

> No labor problems have arisen in five years—following two major strikes which occurred prior to my assuming my current position as manufacturing manager.

Despite these successes, I plan to relocate with another firm, since my next promotion would involve a move to corporate headquarters in another part of the country. For personal reasons, my family wants to remain in the East.

In relocating, I am seeking a position as Director of Manufacturing for a medium-sized firm or manufacturing manager for a larger firm. As indicated on the attached resume, I have experience in all phases of manufacturing and quality control in the appliance and electronic industries; and have supervised more than 500 people. My salary is $65,000. I am however flexible on salary since the position and location are more important to me, and I'm sure a reasonable figure can be arrived at if both parties are happy with one another.

If one of your clients seeks a person with my background, I look forward to discussing your client's needs with you at your earliest convenience.

                          Sincerely,

Box 4871

Gentlemen:

This responds to your ad in the April 12th edition of the
<u>Chicago Tribune</u> in which you express your need to locate
an experienced <u>Sales Promotion Manager</u>. As the attached
resume reveals, I've had 8 years of experience in the
Sales promotion field and for the past 3 years have been
<u>Sales Promotion Director</u> for Chillbest, Inc., a regional
white-goods manufacturer with annual sales of over
$300,000,000. In this position, I report to the vice-
president of marketing and am responsible for a $4,000,000
sales promotion budget. Specific areas of my experience
that might be relevant to your needs include:

- <u>Development of Trade Incentives</u>--Created the
  first "Matching Dollars" promotion used in the
  white-goods industry in which dealers received
  a promotional incentive equal to the rebate
  check sent to consumers who bought from their
  outlets. This resulted in massive displays of
  our brand and increased sales of the Chillbest
  line by 20%--at the expense of our 2 major
  competitors.

- <u>Creation of Theme Displays</u>--Secured tie-ins with
  3 major frozen foods companies (Zero, Frosty,
  Brrrr brands) to support our "Colder the Better"
  refrigerator which features more reliable freezer
  controls. These displays offered "frozen food"
  sweepstakes prizes valued at more than $200,000
  which were delivered at <u>no</u> expense to our company.

- <u>Preparation of Sales Promotion Materials</u>--Direct
  activities of a 6-person staff which each year
  develops more then 18 theme and technical promotion packages. Four packages in the past year
  were cited by the Downstate Sales Executives
  Club for "originality and sales effectiveness."

As indicated in my resume, I am a graduate of Missouri
State with a major in business administration.

At your earliest convenience I'd like to learn more of
the specific sales promotion needs of your company at
this time.

                    Sincerely,

Gentlemen:

This responds to your ad in the May 22 edition of the
Washington Post in which you outline your needs for a
creatively oriented director of marketing for a company selling to drug and department stores.

My experience has been in marketing products to these
two classes of trade and I have worked at three levels
of marketing management. Some of my contributions are
outlined below:

> Organized and directed a marketing department
> to introduce a new quality line of health-care
> products.

> Programs instituted by this marketing depart-
> ment contributed to these results: Several
> products were in the strong #2 position in
> test markets just sixteen months after intro-
> duction. Several others were in #1 positions
> in the quality segment of the categories in
> which they compete.

> In response to market needs, this marketing
> group also developed and readied for intro-
> duction five conceptually new products, the
> first developed by the company in nine years.
> These products accounted for 20 per cent of
> annual volume in their first year.

Earlier in my career, as a marketing manager at another
major company, I took over a gradually eroding
$10,000,000 food product. Two years later the brand
had its first sales increase in five years (+ 12 per
cent): Turnaround reflected a shift in advertising
strategy. Sales increase occurred without a price
increase and with concurrent reduction in media
support.

By way of biography, I was graduated with honors from
Stamford Business School, and with high honors from
Michigan University.

I look forward to discussing further details of my
experience with you in a personal interview.

                              Yours very sincerely,

☐   *First,* your prospective boss knows you're the kind of a person who recognizes business problems—and, hopefully, his problems.

☐   *Second,* even before the advertiser turns a page, he knows you're a person who can do things he would like to see accomplished at his company. He doesn't have to grope around your resume looking for proof of your worth.

☐   *Third,* the advertiser will realize you cared enough about the opportunity presented in the ad to write a *personalized* cover letter rather than a transmittal letter like those he'll see the rest of the day.

☐   *Fourth,* your letter is a demonstration of your ability to write well-documented, businesslike correspondence in support of your position. The advertiser knows you could do the same thing for him.

Certainly a letter such as this requires a little more work to compose than the typical transmittal letter. But once developed, you can use it without change to respond to every classified ad that states the same job title! Judging by the reports I've received from job-seekers who have written letters like the one above, the extra effort has definitely been worth it.

Let's turn briefly to one job-search letter format I recommend you *don't* write, and that's a "curiosity rousing" response to blind ads. This kind of letter has only one purpose in mind: to whet the appetite of the reader; to force him to invite you to his office, where you can present your credentials in person. According to the curiosity-rousing formula, you do not include a resume with your response, nor do you even offer the requested information in a letter format. Instead, you acknowledge the position you are applying for, provide a synopis of your work experience *without naming the companies you worked with;* and provide a list of your key worthpoints written in somewhat vague terms. An example is on page 175.

If your worthpoints are good enough, the letter may get a very positive first reading. Whether it gets you in the door is another question. Why am I a doubter? Simple. I had a number of clients try the technique. They forwarded a vague description of their backgrounds and worthpoints. In almost every instance, those who heard back got this type of response:

Dear Job-Seeker:

Thank you for your letter generally outlining your background and contributions. It's possible we would like to meet you once we have more specific information on your background. In this regard, please forward a recent resume. Naturally, it will be held in the strictest confidence.

Yours very truly,

The fact of the matter is this: Today curiosity is usually not sufficient, in and of itself, to assure you either a response or an interview. If this technique worked a decade ago, its novelty has now worn off, and advertisers are apparently less impressed with coy candidates than with those who deal from the top of the deck. What should be of even greater concern to you if you use a curiosity-rousing letter is that while you are sending in your resume in a response to the advertiser's request, who knows how many other candidates may already be entering your prospective boss's office!

Thirteen

How to launch your better job campaign

By now many of you must be chomping at the bit. You've reviewed your career year by year, picking out the worthpoints that will sell you best. You've drafted—and edited—a resume you are proud of. You've answered an ad or two, using the technique of responding to each of the needs the advertiser has outlined. You may even have rehearsed how you will relate your worthpoints at an interview. But you know that to get the job you want, this level of activity is not really enough. Your goal is to locate every potential job opportunity that currently exists for the talents and experience you have to offer. You are now ready to get your job-search campaign into high gear! Here are some thoughts on how to do it.

1. Recognize that production of materials for your search is a big undertaking, and get started on this assignment as soon as you possibly can

Unless you are a perpetual job-changer, you may be unaware that there are a lot of purely mechanical aspects to mounting an effective job campaign. You'll need to write letters. That means you first have to order stationery! There is nothing in the book that says you must use personalized writing paper, but it looks far more professional than a name and address typed on a sheet of erasable bond. And your goal is to do everything you can to create an impression that you are, in fact, a pro in everything you do during your job search.

Ordering stationery isn't hard to do, but it does take time to get it—anywhere from one to four weeks. So you've got to make time to order it now, or it could delay your job-search campaign later on. Fortunately, almost any business stationers can order it for you, but you might want to consider getting stationery by mail from one of the national outfits like The Stationery House in Hagerstown, Maryland, or The Drawing Board in Dallas, Texas. These companies, and others like them, sell on such scale and avoid the markup the local printer must make, and so might save you money. You can call either for a catalog.

Once you've ordered your stationery, you'll need to find someone who can type your letters and resume for you. Perhaps you or your spouse are good enough to do this. But even if you are, don't make the mistake of trying to do your typing on a home portable. If you plan to be your own secretarial service, at the very least rent a business typewriter like the IBM Selectric, or other carbon-ribbon machine. If you plan to write to prospective bosses on your own, be sure you can turn out letters that look as if they are professionally typed. The impression your correspondence makes when it is first opened by a possible employer can be as important as what you say in your letter. Again, you want your prospective boss to think to himself that he is dealing with an individual who does everything first class, because that's the sort of person he'd like working for him.

If you decide to be your own typist, your cost of turning out top-quality letters won't be more than $40 a month—the cost of renting a business typewriter. When you consider it, it is a small investment to make in getting your next job! But don't forget, if you plan to type your job-search letters on your own, it will take a good deal of your time. You don't want to delay a follow-up note because you simply didn't have the time to get to it, or to answer an ad a week or two later than you should have, just because you had no time to sit down to type it. That's why you may well opt for an outside secretarial service. If you do plan to get help, take the time to call around. In our town, you can pay as little as $1.50 per page and as much as $3.50 for the same quality work. It would pay you to make a few calls—and visits to see examples of typefaces, and just how professional the typist's work really is.

You'll need to locate a good quality printer, too. There's nothing that says you can't go to the closest local printer you can find. But you could end up paying a great deal more unless you look around. Today there are a number of printing chains that specialize in short-run offset printing. Outfits like Sir Speedy, Insty Print, Postal Instant Press, and others, are geared specially to individuals, and many specialize in resumes. As with all things you can buy, not every service does the same quality work. It would really pay you to look at samples of printing from several outfits before you make up your mind. One caution in this regard: some local printing outfits are using Xerox high-speed copiers as printing devices. They're never of as good quality as photo-offset. Don't try to save a couple of bucks at the expense of creating a "what, me worry?" look about the resumes you send out.

Many executives prefer their resumes to be "composited." This is a reasonably priced technique (approximately $50 for two pages) that makes your resume pages look as if they were 'set' in type like a book rather than looking as if they were typed. This technique has two advantages: it looks more professional, and you can get more information on a page. If you plan to have your resume composited, you'll have to locate a good compositor, as well as a typist. Often you'll find compositors listed under "letter shops" in your yellow pages.

Letter shops can be useful in mounting an aggressive campaign in another way, too. Many letter shops have automatic typewriters as well as composing machines. An automatic typewriter is one that can be used to create "individually typed" letters without individually typing them. IBM, Xerox, I-M, Lanier all make such "computer" typewriters, and any is suitable as long as it utilizes a carbon ribbon. (Some of the older models do not.) If you plan to conduct a broadcast campaign—and most job-seekers should—you may well want to locate a letter shop with an automatic typewriter so that your letters to companies look as though you had typed each individually. In this regard, shopping for the right letter shop can be very much worth your while. For example, automatically typed letters are available for 47¢ each (one page, in quantities of two hundred of the same letter) from one outfit in New York City, and for two dollars per page from another outfit only a few blocks away.

You may also wish to locate a good "mailing" house. These outfits will stuff your letters into envelopes, seal them and stamp them automatically for you for a few pennies per envelope. Some mailing houses have compositor and automatic typewriters in-house so that they can conduct your direct mail campaign for you from first to last. You may want to explore that possibility to save yourself running around from printer to mailer, although you may pay for this convenience.

If you use assistance at every stage of your job search, you could well spend upwards of $500 on all of the services I've described. If this seems like an enormous investment, remember it is in your career, and getting the right job is well worth it. Of course, you don't have to spend anywhere near that amount if you are willing to handle the mechanical aspects of your search on your own. As an example, if you don't want to use an automatic typewriter for your broadcast letter, you can have the body of your letter run off by a photo-offset printer, and then slip each printed letter back in your typewriter for addressing. But if you go this route, you've got to spend the time to locate an offset printer with a machine good enough to duplicate your original letter so well that when you do type in the address, it looks as if the entire letter came out of a typewriter. The important thing to keep in mind is that the less you spend, the more time you've got to allocate to the purely mechanical aspects of your search—the stuffing, stamping, sealing, etc. The choice is yours. Just be prepared with the time or money if you want to do the job right.

2. Organize your time in a way that will maximize the results of your search

You obviously can't do everything at once in your campaign, so it pays to concentrate on those things necessary to produce the greatest return for your time spent. In this respect, the following priority schedule makes a good deal of sense:

☐ AS A FIRST PRIORITY, GET AS MANY PROFESSIONALS WORKING ON YOUR BEHALF AS YOU POSSIBLY CAN   The more executive recruiters or ethical employment agents who are on the lookout for the right job for you, the more you can multiply the speed with which you can land the job you want. Getting the job-search professionals to work on your search for you is not unlike getting your home "multiple listed" when you plan to sell it: you have a lot more leverage than if you try to sell it on your own. In the following chapter, you'll learn who are the ethical professionals to approach for help, and how to find them. Suffice to say for now, you should get them working for you as soon as you can. To do this, you'll need your resume printed and mailed out in quantity, so the mechanical production I spoke of earlier must be organized at the start.

☐ AS A SECOND PRIORITY, GO AFTER THE JOBS THAT ARE "HERE AND NOW" As soon as you learn of any job opening suited to you, no matter how you learn of it, take action to make sure you are considered for the position. To locate as many "here and now" jobs as you possibly can, you'll need to start reading local papers, national newspapers like the *Wall Street Journal*, appropriate trade journals, and the like, and to read as many as you can get your hands on. The point is simply that once you've made sure you've got the professionals working for you, make sure you're in touch with all the sources that can help you locate jobs on your own. And don't skimp on subscription money. You can cancel your newspaper subscription the day you get a new job. In the interim it's worth every penny for the leads it creates.

☐ AS A THIRD PRIORITY, GET YOUR FRIENDS AND ASSOCIATES WORKING ON YOUR BEHALF The thing to keep in mind is that when you've got your campaign to recruiting professionals in full swing, and have lined up your "here and now" leads, you've reached the point in your search where you should turn your full energies toward getting as much nonprofessional help in landing a new job as you possibly can.

☐ THE LAST PRIORITY ON YOUR CAMPAIGN LIST IS TO SEEK OUT JOB OPPORTUNITIES THAT DON'T EXIST UNTIL YOU, YOURSELF, CREATE THEM Obviously, *developing* a job for your talents with a company that isn't actively looking for someone like you has got to be a long shot! But this type of activity has yielded many job-seekers good positions, and it's worth exploring. The only thing to keep in mind is that the odds of creating your own position are pretty steep, so it must take a back seat to your other efforts to get a team working to locate jobs that actually exist, and to pursue, on your own, the opportunities that you know are available. By now, you may have drafted your "cold-turkey" letter to companies you'd like to work for, and the next chapter will spell out how to reach them. My point in discussing them here is simply to caution you that as you lay out your campaign, this phase of it has to take a back seat to the other activities I've outlined.

3. Establish a specific timetable for each step in your job-search campaign

In the introduction to this book, I suggested you set yourself a realistic target date by which you'll have the job you want. Now I suggest you establish a specific date for each phase of your job campaign. If you haven't already completed a draft of your resume, what date will you have this done by? When will your stationery be ordered? Be ready to be picked up? When will your resume be mailed to recruiters? And so on. There are so many "little" things that you have to do to get the job you want—from stamps to lists to ordering newspapers, etc.—that unless you make yourself a schedule, it would be possible to overlook the one thing that could make the difference between landing an offer and just missing it.

4. Log your progress every day without fail

Even though it may seem like an inordinate pain in the neck, keeping records regularly will actually save you time and help you to make critical campaign decisions. Keep records of professional recruiting firms you've written to, responses received, interviews you've set up. Names of people you've interviewed, particularly if you've spoken to more than one individual at the same company. Position of each person you've interviewed. Mistakes you think you've made along the way. Dates of job offers, if and when you get them, and turndowns, too. Ads you've answered. And the time to record these items is when they happen. It is almost impossible to reconstruct the progress of your job search by writing down key events and names a month later. Most people and dates are long forgotten by then. Although keeping records is, admittedly, a pain, in the end you'll find doing so is worth it for several reasons:

☐ There's nothing more flattering to a person who calls than to recognize instantly the organization he's with, how long ago you met him, and the place you both met, if it was outside the office. (I'll confess that in the past there were times when I received calls from possible bosses whom I had met just days or weeks before, and whose names sounded totally unfamiliar to me. After a few goofs, I kept a handy list by the phone; it included everyone I talked to during my search, and the company each represented. When someone called, he knew he was important to me.)

☐ Knowing exactly when you saw a company last can help you determine its interest in you, help you determine whether you are still a live prospect in its eyes. If, for example, you've had three interviews spaced within two weeks, and then two weeks go by without a call, you had better believe the company has some doubts. Perhaps the job has been redefined. Perhaps a newly met candidate interests the company more. Knowing you are no longer a prime candidate may result in your redirecting your efforts. It's better to know than to live with false hope.

☐ You give yourself the opportunity to evaluate the effectiveness of each element of your campaign at *any* point in time. Take letters, for example. Six years ago, a job-seeker sent out two different letters, each to fifty companies he thought he'd like to work for. The first letter yielded seven interview opportunities, the second, two. His first letter apparently worked better than his second. Not surprisingly, he used the first letter exclusively in subsequent correspondence. If you keep records, you can change your program at any time to make it more effective.

Sometimes I'm asked if there's a best way to keep records during a job search. I suspect each person has his own favorite way of doing this. If you're open to suggestions, however, why not consider using a three-ring binder exclusively for your job search. If you do use a binder, it's a great place for everything concerning your job search, particularly if you organize your notebook with tabs. What should you include in each section? Some possibilities:

☐ YOUR OBJECTIVES The ones I suggested you write out in the introduction. Keep them up front where you can look at them once in a while to hold yourself on target.

☐ YOUR RESUME Keep each of the drafts you make. Many a job-seeker has decided that his latest version wasn't as effective as an earlier one. Keeping copies in a notebook can help you backtrack if you have to.

☐ YOUR WORTHPOINTS If you've spent a few days developing lists of what you have to sell, keep them in one section. You may have items on your list you didn't include in your resume. Keep the list handy for revising your resume and for studying prior to an interview. You never know what obscure experience you've had might mean in a particular interview.

☐ YOUR INTERVIEWS A record of who you met, the dates, and most important, how things went. Record the tough questions so that you don't forget to develop good answers for them. Jot down reactions people had to your worthpoints, so you know whether to reintroduce them at another interview, or how to describe them differently to get greater impact. If you've persuaded a friend, or friend of a friend, to interview you, this is a good place to note his reaction.

☐ YOUR JOB-SEARCH CORRESPONDENCE Keep a copy of each of the drafts you make of answers to ads. You'll probably find that the way you state one particular worthpoint in one letter appeals to you more than the way you state it in another. Go over your drafts and pick out the "ideal" phrases and paragraphs every so often. No sense writing every response to an ad from scratch when you have "models" to work from in copies of previous responses. This section of your notebook is also a good place to keep the actual ads you respond to. Many of my clients clip the ad they've answered along with a Xerox or carbon copy of their reply. That way, if the letter results in an offer of an interview, they know exactly what the advertiser was looking for in hiring someone, and exactly what was said by the candidate in his letter that secured the interview.

☐ YOUR COLD-TURKEY CAMPAIGN This section of your notebook is the place to keep copies of each of your letters to potential employers, particularly if you are testing one against another. Unfortunately, I've known some job-seekers who have tested several letters, then discovered they didn't have a copy of the winning letter on file, and had to reconstruct it in expanding their cold-turkey campaign. It's never the same!

This section of your notebook is a good place for recording the names and addresses of each potential employer you come up with. Keep them all together and note whether they reply to your cold-turkey letter, and who, and how many invite you to interviews, so you can see how well your letter-writing campaign is working.

☐ **YOUR SOURCES OF SUPPLY** As you uncover printers, stationers, typists, etc., why not jot down their prices and phone numbers in this section of your job-search notebook? It's a lot easier to get in touch with people who can help speed your job search if you know where you've recorded information about them, than to search through scraps of paper in your wallet, hoping you can retrieve the information you jotted down.

☐ **YOUR TIMETABLE** This is the place for the schedule of specific dates you established, and a good section to look at once a week to determine if you have kept to your original timetable, or whether it needs revising.

In suggesting that you develop a job-search notebook, keep in mind that it is by no means mandatory to the success of your job campaign. A notebook is a simple way of making sure you have all the information at your fingertips that is needed to conduct a businesslike job search. Undoubtedly there are other ways. Some people use calendars only, and file other important papers. So be it. The important thing to keep in mind is that you develop a comprehensive, easy-to-use system that helps you run your search efficiently. It may take a little extra effort to set up, but in the long run it should save you time and energy, and help you to make more realistic decisions as you pursue your goal of landing a better job.

Fourteen

Sources of job-search assistance any job-seeker can turn to

Several years ago a building contractor started an addition to my house, and, after accepting a check for several thousand dollars, disappeared into the night. Naturally, I got hold of a lawyer who wrote a compelling complaint and a summons for the contractor to appear in court. Unfortunately for me, the unscrupulous contractor had vanished and the summons was simply not deliverable. In effect, despite the quality of the summons and complaint, these legal documents were worthless because they were never seen by the person they were addressed to. This story has a telling parallel in any job-search campaign. Your resume is a useless document, no matter how well it sells you, unless you can get it into the hands of every executive who needs a person like you. It doesn't make any difference if you are head and shoulders above any other candidate for the job. Unless you are known to the prospective employer, you'll still be looking long after a lesser candidate has been welcomed aboard.

One principle of getting the better job you want is simply to maximize the number of exposures you make to prospective employers. How do you go about it? Obviously, by answering every ad for which you are reasonably well qualified, and by writing cold-turkey letters to companies you'd like to work for. But you may be hitting only the tip of the iceberg with such techniques. Many positions are never advertised because companies prefer, instead, to hire professional recruiting firms to look for candidates discreetly. Many other positions are advertised so subtly—with a one-line listing of the job title by a professional recruiting firm, along with a telephone number—that unless you make an effort to scrutinize such ads, you could easily overlook them. It all boils down to this: unless you make it your business to make your campaign known to professional recruiting firms, you may be missing an important source of possible positions that you might want to secure. And not doing so could be one of the biggest mistakes of your job search. After all, professional recruiting outfits are in business to bridge the gap between a prospective employer's needs and your talents. They make their living by unearthing positions that need filling and convincing employers that they can fill these openings more effectively than if the employer advertises on his own. So no job-seeker should fail to make use of these professional recruiters. They are an additional channel to prospective opportunities; they are available and willing. Without them, you can't maximize your exposure to the market for your talents.

Who are these professional recruiting firms? How can you reach them? Unfortunately, they range from highly professional prestigious firms to one-man backroom operations that exist only by the grace of Alexander Graham Bell. So it's really not possible to secure one comprehensive list of people in the business of professional recruiting and to send your resume to them. You have to deal with each type of recruiter in a way that will yield you the best results. Here is a rundown on the kinds of professional (and not so professional) recruiters you are likely to come up against during your job search.

1. Executive recruiters

The most prestigious of the professional recruiters, these organizations are employed by those companies seeking executives to fill vacant executive positions typically at $30,000 and up, although many limit their searches to executives making $50,000 and up. Executive recruiters are generally on retainer but earn additional incentives (up to 25 percent of your first year's salary) when they place you. Professional executive recruiters rely heavily on repeat business from the companies they represent and are very thorough in checking on the backgrounds of the job-seekers they discover. Their thoroughness can be a nuisance to job-seekers when they request a detailed written letter to accompany a resume, or the names of fifteen or so references from the past. This is particularly bothersome when an executive recruiter requests this information without having a particular client vacancy to fill. But you'd better live with the inconvenience since executive recruiters can be key people in your life. Typically, executive recruiters themselves have risen in the ranks of business and are personable and highly articulate. Frequently senior company officials retire to the prestige-paneled offices of executive recruiting firms and use their former business contacts to secure the right to represent companies in finding executives to fill key positions.

Because they represent companies, executive recruiters do not promote job candidates. They will put you in contact with a company they represent only if a genuine job opportunity exists. Thus, sending a resume to an executive recruiter won't often get you in the door of a potential employer. Executive recruiters do maintain active files, however, and it can't hurt to have your resume in them. Executive recruiters' active files are definitely not circular. I know of a dozen cases in which executive recruiters have located candidates two years or more after they first received the resume. In most instances it's too late: the candidate is at peace with the world. But not always. An executive recruiter may catch up with you just as you are ready to move again.

Which executive recruiters should you write to? All of them. Why? Because executive recruiters typically are on an exclusive retainer to fill all jobs for the particular company they represent. Thus, when you send your resume to all executive recruiters, you run very little risk of having your resume sent to a company from several different sources. At the same time, you broaden the base of companies that might possibly be looking for a person like you. How can you locate those executive recruiters that could help? The most comprehensive list I've seen was developed by the American Management Associations and is available if you send $2 to the Management Information Service of the American Management Association at 135 West 50th Street, New York, N.Y., 10020. Another excellent list is available for $2 from the Association of Executive Recruiting Consultants, Inc. (AERC) at 30 Rockefeller Plaza, New York, N.Y., 10020. Executive recruiters seem to merge and change addresses fairly frequently.

Even if a friend has a list from several years ago, I suggest you write for an updated list. Last year's may be 20 percent out of date. A two-year-old list, even more so. While I urge you to get to every genuine executive recruiter that you can, one caution: several directories of executive recruiters are published that are not very discriminating in which firms they choose to include as "executive" recruiting firms. A review of such directories yields many an employment agency, particularly in smaller communities. Since employment agencies must be handled differently from executive recruiters, writing to every name in such directories could pose problems. That's why I suggest you use the directories above, and be cautious of any directory with nine hundred or a thousand names of recruiters in it. There aren't that many real ones.

2. Management consultants

These firms are primarily in business to solve systems and organizational problems for their client companies. As part of their assistance program, many management consultants do provide assistance in locating executives. Initially this service was limited to finding executives for positions that developed as a result of restructuring the organization according to the consultants' recommendations. Today, however, a number of management consultants maintain full-time recruiting departments as a separate profit center and do recruiting for clients regardless of whether they are doing other manpower consulting. Management consultants, like executive recruiters, work for the company, not the candidate, and are interested in people only when they have specific job openings to fill. As with executive recruiters, management consultants rarely if ever overlap each other in representing a client company, and you need not fear duplicate distribution of your resume if you send it out to a number of management consultants. You should recognize in approaching management consultants that for many of them executive recruiting is a secondary service. As such, they are not aggressively seeking people like you. So don't rely heavily on them for results. At the same time it can't hurt to contact any major consulting firms in your area to make sure they know of you in the event that something comes along while you're still looking.

3. Certified public accountants and major banks

In one sense CPA firms and banks are consultants in their own disciplines. As such, client companies have turned to them for help in locating qualified executives in their own fields. Recognizing that recruiting is a lucrative business, many such firms have also established search departments as separate profit centers. The "big-eight" accounting firms like Arthur Andersen, Touche Ross, and Price Waterhouse, for example, offer executive recruiting assistance to their clients—and seek out individuals in *all* disciplines. Similarly major banks such as Citibank and Bankers Trust in New York are set up to handle recruiting assignments for their clients. It would pay you to contact the *Executive Recruiting Departments* of the major CPA firms in your area as well as the *Executive Recruiting Officer* in major banks in your locale.

4. Employment agencies

There are several different kinds of employment agencies. But there are some characteristics that are common to all. Employment agencies generally don't try to fill positions as high up the organizational ladder as do executive recruiters, and are often geared to entry-level jobs. So if you earn forty thousand dollars annually, employment agencies probably won't be as helpful as executive recruiters. Don't overlook them, even if you do make a lot. They can still help on occasion.

The biggest difference between executive recruiters and employment agencies is that the latter do *not* work on a retainer basis. They make their money by introducing you to the company that hires you (up to 25 percent of your first year's salary). Employment agencies rarely have an exclusive contract to fill a job opening. Many seem to learn about the same job openings at the same time, and competition is fierce to be first to introduce a logical candidate. What does this mean to you? If you send your resume to a large number of employment agencies, you run the distinct risk of having it sent by several different agencies to the company seeking to fill a position for which you are qualified. Overexposure can make you look as if you are desperately seeking a job, an impression you don't want to convey even if you *are* desperately seeking a job.

The fact that employment agencies only get paid if they *place* an individual results in another problem, too. Many job-seekers complain that they are sent out by employment agencies to interview for jobs that are really not matched to their level of experience. Naturally the candidate is resentful of the time and effort wasted in going to see a prospective employer about what he thought was a legitimate job only to discover later it was a job he wouldn't have crossed the street to interview for. Why do the employment agencies sometimes send job-seekers on a wild goose chase? The most logical answer is that they hope if the candidate is hard up enough, he will take the job even though it's not right for him, and the agent will be that much richer. So ask specifically about any position the agent wants to send you on. Don't let him suggest you see such and such a company without knowing exactly what your interview is about. It will take your time and your money to get there.

A decade ago an employment agency made its money from the employee, who paid a fee to the agency that landed him his job. Today things have changed. Prospective employees balked at paying fees, since they were obviously less well heeled than the corporations that sought to hire them. Employment agencies realized this, and today virtually all feature "fee paid" positions, in which the hiring company agrees to pay the agency's fee. It should come as no surprise that fees are higher now that companies are paying them. You should keep a wary eye out nonetheless since in some fields—education, for example—agencies still charge the employee a fee. If you are not sure, your best bet is to ask. No sense paying to get a job when so many companies are willing to pay for the privilege of finding you. With these generalizations in mind, let's look at three types of agencies you will probably run across.

☐ AGENCIES THAT REPRESENT CANDIDATES AS WELL AS COMPANIES   Some smart professional agencies today represent candidates as well as companies. In addition to "filling job orders" (the industry jargon for finding people for positions the agencies have scrambled to learn about), a small number of agencies aggressively promote candidates that they believe have exceptional backgrounds and should be placed easily. One way it works is like this: A job-seeker submits a resume that impresses the agency. The agency invites the candidate to look up the names of the fifty or so companies he would like to work for, and the names of the persons at these companies the person might report to. The agency then phones these companies, singing the praises of the candidate in question. (As a third party it can do this. You can't.) Naturally the candidate has to have some special qualifications that make the agency think he's particularly saleable. In instances where the agency represents the candidate, the agency tries to get a verbal commitment from him that he will deal with it on an exclusive basis while it is promoting his cause. This is because the agency gets paid by the hiring company and wants to be sure that its candidate lands at one of the companies it puts him in contact with. The exclusive arrangement assures the agency that it will be paid a fee from some company or other making the time and expense associated with promoting a particular candidate worth while.

Getting an agency to act as a third-party endorser for you at the companies you'd like to work for may in some cases be beneficial in your job search. On the other hand, it's not a sure thing. The aggressive agency that promotes you may get you interviews with companies that have no immediate openings but are willing to meet you—if for no other reason than to get the agency off the phone. In these instances the interview may be a total waste of time. But, since you know how to sell yourself in person, you may well convince a company with no opening that it should make one just to get you. If you think you are exceptional, and you run across an agency that wants to act as your spokesman with the companies you'd like to work for, by all means give them a week or two to try to open some doors for you. But no more time than that! Their interest in you will undoubtedly wane in this period if you're not placed by then. *Don't* rely on them any longer. Get on with the job yourself and see other agencies.

Some agencies promote candidates without their knowledge. One nationally franchised firm with headquarters in Chicago, for example, regularly *floods* the mails with reprints of the resumes received from candidates they think are particularly appealing. The agency theorizes that if every major company gets a copy, maybe one will have an opening for the candidate and they'll be richer. They're not concerned that it can weaken the candidate's desirability (and negotiating position) if the second resume arrives while the candidate is already meeting with one of the companies they mail resumes to. If, in your case, an agency asks for a good copy of your resume to reproduce or asks if they can mail out a few copies of your resume, ask them: "How many and to which companies?" Don't risk overexposure; don't work with this type of outfit.

☐ MULTI-INDUSTRY AGENCIES   If an agency limits its sights to a single industry, it obviously limits the number of candidates it will appeal to, and the number of companies it can service. It follows, therefore, that the biggest, most profitable agencies deal with a multitude of industries. Typically, when agencies are large and successful, the staff is broken down by industry, with one person concerning himself exclusively with the potential openings in one or more industries, depending on the size of the industry. Why should this concern you? Because frequently the owners of large and successful agencies hire young, inexperienced, low-cost staffers to serve as industry specialists. How does that affect you? Very directly. Young, inexperienced, industry specialists are less likely to have high-level contacts than mature, experienced professional recruiters who have spent a lifetime developing contacts and are now in senior positions within the organizational ranks. The young industry specialist is not necessarily inadequate to the task. But, let's face it, more often than not the young specialist has contacts with personnel directors, not vice-presidents, and he might thwart your introduction to the right person, despite his good intentions. What should you do with this piece of information? When you talk to employment agencies, evaluate the person who is the intermediary between you and a successful job. If you don't think he can get you an introduction at the highest possible level, ask him specifically not to make contacts for you with any company without previously calling you. Tell him you want to decide on each company yourself before exposing your resume. Remember, more often than not several employment agencies will be trying to fill the same job slot. It's likely that you will meet someone from another employment agency who knows of the same opening, and in whom you have greater confidence. It would pay you, therefore, to have personal interviews with the large multi-industry agencies. See who in the organization is promoting your cause before you have your resume sent out to the wrong person.

☐ INDUSTRY SPECIALISTS Some smaller, one- or two-person agencies specialize in a single industry. More often than not, the proprietor spent a few years in the industry prior to entering the professional recruiting business. He has an idea of the industry jargon. He knows the industry pulse, the good-to-work-for companies and the bad. He doesn't have to look up Dun and Bradstreet to talk about the key people in his field. He knows the cast of characters by heart. Obviously, this type of professional agent can bring more pressure to bear to get you interviews with hiring officials than can the younger, less experienced agency representatives. Your friends should know the names of these industry-specializing agents, since they are the ones who usually get results. Ask them first. If your friends can't help you, you can probably spot these agencies by their ads. Go over eight or so back issues of the Sunday classified section, which you can pick up in your local library. Look through them. Note those agencies that consistently advertise for specific positions in your field. Be wary of those agencies that advertise for general positions in your field, or whose ads are the same week after week (e.g., "Senior purchasing jobs—$15–25M"). This type of ad could be placed by agencies trying to lock up potential candidates without really having positions for them to fill. Send your resume only to those agencies that consistently have specific jobs in your area to fill, and follow up with a personal interview. In person, you'll sense whether or not the agent is capable of making high-level contacts.

Don't send your resume out to several dozen agencies at one time. Limit your contacts to those that appear able to help you most. See a half-dozen initially. If they aren't producing interviews after two or three weeks, see a few more. You'll save yourself postage and overexposure. Spacing out agency contacts will help you even out the number of company interviews you have each week in your job campaign. If you contact too many agencies at once, you'll end up with exhaustion in the first two weeks, and have too few company interviews in the weeks that follow, which is bad for your ego, if nothing else.

WHOM ELSE CAN YOU
GO TO FOR HELP?

There are a number of nonrecruiting firms that make their livelihood by helping job-seekers to land successfully. Since their ads are sometimes interspersed among those placed by management consultants, executive recruiters, and employment agencies, you should know about them. Here's a run-down.

1. Career consultants

This group of highly successful and profitable firms advertises in or close to the executive-recruitment pages. And for some executives this type of firm provides a valuable service. Career consultants help undecided executives select the right career goals by means of aptitude and interest tests and personal counseling. They provide individualized assistance in resume preparation and interview techniques. And in many cases they do their job well. It does cost, however. A young, low-priced executive ($18,000) can expect to pay $1,000 for this service. A senior executive ($60,000 or more) can end up paying through the nose for such assistance. I know of cases of $4,000, $6,000 and even more. And it takes time. Counseling frequently runs over a period of months. If you have the time and the money and don't know what you want to do next, there's no question that a career consultant (or executive assessor, as one firm likes to call itself) can be of service.

From my vantage point, if you've read this far in the book, done your homework, and are anxious to pursue a career consistent with your current background, putting your entire campaign in the hands of a career consultant will be of limited value to you. The advertising by some career consultants is frequently unclear, and if you are not on your toes you might think you are looking at an advertisement placed by an executive recruiter. One frequent statement by one of the largest of these firms *suggests* that it has access to thousands of good positions that are not advertised. It well may, but none of the candidates I've met with who have worked with such firms has ever been told specifically of any! If you are not interested in career counseling, look for the line buried in the ad in two-point type that says: "Not an employment agency or job placement service." If you do pursue help from a career consultant, a second word of caution: You might be confused by what your career consultant says at your preliminary interview concerning your fee and what it will get for you. To avoid any confusion, let me tell you in advance: Your fee does not guarantee you a job. (Career consultants are not in the recruiting business, so they don't have positions to advise you of.) But your fee is payable whether or not you land a job. Think it over before you sign on the dotted line.

2. Resume peddlers

As you read through the executive-employment section of the paper, you may come across several ads that offer to expose qualified candidates to hundreds of companies with positions that need filling now. The advertisers who promise this generally have very impressive titles. If you send your resume in to one of them, you probably will be invited to a personal interview. There you'll be told that this firm exposes the resumes of exceptional job-seekers in a unique manner. Here's how: The resume peddler reduces all resumes to half-page summaries (anonymous) and publishes a book of resumes periodically (usually one each month). Some peddlers mail out their resume summaries to personnel directors at a select list of companies. Other peddlers maintain field representatives who make calls on personnel directors, carrying with them binders filled to the brim with such summaries. You'll be advised that there is a modest charge for summarizing your resume and including it in the book. It runs around $100. And it's rebatable if one of the companies contacted by the resume peddler meets you and hires you. From my experience, the resume peddler has a better deal than you do. He makes about $97 on your resume summary, while your chances of selling yourself with his resume summary (which is devoid of all your worthpoints and is but a mere skeleton of your work experience) seem to be pretty slim.

Recently I learned of a new version of this service that has gone electronic. Not only is your resume summarized and published anonymously, but a ten-minute videotape interview is made of you. You have a chance to sell yourself to an out-of-town client who is impressed by your background. Of course, a videotaped interview has several drawbacks. First, you can only talk generally about your background because you don't know who your prospective employer is or what his specific problems are. Second, this electronic interview obviates the necessity of a meeting in person, which is what you wanted in the first place. I wouldn't place a high priority on the results of resume peddlers in your job search. But the decision to use them is, of course, up to you.

3. Professional resume-writers

There are a number of firms that help job-seekers prepare their resumes for a relatively modest fee (from a low of $50 for the young executive to several hundred dollars for the well-heeled vice-president). These firms employ professional word-crafters who can take your experience and make it sound good. Each firm has its own resume format, but most today include worthpoints in some form or other, so that a resume prepared by such a firm could be of value to you if you are absolutely unable to prepare your own. Several things about the resumes I've seen from these firms concern me, however, and I must pass my concerns along to you.

For some reason, unknown to me, page one of such resumes usually includes a glowing description of the person, using words that sound as if they came from a military commendation. In a resume, words like these make you seem to be tooting your horn. As you know, it's much more convincing to let your deeds speak for you. Your eloquent description of your magnificence suggests only one thing: that you might be an egotist.

Professional resumes tend to look and sound like one another. At one time I received five professionally written resumes from five candidates who answered an ad placed by my firm. Although the people in question had substantially different backgrounds, each sounded as magnificent as the other. As such, professionally written resumes can be spotted a mile away. In submitting such a resume, you obviously run the risk of having your prospective boss think you can't write. That's a dangerous shortcoming when you are being compared to other candidates who can.

From my point of view, it's worth sweating a little to write your own resume. And then, if you're so inclined, have it critiqued by a friend or professional in your field, or by a reputable authority. If all fails, you should get help. But at all costs avoid the professional resume houses that accept mail inquiries. Any resume-writer who can write your resume without meeting you has got to be a mind reader or a charlatan. In my book, he's a charlatan.

DON'T FORGET YOUR FRIENDS

You don't need me to tell you that your friends and former business associates can be an extremely important source of information concerning currently available jobs and those that might be coming up. So just a couple of points.

Friends who have recently switched positions are an extremely good source of leads. Once they are installed in their new affiliations, they are very happy to review the positions that they weren't interested in, and the professional recruiters who provided the most help.

People who are looking for new jobs along with you can also be good sources of information. Once they've been turned down by a particular company, there's no reason not to tell you of the job opening. And you might be right for it. In return, tell them of the jobs you're no longer interested in. Don't overlook your competition.

Your address book, business-card file, and out-of-date appointment book are great sources of contacts. The best of us forget some of the people we've met along the way. If you keep old date books (or appointment books) you're bound to turn up a business acquaintance you'd forgotten about. And he may be just the one who knows of the job you want.

Acquaintances can be an enormously important source of job opportunities. According to a 1973 Labor Department survey of where managers got their last jobs, 18.7 percent secured them through friends, another 6.6 through relatives. Many job-seekers, however, advise me that they contact friends who "say" they'll help, and then nothing ever comes of it. If you sent your resume to personal friends or business associates and discovered that doing so led you nowhere fast, it wouldn't be surprising. When you phone a friend and ask him to pass your resume on to someone he knows, you are putting the responsibility on his shoulders to find you another job. Naturally some friends will fall down on this assignment. The fact is there's no reason why you have to saddle friends or associates with the chore of setting up interviews for you. Another alternative that works extremely well is to ask them—preferably in person over lunch or a drink—to do something that's a lot easier: to give you the *name* of someone they think you should meet in your field. Use your friendships as a source of names and then you take responsibility for establishing the contact. It puts much less of a burden on your associates and gives you better control over seeing to it that interviews actually do get set up.

At this point you may be wondering how you, the friend-of-a-friend, will get past the protective secretary when you try to set up your own interview. Here's what to say:

> "May I speak to Mr. Smith, please?"
> "May I ask what it's in reference to?
> "Well, Bill Jones, a good friend of Mr. Smith's, and a close friend of mine, suggested I call him. Has Mr. Smith heard from Bill yet? If not, I'm sure you will in the next day or so."

At this point the secretary should let you through to Mr. Smith. After all, she doesn't want to take responsibility for turning down a request by a friend of her boss. When you reach Mr. Smith, use the same technique. Unless Bill Jones isn't on good terms with Mr. Smith, it will be hard for him to refuse to meet with you when you tell him his friend recommended him as a person "who could give you some advice and counsel" concerning your career and your resume. And when you ask if he could spare just twenty minutes of his time to meet with you, how can he legitimately turn you down and still face Bill Jones in future? When you do meet Mr. Smith, tell him your job objective and ask him if he thinks your resume supports pursuing it—or if you should change your resume in some way. In so doing, Mr. Smith will discover your objective and find himself reading your resume. Naturally you hope Mr. Smith will have a position in his own organization suited to both your objective and background. If he doesn't—and the odds are against it unless your friend, Bill Jones, had directed you to a *specific* job opening he knew of—ask Mr. Smith if he can think of the name (or names) of someone you can contact using his name as a reference. In this way, you keep the friends' and associates' introductory chain going.

Will this approach work for you? Only if you have the guts

to use a friend's or an acquaintance's name as leverage in securing interviews. If you do, it might be your best job source. According to one authority in job search, whom I once debated on TV, a friend's campaign is such a good source of opportunities that he doesn't recommend any other avenue. I don't agree on such a limited approach, but at the same time, I strongly recommend it.

Fifteen

Where will your next job lead you?

Whenever I'm asked to lecture on career planning, a "good news-bad news" story comes to mind. It's about an airline pilot who addresses his passengers over the intercom. His good news: a twenty-knot tail wind has picked up the airplane's cruising speed to 600 miles an hour. His bad news: the plane's navigational equipment is out of order and he has no idea which way the airplane is going! Sad to say, there's all too much similarity between this pilot's situation and that of many job-seekers. They are successful in securing what they think will be "a terrific new position." The only trouble is it doesn't relate in any way to their long-term career goals. The following three real-life case histories illustrate the problem.

☐ A young man accepts an internal promotion in a small Midwest office of a New York-based advertising agency because of the title that goes with it. A couple of years later he discovers it's almost impossible to get back to *any* advertising firm in New York from this remote outpost. His goal of becoming vice-president of a large New York agency is thwarted.

☐ An executive in his mid-thirties leaves the position of purchasing manager, the number-two slot in a large purchasing department, because he feels he can make more money in the next fifteen years by accepting a job in brand management. After a couple of years he is told by his boss that he has "no future in brand management." Only then does he discover there is no way to work his way back into purchasing at the same level he had reached a couple of years before. His goal of becoming rich at an early age is tossed out the window.

☐ A young vice-president with a large, well-known consulting firm leaves to join a new, two-man consulting firm set up by a former associate in his old company. He makes his move based on the lure of stock participation in the new firm. Sixteen months later the fledgling firm collapses. The executive then finds out that his experience with the unknown company is not saleable. He cannot relocate as a vice-president with a prestige firm such as the one he was formerly with. (This young vice-president had the potential of becoming a partner in his original firm if he only waited it out. He might not have owned as many shares, but they would have been worth more, and his goal of equity could have been achieved.)

In each of these true cases, the job-seeker made the same error: failing to assess alternative opportunities, not only in terms of their immediate benefits but in terms of their appropriateness as stepping stones toward his long-term career goal. What can you do to avoid this type of pitfall in your own job search? Several things.

1. Establish an overall career goal for yourself, as well as a goal for your next job

Your career goal should be reasonable—one which a person in your position can hope to achieve within the next fifteen years. What do I mean by reasonable? Well, it might be reasonable, for example, for an aggressive young person who has just graduated from business school to hope to become the president of a two-hundred-million-dollar division of a billion-dollar company within fifteen years. But, should this same business school graduate hold the title of financial planning analyst twelve years later, continuing to pursue his original career goal of becoming a company president may not be realistic. How can you tell what's reasonable? One way is to develop a series of progressive job titles you might have to pass through in order to get to your long-term goal, and then assign a time frame to each. Let's say you are the financial analyst above, and that you are now thirty-five. What steps could you take in order to become president of a two-hundred-million-dollar company. One logical progression might be:

☐ *Assistant Treasurer*, responsible for financial planning, reporting to a treasurer (you might shoot for this step up when you relocate at this time).

☐ *Assistant Treasurer*, responsible for the financial aspects of acquisitions and divestitures. (This job provides you with a second discipline that broadens your exposure within the treasurer's function and is most likely to result from an internal lateral move.)

☐ *Treasurer*, responsible for all treasury functions with assistant treasurers reporting to you in the areas of planning, acquisitions, investor relations and bank relations. (This is your first exposure to two other critical treasury functions. More than likely it will have to result from a promotion.)

☐ *Chief Financial Officer*, with treasurer and controller reporting to you. (At long last you have exposure beyond the treasurer's department.)

☐ *Chief Administrative Officer*, now with finance and general administration reporting to you. (A job change or a promotion broadening your exposure still further.)

☐ *President*, in a division in which a background in financial management is more important than, say, a background in marketing, sales, or operations. (A job change or a promotion.)

If you feel this is the most logical progression you can take, you next have to decide *how long it will take you to pass through this progression* and whether there's time left to reach your goal. Your "most logical" timetable might look like this:

	Duration	
	Short years	Long years
Assistant treasurer-planning	2	3
Assistant treasurer-acquisitions	3	5
Treasurer	4	7
Chief financial officer	5	8
Total required before trying for president's job	14	23

If this timetable seems reasonable, this means the earliest you could go after your president's title is when you are already forty-nine! What's more, you might be in your mid-fifties before you really have enough of the right experience under your belt to shoot for your long-term goal. At this point in time, then, you might well come to the conclusion that your original goal just isn't in the cards. After all, you've been out of school twelve years and you are still a financial analyst. There's always the possibility that you might skip a step, of course, like moving directly from chief financial officer to president. But you have to ask yourself the likelihood of this occurring. And it's not much. The secret of this simple exercise in climbing the corporate ladder is to be totally realistic. No point in fooling yourself that you can skip certain rungs, or that you won't need as much time in each as the average person. If you're totally honest with yourself, you can avoid some pretty unrealistic decisions in going after your next job and each job after that.

2. Be specific about every element of your long-term career objective

It's not enough to say that in fifteen years you want to be president of a two-hundred-million-dollar division. You need to establish what satisfactions you expect such a long-term career objective would bring you. For example:

☐ WHAT TYPE OF COMPANY IS RIGHT FOR YOU IN THE LONG-TERM? If you are now with an industrial manufacturer, is this the type of firm where you want to be in fifteen years? If you have a technical background, this may be the *only* type of company you'd wish to work for! But perhaps the reverse is true. Maybe you're like two of my clients, both vice-presidents who wanted more than anything else "to get out of Wall Street." Becoming president of a Wall Street firm would have pleased many other executives in their situation, but not these two individuals!

☐ WHAT JOB RESPONSIBILITIES DO YOU EXPECT TO SECURE WITH YOUR LONG-TERM CAREER GOAL? One of my clients was the president of a $130-million company. Sounds like he'd be making "final decisions" about everything, doesn't it? Not true. His company was a division of a very tightly held conglomerate. He was president in title but was definitely a number-two person when it came to decision making. What do you want your long-term career goal to bring you in terms of job functions and responsibilities? To shoot for a "title" in fifteen years may not be enough.

☐ HOW MUCH MONEY DO YOU EXPECT TO MAKE? Is money a factor in the long-term goal you've set for yourself? If it is an important element in your objective, it could affect the type, size, and location of the company you plan to be president of! The very large corporations generally pay their senior people more for the same job title than small- or medium-sized firms. Typically, East Coast companies pay more than those in the Midwest for the same title. If money is a major goal, you can't just hope to be president of *any* company. And, possibly, you don't *need* to become president of a company! There are lots of other ways to make as much as a company president. Should you be considering alternative career objectives, it might affect the position you are going after this time.

☐ WHAT SIZE COMPANY? In fifteen years' time will you be comfortable in a large organization? Do you think you will prefer the informality and breadth of exposure you might have in a smaller outfit? I've seen executives who were miserable because they switched from small to large outfits and vice versa! You can't avoid this element of your long-term objective because it will have an impact on every company you interview between now and the time you achieve your ultimate goal.

☐ LOCATION If you had more than one offer the last time you conducted a job search, it's a pretty good bet you took into account the location of each company as you made up your mind which outfit to join. Almost every job-seeker does, and you probably know of an executive or two who refused a promotion in his company or a fantastic job offer with another organization because in each case a move to another part of the country went with it. Location is a pretty universal consideration with each job change, but it is something worth considering in relation to your *long-term* career goal as well.

How can you consider location in a job you won't be going after for fifteen years? Good question. Obviously not as easily

as in your current search. But supposing you are currently
deciding between two equally good job offers as plant super-
intendent. One of these jobs is in San Diego, the other in
Philadelphia. Because you're a sun-lover at heart, you're
sorely tempted by the offer in San Diego. In the short run,
why not take it? Okay, supposing your long-term goal is to
become director of manufacturing with a firm exactly like the
one you plan to join, and supposing corporate headquarters
of this firm is in Chicago, and supposing you hate windy cities. You are setting yourself up for a difficult confrontation in
ten to fifteen years when, in order to achieve your long-term
career objective, you need to make a sacrifice and move to a
city you don't really like. Now supposing the other company
offering you a job has its plants *and* its headquarters in
Philadelphia. There could be no potential conflict. Of course,
you say, a lot can happen in the meantime. You could
change jobs three or four times and be with an outfit in Mi-
ami by then. True, but if the two outfits you are considering
are both ideal, why set yourself up for relocation some time
down the road?

☐ IMPACT ON YOUR PERSONAL LIFE   Certain long-term
career goals demand more personal sacrifice than others. For
example, some will require pulling up stakes and relocating
every three years or so. Maybe you're willing to make a
move now, but will you be willing to make another move in
three years' time or in six, as your family gets older and you
establish roots in a community? Some careers demand that
you wed yourself to your job fifteen or twenty hours a day.
Maybe you don't mind that in your next job, but will you
want to devote your days, nights, and weekends to your job
in a decade's time? Certain jobs require that you have special
types of experience in order to get to the top. You might be
considering an outfit in which the senior people have all had
several years of field sales under their belts. It's possible that
selling is not your bag. Are you willing to sacrifice a couple
of years of your life doing something you don't care for in
order to have a crack at a long-term goal that you do?

While you might take a job now knowing that it demands
personal sacrifice for a couple of years, it's a mistake not to
consider the extent of personal sacrifice demanded over the
next fifteen years. You may think you can handle the moves,
hours, and frustrations that go along with your long-term ob-

jective, but can your family? Judging by the number of mid-career executives I've counselled who were coping with both a job change and a divorce at the same time, I've got to believe you should involve your spouse in your long-term career objective to make certain that it's worth pursuing. If you don't, you might be reexamining your career *and* your personal life in a decade.

3. Use your long-term career objective as one factor in assessing all job opportunities that develop as a result of the job search you are now undertaking

If you're fortunate enough to have two or three job offers by the end of your campaign, you'll no doubt evaluate each of them according to the benchmarks discussed earlier in this book—salary, title, responsibilities, and such. At this point I suggest you review your alternatives a second time, keeping your long-term career objectives in mind. You might find this second look leads you to different conclusions than the first.

Example. Your long-term goal is to be that president of the two-hundred-million-dollar division of a billion-dollar company we spoke of earlier, and that you have two alternative job offers at this time. The first is as *controller* of the Alpha Corporation, a ten-million-dollar manufacturing company. The second is as *section chief* reporting directly to the controller in the corporate accounting office of the Beta Corporation, a billion-dollar holding company with a number of two-hundred-million-dollar divisions. To complicate matters, the offer you got from the Alpha Corporation was for three thousand dollars more a year than the Beta offer. Which one should you take? If you consider the job titles and financial rewards of the two jobs, your first impulse is probably to accept Alpha's offer. If you take into account your long term objective, however, chances are you might opt for the job with Beta. Why? It's almost impossible to move at a senior level from a ten-million-dollar company into a billion-dollar corporation. But if you go to work for a billion-dollar corporation, it might well promote you at some point from corporate headquarters into one of its $200,000 divisions as a controller. This position as controller can then serve as your stepping stone to general management of this division.

Another example: You're a salesman with about three years' experience working for a large national company.

You've conducted a job search and have two offers pending. The first is with The Super Foods Corporation, another large national firm known for moving its sales people rapidly from territory to territory as they progress towards senior sales management. The other offer is with The Mid-City Distribution Company, a local foods wholesaler. The salary offer is the same at both companies, although your prospective boss at Super Foods has told you if you make it to territory manager you can make a lot more than with a small firm. There is an opportunity to move into sales management with both firms in the next three years. Which job should you take?

At first blush, the opportunity with the large national firm might seem the best opportunity, particularly if your immediate goals are to have responsibility for larger and larger sales territories, and to make as much money as you can in the next fifteen years. But now let's complicate matters. Let's suppose your spouse is a real "family" person with many friends and relatives in the city you now live in. Let's suppose, too, that your spouse has a good job. It doesn't pay as much as yours does but your spouse has been with the outfit for a number of years and would like to stay with it for a good long time. If you join Super Foods, your long-term success with this firm is likely to have a strong negative impact on your personal life. The choice boils down to career versus family in this case. It's impossible to separate the two. But only if you consider your long-term career objective would you come to this realization!

4. Consider the "saleability" of all alternative job offers just in case things don't work out—

Ask yourself which would bring you closest to your long-term objective. Few job-seekers accept a position with a firm thinking they're going to "bomb out" within a year or two. It's the sort of negative thinking most of us shut out of our minds. And yet, experience has shown that many job-seekers will be changing jobs in less than three years' time. If you assume a pessimistic outlook for just a few months as you consider the alternative offer your search has netted, your choice of which company to go with could be affected. Let's say that your long-term career objective is to become vice-president of manufacturing in a large corporation, and that you have two offers. One is with Universal Fabricators; the other is with

Taylor Tubing. Both jobs are as *supervisor* in a manufacturing plant. The biggest difference between the two jobs is that Universal manufactures twenty diverse products, and as a result, has a wide variety of manufacturing machinery in its plant. Taylor Tubing manufactures only tubes, and uses a group of highly specialized machines for this purpose. In making your decision between Universal and Taylor, your first conclusion might well be to take the job that paid best, was closest to home, seemed to have the nicest people.

If, however, you consider the possibility that despite your good intentions you get fired in a year, your long-term career objective might be the critical factor in deciding which alternative will do you the most good. In three years' time, which of these two jobs would be most saleable as you work towards that vice-presidency of manufacturing? Given that both companies have a good reputation, Universal Fabricators, which uses a variety of manufacturing equipment, might give you more to sell in your next job search. Even if you are offered a thousand dollars less by Universal and have to commute ten additional miles to work, it still might be in your best interest to go with Universal since it provides you with the most saleable foundation for your long-term career goal. How important is the saleability of any particular company to achieving your long-term objective? Based on the hundreds of job-seekers who have told me, "I never would have taken that job, had I thought about having to sell that company later on!" its importance is far greater than some job-seekers realize.

TO THE JOB-SEEKER IN SEARCH OF A SECOND CAREER

Many executives, particularly men in their late thirties and early forties, have second thoughts about their careers, and consider embarking on new and different paths at this stage of their lives. Often, these executives haven't succeeded in achieving their original long-term objectives. They figure that perhaps it's because they were wrong in choosing their first career paths, and that they would enjoy greater satisfaction if they pursued totally new goals, more consistent with their current interests and avocations. If you are an executive in this situation, one word of caution: in choosing alternative career paths, keep in mind the saleability of your new pursuits in the event that you find yourself wanting to get back to the track you were originally on. There's an enormous risk associated with switching careers if, as so many executives discover, you later wish to switch back. To minimize this risk, consider job titles and organizations that are consistent with your *new* goals but which still might be saleable in helping you secure a job later on that is more consistent with your original career objective.

As a case in point, consider this true story. At age forty-five, the vice-president of an East Coast supermarket chain, whose responsibilities were primarily in the areas of distribution and warehousing, got fed up with the rat race and decided to go into business for himself. He had a number of options. One was to become a partner in a small consulting firm as the firm's expert in warehouse and distribution management. Another was to join a small food broker in his home town. (The salary in the brokerage firm would have been significantly less than he was used to making although there was a promise of equity in the next two or three years.) This executive decided to pursue the third alternative available to him. He went into the real estate business with a local broker and tried to sell both industrial and residential homes. Three years later his agency went bankrupt. The executive was forced to find employment again, his resources having dried up. He decided to try to get back into supermarket management. He had a devil of a time doing so! Why? His experience in the three intervening years were totally unrelated to distribution, warehousing, and food retailing. The sad fact is that either of the other alternative career opportunities could have brought him the satisfaction of being in his own small business. If things hadn't worked out in either of these positions, he would have been far better off because he could have "sold" his experience as he attempted to secure a position similar to the one he left three years before. This executive's search lasted much longer than it needed to, and involved far more explaining than would otherwise have been the case.

Unfortunately for all of us, hindsight is a lot sharper than foresight. If you are so fed up with what you are now doing that you've made up your mind to switch careers, you may feel absolutely sure that you'll never go back to your original career. But if you keep in the back of your head that the possibility does exist and ask yourself whether the career change is "reversible," you may save yourself such much needless frustration later on.

At the same time, I urge you not to take a position that "compromises" going into a second career just because it's the safer route. If going into a new career is so important to you, try to get the best job possible in this new discipline. Just recognize that you might not be able to get back to your original path. If you are committed to a totally new pursuit, be certain the position you take *now* provides you with enough satisfactions to have made the switch worthwhile. If you didn't achieve the success you hoped for in your original career path, maybe you won't achieve the success you're counting on in your second career. So the job you take at the end of this search must provide you with sufficient rewards to be happy with it even if you don't manage to make any further steps upward in your second career.

Sixteen

Eight ways to avoid
the hidden hazards
of job hunting

When you've come this far, there's not much more counsel anyone could offer you on the strategy and plans required to locate and land the job you want. While there may be some specific questions left in your mind (and I've tried to answer the most frequently raised questions in the Appendix that follows), you know the rules of the road of successful job campaigning.

There's one additional topic that deserves your attention, however, before you close the pages of this book, and that's what I call the hidden hazards of job search—those small errors of judgment that could prevent even the world's finest candidate from landing the job he wants. This chapter is devoted to eight simple rules that can help any job-seeker avoid those inadvertent mistakes that I've seen otherwise excellent job-seekers make. Fortunately, if you follow the rules, it's easy to avoid the hidden hazards that cause some job-seekers so much frustration. All you have to do is be aware of the rules of the road at the start and don't lose sight of them as you conduct your search.

1. Begin your job search before there is pressure to do so

Shortly before this book went to press, Ben K called me at about 9:30 one night to set up a "crash" appointment. For months Ben had attended off and on a series of job-search seminars I had given in New York. I asked what made him wait until this particular moment to call. "Well," said Ben, "I got canned this afternoon, so now I want to put my campaign into full gear."

The sad fact is that Ben should have put his campaign into full swing six months earlier! How do I know? When I questioned Ben, he advised me that a year ago his boss told him: "You're not working out the way I hoped you would." Delaying his search has cost Ben a great deal more than he realizes. By the simple fact of being out of work, Ben is now less of a candidate in demand. As I suggested in the chapter on sources of assistance, recruiters much prefer to steal an executive away from a company, than to recommend to their clients someone who is out of work. (It seems as if they did their job better.)

Another thing, by delaying his job search until it was too late, Ben may have to reduce his job-search goal. At this point, Ben needs a job in a hurry. He has a family to feed and a mortgage to pay. He's under pressure to accept the first offer that comes along. So Ben may take a position that is really second best simply because he is afraid to hold out for the right one. Unfortunately in cases like this, the first job that comes along isn't always the one to take, and Ben could be back in the marketplace six months after he gets a job because things didn't work out the way he expected them to.

What steps should you take to make sure that you start your search on time? First of all, *realistically* appraise your position with your present company on a periodic basis. If you haven't been promoted in several years, or at least have not had regular increases in responsibilities and salary, sooner or later the boss is going to start thinking of replacing you with someone younger and less experienced but who, in his mind, has greater "potential." *Don't wait until that happens!* Even more important, if you're not getting along with your current boss as well as you once did, read the handwriting on the wall. Or if the business you are in is not doing as well as it used to do, and layoffs are taking place in other departments (perhaps even in your own) don't assume that it will never happen to you. It just might. Most people find it tough coming to grips with the fact that they have to go and seek out a new job. There's comfort and assurance in just having the old one, even if the boss has become unpleasant of late, and even if the raise you'd counted on never materializes. But on balance, facing up to the task of conducting a job search is far better than facing up to it too late.

2. Conduct a complete job search—anything less is not enough

Several months ago I met with the former president of a $130 million-dollar subsidiary of a major U.S. corporation. Eleven months before, this president was told, after twenty-five years with the same company, that his services were no longer needed. He was given eighteen months' salary as severance and let go. When I asked this former president what he had done during the eleven months since then to secure a new job, he advised me that he had sent his resume to approximately two dozen top-flight recruiters and had lunch once a week with friends who he thought might know of chief-executive-type positions. With further prodding I learned that this executive had secured no offers during the previous eleven months with these techniques. Why hadn't he done more to secure a new position? Undoubtedly, one reason was that he was financially secure for the moment. But in actuality this former president thought he was doing all that was necessary to secure another job at his level.

This president's experience is not unique. A vice-president of a leading Wall Street firm advised me that she did not answer blind ads in any newspaper. It wasn't that she worried that she might be answering an ad for her own job. After all, in this case, her company already knew she was leaving—it had planned her departure. She did not respond to blind ads simply because she had a hangup about them. A third case: when a former strategic planner for one of the largest conglomerates in the U.S. asked me to evaluate his search strategy, I discovered he had limited his search just to answering ads. When I asked why, he told me that he planned to do other things when he felt he had "exhausted the possibilities through answering ads."

Job-seekers who do a piecemeal campaign prolong their job search, cause themselves needless frustration, and worse still, lose out on opportunities with leverage to gain better positions. Why so? Because the candidate who touches all bases simultaneously has a far greater chance of getting the job he wants at the salary he would like. According to a U.S. Department of Labor study involving ten thousand executives and professionals, job-seekers discover their next job from a wide variety of sources, as the table below indicates.

Methods by Which Current Jobs Were
Obtained by People in Managerial Occupations*

Applied directly to company	24.2%	Private employment agency	10.9%
Asked friends about jobs	18.7%	State employment service	2.5%
Asked relatives about Jobs	5.7%	School placement office	1.9%
Answered ads in local papers	16.5%	Civil Service test	3.1%
		All other methods	15.5%

* Dept of Labor, January 1973

What it boils down to is this: If you concentrate on personal referrals, you limit yourself to only one out of every five possible job opportunities.

Ideally, you should try to get several different job offers at once—for several reasons. First, it gives you the opportunity to "play one against the other" to negotiate for the best possible opportunity. Second, even if salaries are the same, it gives you the opportunity to decide *which* job to take, rather than to have to settle for the only one at hand. Third, not every job-search technique works as well for every candidate. Some work best for some; others work best for others. So no job-seeker can afford to overlook any opportunity.

3. Set realistic goals even if it hurts the ego a little

Can a person who works with a consulting firm specializing in strategic and financial planning hope to secure a line management job in a manufacturing firm? Can an individual who's been out of work for six months hope to land a job paying 20 percent more than he did on his previous job? Can a vice-president of sales with *no* general management experience hope to find a position in general management? Of course he can hold out for whatever he damn well pleases! There is always a chance he'll succeed, but there are a lot more chances he won't. Particularly, if he has set a time limit for his search. Still, the cases above are *real*. They involve people I've worked with in the past year. If all were frustrated in securing their goals—frustrated enough to come to consult with me—all brought much of the frustration on themselves. I'm not suggesting these job-seekers should not have established goals for their job searches that meant a happier, more rewarding life ahead. But these should be attainable goals. Otherwise they can throw an entire job search off the track.

What can *you* do to insure that your goals aren't unrealistic?

☐ Make sure your search isn't built around several conflicting goals. For example, if you won't move from your current home, you limit your job-search opportunity significantly. So holding out at the same time for a major increase in salary may not be realistic. On the other hand, if you're willing to go to Timbuktu, perhaps you'll find a company there that is willing to pay you the 30 percent increase you are seeking. If you insist on both goals you can count on a tough search. So don't start complaining if it seems to take forever.

☐ Don't expect miracles. Expect to do as well as what others in a similar situation to your own achieved, but not much beyond. Yours is not a special case!

☐ Put a priority on your goals. If getting a job fast is all-important to you, then recognize that this probably rules out getting a much higher salary.

☐ Review your goals periodically during your job search. It may be that what seemed a realistic goal at the start of a campaign is an unrealistic one two months into it. Hanging on to an objective when eight weeks of searching has shown there is no real likelihood of your achieving it is senseless. The tough thing, however, is to admit it.

4. Be willing to invest enough in the best investment you could ever make—yourself!

In my lecture on job-seeking strategy and planning, I deal a little with the administrative work of job search—such as finding a source to type and print your resume and broadcast letters. In this class I'm invariably asked: "Can I type my own resume and letters? I've got a pretty good machine." Or "Do I have to have my resume printed? I don't need more than a hundred copies. Can I put them on the Xerox in the office?" Or "Do I really need to buy letterhead paper? Can't I just type my name at the top?" My answer to all these questions runs about the same: "Hey, who are you investing in? Aren't you worth the money to have your resume professionally printed? Aren't you important enough to yourself to invest the thirty dollars or so in stationery it takes to look like a first-class candidate?"

Anything you as a candidate do to cut corners in your job search is likely to cost you money if skimping means it takes you longer to land a job. If your resume typed on an available portable is less impressive than one typed on an IBM Selectric and submitted by your competition, then saving a few dollars may result in keeping you out of work. *Anything* you do that presents you in less favorable light than necessary might keep you from getting the one job that could make your career. John Malloy, in his book *Dress For Success*, makes the point that if you look successful, you have a better chance to be successful. His point actually applies to every aspect of your job search. Do without going out to dinner. Eat macaroni and cheese twice a week. But don't be cheap about your resume, your letters, your mailing lists. The money you spend in job search is the best investment in your future you'll ever make.

5. Revise your job-search strategy, plans and materials if and when your original target becomes an unrealistic one

Many job-seekers come to me to critique their resume at some point in their search. Often they'll present me with a resume that is everything a resume shouldn't be—laden with puffery and lengthy job descriptions; sloppy to look at and poorly organized. When I tactfully point out where improvement is needed, frequently I'm met with: "Well, I'll revise it when I run out of these. I made up two hundred, you know." Were these same people to own their own businesses, would they continue to run an advertisement once someone had shown them why the ad wouldn't pull a good response? Of course not! But somehow it's different when it comes to job search. People use resumes that don't work just because they have them; they send out the same letter in response to ads even though they rarely get invited to interviews; and they make several mailings of the same broadcast letter even though two hundred letters in their first mailing produced zero results. What prompts job workers to stick with the status quo—to fail to make the effort to revise their broadcast letters, resumes, or answer-to-ad formats—is beyond me! The cost of doing so is minimal and the consequences of not changing an element of the campaign that doesn't work are obviously serious.

Continuing to go after a particular position when it becomes evident with time that it is not attainable is just as ludicrous. One example brings the point home. A group vice-president, fired after twenty years with a conglomerate, set out to secure the presidency of a medium-sized company. Logical goal? Yes, if you stop to think that he had "run" several medium-sized companies within the conglomerate. But eight months later, when he was still out of work, he was still pursuing this goal and turning down opportunities at the group VP level. When he came to me at this point, I had a feeling I ought to check his references for him. Five out of five recommended him highly as a group VP. Not one felt he could handle the number-one spot—and incidentally, all five references were at the presidential or board chairman level. When I reviewed my findings with the group VP, he was interested in them. But he still pursued the presidential slot for another six months exclusively. His success was no greater than before. When he finally revised his goals mentally, and pursued a goal that was attainable, he landed an excellent position—as executive VP for a $60-million company—in about two months. Obviously it takes a certain amount of self discipline to redo a resume; more to revise your estimation of your career potential. Still, you should do one or the other, or both, if after reviewing your search results at the end of eight, twelve, or sixteen weeks, you discover you are not as marketable as you assumed you would be.

6. Try your damnedest to get every job offer you can including those you're not sure you want!

Recently I met with a very frustrated job-seeker who complained he had not been able to get a good job after a four- or five-month search. As we explored the reason for his lack of success, I asked him how he'd done in one of his interviews. "Very badly in that one," he told me, "but I wasn't really interested in that position so I didn't try to do a particularly good job." Either he was making the excuse for having done badly for my benefit, I thought to myself, or his sour attitude had actually come through in the interview. Why discourage offers *before* they are made? That can be fatal to the success of any job search for several reasons:

☐ **YOU CUT YOURSELF OFF FROM AN IMPORTANT NEGOTIAT-ING TOOL**   Even if you would never take the job in question, if you can get an offer it could help you get the job you *do* want! If a company with a job you are interested in knows you have an offer from another company, it may be more interested in making a better offer of its own. Why give up this potential clout?

☐ **YOU NEEDLESSLY BURN YOUR BRIDGES BEHIND YOU**   This is not a safe thing to do in a prolonged job search. Maybe the job you're interviewing for doesn't appeal to you at this moment in time. You don't know that it might not turn out to be your most appealing alternative later on.

But can you stall your second-choice employer until your first-choice employer comes through with an offer?, you ask. Not always. But I've known candidates who've successfully managed to hold off companies for four weeks or more once an offer had been made, while they tried to pry loose another, better offer. And I've known several job-seekers who worked hard to get offers from their second-choice companies knowing full well they'd turn them down at that point in time. But getting the offer in the first place established the company's keen interest in these candidates. Several months later these candidates reapproached their second choices after failing with their first. In one of them the job was still open and the original offer was made again!

☐ **YOU SPOIL A PERFECTLY GOOD DRESS REHEARSAL**   Regardless of whether you want a job or not, the interview is an excellent opportunity to see how well you can make people want you! If you practice responding to the needs of the potential employer in such a way as to get an offer (even when you don't want it) you'll know you've mastered the technique that can get you an offer with the company you *do* want to work for. Becoming an effective interviewee isn't a breeze. So why not practice with those companies you really aren't interested in?

☐ **YOU MISS OUT ON AN IMPORTANT PSYCHOLOGICAL AD-VANTAGE IN YOUR CAMPAIGN**   Everyone likes to feel that he is needed. In this respect, getting a job offer can be extremely important in building yourself up psychologically. This is particularly true if you were fired, or if your job is about to end. This psychological boost may be the very thing you need to score well in your next interview with a company that you *are* interested in.

7. Follow up every lead you get without exception

Many job-seekers are reluctant to follow every blind lead from every referral they get. You can't blame them. After a while, most job-seekers realize that many leads are dead ends and a total waste of time. On the other hand some leads are bound to be superproductive. Without benefit of a crystal ball, you can't tell which is which. So if you're going to land quickly, you'll have to follow every lead, even if you're convinced beforehand that it's a loser. The least likely person may well be the one to get you your job or lead you to the man who does.

A young financial executive I counseled was told by a prospective boss that he didn't have sufficient qualifications for an opening he was being considered for. But the prospective boss was kind enough to suggest that the young man talk to a CPA friend, and the young man followed through. The CPA had no job to offer either. But a couple of weeks later one of the CPA's client's asked him whether he knew of a person with precisely the qualifications of the young financial executive. The client firm never placed an ad for this job opening because the young man was introduced by the CPA and landed the job. Leads have a way of snowballing. But you have to keep the snowball rolling. Don't overlook any referrals.

One further thought on follow-up: If your prospective boss suggests calling back in a week, do it in precisely seven days. Don't take a chance on his being out of town on the eighth day.

8. Don't overtax yourself—remember job search is a full-time job you must do in your spare time

Nine months ago an executive I had coached dropped by. He looked haggard. When I asked if he had a problem, he pointed to his appointment book. Believe it or not, although this executive already held a demanding position, he had squeezed fourteen job interviews into the previous week. Every lunch hour was taken up. It so happened that this man had to travel to get to his interviews, and so he had skipped lunch as a result. He had four 8:00 A.M. appointments, so he skipped breakfast. He had several midafternoon and evening appointments as well. No wonder he was haggard, and hungry to boot. I asked the executive why he made so many interview appointments in such a short period. He explained that in the previous three weeks he had sent out one hundred letters to professional recruiting firms, one hundred more letters directly to companies, and, on top of this, had answered thirty or so newspaper ads. He was overwhelmed with interview offers. Obviously he didn't pace himself well.

There are two reasons why you should not try to do too much in too little time:

☐ You could lose your job. If you're out of the office too often, it could be noticed. If your boss knows you're leaving, he might fire you and be done with it.

☐ You can't do a professional job if you're going too fast to keep up. Undoubtedly you'll forego follow-up letters simply because you won't have time to write them. You'll probably have greater difficulty remembering names and faces because you'll meet so many people in so short a time span. Chances are you won't have an opportunity to look up the annual report of each of the companies you interview simply because you are running so fast.

It would be nice if I could suggest the precise number of letters you should write each week. That largely depends on your own available time, the amount of help you have to assist you in the physical details of your campaign, and the interest you generate as a result of your contacts. To be safe, you might start by sending out fifty or so letters to professional recruiters to determine the level of interest in you.

Keep in mind that each interview you set up with a professional recruiter will probably result in one or more interviews with company officials within two or three weeks. Each company you meet with once may want to meet with you again. Your best bet is to let the number of interviews you can reasonably handle guide you in determining the number of letter or phone contacts you should make. You'll have to experiment. Just take it easy at the start.

As I suggested at the beginning of this chapter, there isn't a hidden hazard in job search that's not easily avoided. The problem is that all too many job-seekers think their situation is different and so the hazard won't apply to them. The fact of the matter, however, is that the pitfalls I've suggested are those that job-seekers fall into every day. And I've seen the results: perfectly capable people out of work for months and even years, or in jobs that will undoubtedly set their careers back. And so this parting thought: Don't just use the tools you've learned about in this book to look for another job, but use them as part of a systematic, well-organized campaign that you tackle in dead earnest. The potential result of any job search is the best job you've ever had. It's worth your best efforts to secure it.

Appendix #1

Does anyone have
any questions?

At each of my classes on job search, I invite participants to bring up any problems they feel need more discussion. Some questions come up again and again. This chapter is a potpourri of such inquiries, along with the "best" answer I know of. Some of them may be pertinent to your situation, and give you the direction you seek.

1. Job titles in my company are very different than equivalent job titles in the balance of my industry. In my resume should I change my job title to reflect what the industry title is? Or shall I state it exactly as it is in the company I work for?

It could be a mistake to change your title without someone at the company you're working for knowing and approving of it. This type of thing could put your boss's nose out of joint if he is at some point asked to give you a recommendation. On the other hand, if your boss knows you are leaving, and understands the dilemma created by the unusual job title at your company, he's likely to go along with your making a change of this nature if you *ask* him to do so beforehand.

2. I attended a very fine, well-known school, but the companies I've worked for since are ones nobody ever heard of. Should I put "Education" first on my resume even though you recommend this section be used toward the back in most cases? That way I could establish my most prestigious credentials up front.

Suit yourself. The decision should depend on the prime target for your talent. The other day a client of mine who is a graduate of Stanford Business School and the U.S. Naval Academy asked the same question. His career has been totally in venture capital for real estate development. At the current time he sought a position with a real estate developer who needed a highly qualified individual in equity financing. I asked him what types of people were the prime targets for his talents. Were they the kinds of executives who would be impressed by Stanford and Annapolis? Or would they be the kinds of people who would be turned off by these schools? Based on the target audience for his search, he decided to put education last and his current experience first. More often than not, this is the best solution, but if you think the companies you've worked for will turn off your prospective bosses more than your school will, go ahead and try it.

3. I know that executive recruiters don't like candidates who are out of work any length of time. I've been out of work nine months. How can I cover this fact in my resume?

As suggested earlier, perhaps your best alternative is to use the resume you developed while you were still working. That one should have read, for example, "1972 *to Present.*" If you feel you must revise your resume now, do so as though you were still working and date it accordingly. Then when you meet any prospective employer or recruiter, tell him *immediately* of your *current* situation.

Some executives indicate that they have been working as *independent consultants* during this period of time. If they (or you) have, in fact, had consulting assignments, such a course of action is perfectly legitimate. Naturally, any experienced recruiter you meet is going to ask why you didn't go directly from your old company to a new one. One reasonable answer to this question is that you have taken your time looking around to make sure you got the right job.

Some job-seekers have used friends or relatives to "cover" for them during periods that they were out of work. If these friends have legitimate businesses in the job-seeker's own field, maybe this will work out. But a savvy executive recruiter is likely to ask the person in question why he wants to leave his friend's company so soon. If you do plan on soliciting a friend's help, I'd recommend you say you were consulting for his company while you continued looking for a suitable permanent position.

Some job-seekers, too, have the type of relationship with the boss who has just fired them so that they are able to get him to "fudge" the date they were fired. This, in fact, gives them an extra six or nine months of employment even though they were not on the payroll. Unless you have this type of arrangement on paper, and well rehearsed, it's dangerous! Your former boss or his secretary might forget and you'd be caught in a lie. This would kill your chances of getting the job you wanted, then and there.

4. Earlier in my career I held three jobs in quick succession—the total time of all combined was only four years. Is there anything I can do to make it less obvious on my resume?

If the situation occurred twenty years ago, you might consider a paragraph on page two of your resume headed EARLY BUSINESS EXPERIENCE. In such a paragraph, you can "group" your early jobs without using dates for each. For example, you might say:

> 1948–52—EARLY BUSINESS EXPERIENCE. Worked in several training and junior accounting positions including Samson-Jenkins, Inc., Foster-Cummings, Albright, Inc.

Be prepared to give dates in your interview!

5. In order to improve my career opportunities, I plan to begin an MBA program in the fall. Should I include this on my resume?

No. Good intentions don't count in preparing a resume. Good experience is the only thing worth including.

6. The companies I've worked for aren't very well known. Is there anything I can do about this problem?

A couple of things might help some. First, if your titles are more impressive than the names of the companies you worked for why not put your title above the company name or put your title in *all caps;* the company name in lowercase. Make your position as vice-president of marketing stand out, for example, rather than the Ipswitch Construction Company, which no one has ever heard of. A second step you might consider is to describe in one sentence something about your company that establishes what it does in a positive way. You might say, for example, that you are "responsible for all marketing and sales activities of this $30-million construction company with clients including Johnson & Johnson, General Foods, and Proctor & Gamble." Just as with individuals, a company is known by the company it keeps. It could help overcome the problem for you.

7. I don't have ready access to a typist. Should I use a "preprinted" form cover letter to answer ads in this case?

I don't think it's in your best interest. A form letter shows in an instant your lack of genuine interest in the job opportunity. More important, as discussed in the chapter on answering ads, you're missing out on an opportunity to *customize* your response to your prospective employer's specific needs. Not having adequate typing assistance is really a cop out!

8. One of the books on job search recommends that job-seekers use monarch-sized (smaller) stationery. Do you think this size is best for a job search?

The individual who recommended monarch-sized stationery did so because he believed most top-level executives use such stationery, and hence, using this paper made the writer appear to be a top-level executive. This could be true.

Standard-size business stationery ($8\frac{1}{2}'' \times 11''$) offers several advantages, however. First, you can get more on a single page—so your letters don't have to be as long. Second, the standard paper allows for more white space around the paragraphs, making your letter more readable. If you are a tight writer who wastes no words, monarch could be for you. Most job-seekers, however, would be better off with standard-sized sheets.

9. I wrote to a large group of executive recruiters six months ago and heard from only a handful of them.

Would it make any sense to send out a revised resume at this time? I think my revised resume is a lot better than the old one.

If you have the funds to do so, I'd recommend it. Some recruiter firms maintain excellent files of resumes forwarded to them—particularly if the job-seeker sounds like a winner. On the other hand, many executive-recruiter firms do *not* maintain files of resumes, preferring to conduct a survey of possible candidates only when a specific search comes up. A second mailing might well arrive at this executive recruiter's office while he's working on a search. Even if your old resume is on file, you're still better off sending another resume if you feel it reveals your worth better. The executive recruiter is going to be more inclined to present you to his client if your revised resume makes him think you are a stronger candidate.

10. For a number of weeks I have noticed an ad in the paper for a job that I think I would be well qualified for. The job is being advertised by an employment agency that I had previously registered with. They have not tried to get in touch with me, however, about this job. Is there anything I can do about this situation?

Unfortunately, if an employment agency continues to run an ad for a highly appealing job week after week, it could be a ruse to get qualified candidates such as yourself to register with the agency for other, less desirable positions it is trying to fill. Not every employment agency uses this underhanded tactic. But some do, so perhaps you ought not to get your hopes up about the job you've seen advertised.

Let's assume in this case that the job you continue to see advertised is a legitimate one. Your best bet in this instance is stop by to see the employment agency representative in person. Because employment agencies get paid only when they actually place a candidate, some lose interest in candidates who don't get job offers from the agency's clients immediately. If you were sent out by this agency to several of their clients in the past and you weren't offered a job, or worse still, refused it if you were, your resume may well have been filed away and forgotten. If you are truly qualified for the position the agency is advertising, bring them a fresh copy of your resume. Let them know of your interest, and ask them to send it out to their client. Point out to them that they have nothing to lose since you might produce a commission for them if you do get the job. This suggestion is particularly valid if you have *revised* your resume according to the suggestions in this book. A good resume that reveals your worth can make a world of difference in the attitude that both employment agencies and executive recruiters have about you.

11. With regard to my broadcast campaign, I've come across a list "brokerage" firm that has the names of many company presidents. Why not buy their list and let them make the mailing for me rather than develop my own list from scratch?

While many companies successfully use lists purchased from brokers to sell their products, I question whether job-seekers will be successful using a purchased list as the basis for a broadcast campaign. Companies that purchase such lists usually buy ten thousand or one hundred thousand or even one million names. Thus they can afford to write to a few inappropriate names—such as people who are no longer with the company or to executives whose titles or responsibilities have changed and are no longer in a position to purchase the products they sell. The job-seeker who conducts a broadcast campaign can't afford to write to poor names or old addresses. At best, your campaign will involve two hundred to three hundred companies—at a minimum one hundred. Every letter must reach a potential boss if you're to succeed.

Another fact to keep in mind is that some less than ethical list brokers use the same list for every job-seeker—regardless of his experience level and industry background. When the same list is used again and again, it is bound to lose its effectiveness. After a while it's very likely that the president's secretary will file broadcast letters in the circular file rather than show them to her boss. So the candidate who uses a commercial list broker ends up paying more to get his letter in the mail and is less likely to secure interviews in the bargain. Certainly it takes more effort to develop your own list of executives who might hire you than to buy a list of *Fortune* "500" company presidents. But you are far more likely to get a meaningful response if you write to the executive at a company who is in a position to hire you. The product manager, for example, should write to the vice-president of marketing, the senior auditor to the controller, and so on. In a word, buying a list may save time and effort initially but it will reduce the effectiveness of your broadcast campaign.

12. Occasionally, when I answer ads, the companies placing them send letters instructing me to fill out applications that are attached. Some of these applications can be very time-consuming. Is there any way I can avoid filling out such applications?

Fortunately, such requests rarely are made of executive job-seekers these days. But a few companies still insist that standard applications be filled out by lower-echelon applicants prior to the first interview. While doing so is a nuisance, it's easy to understand the company's point of view. When a candidate signs the application, he is declaring that all statements about him are true. This gives the companies legal grounds for dismissing a candidate after he is employed, should the statements turn out to be false. Another reason they are popular with personnel people is that they know exactly where to look for information. Resumes, after all, are all different. So the application simplifies the personnel department's job even though it may complicate yours.

Unfortunately, I know of no perfect way to get around applications. I have known a number of job-seekers who only filled in questions not answered by their resumes, and then attached their resumes with notation that all additional information could be found "in the attached resume." A few have managed to get away with this, although others haven't been called into interviews afterward—and who knows, this approach may have done them in. I've known other job-seekers who have contacted the companies in question, saying they would be delighted to complete the application once they've had an interview to determine if there is a real mutual interest, but that they wish to be considered for that initial interview based on their resume alone. I've known several candidates to get away with this approach, too. The candidates who used the approaches I described and got away with it were strong ones—fully qualified for the jobs, who deserved to be seen without filling out applications.

Aside from these two techniques, I know of no way to avoid the time and effort required to fill out applications. But keep in mind that the choice is yours—whether to fill the application blanks out or not. If you are already talking to a number of companies when the application comes in the mail, there's nothing that prevents you from filing it away until you see that your alternatives are not working out. But if you don't have many job opportunities, it would certainly pay you to complete the application. Except in one circumstance—when completing the application is *likely to hurt your chances of getting an interview. For example, if the ad called for someone with a master's degree, and you didn't have one.* The problem here is that the same person in personnel who would eliminate you from consideration because you don't have a master's degree is the same one who might eliminate you because you refused to fill out the application. Since you're damned both ways, I'd recommend you *don't* fill out the application in this instance. Your only hope is that the person who received your resume and forwarded the application will show your resume to the person who is doing the hiring even though he hasn't yet received your application. If your resume is good enough, maybe you can still get in the door.

13. Recently I was interviewed by an executive recruiter for a position that greatly interests me. A few days later, I learned from the recruiter that I was no longer being considered as a candidate because there were others better qualified for the position. Is there anything I can do to get myself back in the ball game?

When an executive-recruiting firm turns you down, it's almost impossible to get yourself back in the running. I do know of a number of aggressive, determined individuals, however, who tried to do just this. What each of them did was to try to "end run" the recruiter—not an easy assignment when you consider that in each instance the recruiter hadn't revealed the company he represented. What each of these imaginative job-seekers did was to identify twenty or so companies that "fitted" the recruiter's description. After that, most wrote "broadcast" letters to these companies as though they were unaware of the search being conducted by the recruiter. In one instance, the job-seeker phoned companies he thought were the subject of the recruiter's search and after getting through to the person he thought was the responsible executive, asked if a position were open. When he was told one was, he *asked for an interview and got it!* And, while several of the job-seekers who wrote broadcast letters did succeed in getting interviews with companies directly, most did not. The reason: the companies wrote back telling them that their letters were referred to you know whom—the executive recruiter they were trying to maneuver around in the first place! If a recruiter has a close working relationship with a company, once he had turned you down your chances of getting in the door are next to nil. Better off using your energies to pursue other opportunities.

14. About three weeks ago I had an interview for a job I really want. I felt the interview went badly. At the end, the interviewer said he'd get back to me within two weeks, after he had a chance to interview several other people. I've not heard one word since then. Is there any thing I can do at this late date to make things more positive?

Unfortunately, not much. If the magic didn't exist when you met with your prospective employer, it's difficult to create it later on from a distance. The most valuable things you might do at this time are (1) to try to assess why the interview went badly so that you don't repeat your mistakes; and (2) to work hard on getting interviews with other companies.

If your heart is really set on this job, however, and you want to make one last-ditch attempt to get this job even though your interview went poorly, here are two suggestions:

☐ Call the person who said he'd get back to you, and didn't. At the very least you show your courtesy and interest in the job. If his secretary stops your call from getting through to him, you pretty well know you're out of the running. On the other hand, if you get through, he might appreciate your call. Who knows? The other candidates he has met since your interview may not have scored any better than you did! If this is the case, your call may help you get back in the running.

☐ When you speak to your prospective boss, if he seems friendly, ask if he'd like you to tackle an assignment that might convince him of your interest in the job, and your ability. Over the years I've known a few job-seekers who got themselves job offers by using this technique. Not only did the offer demonstrate the job-seeker's interest, but probably just as important, it enabled them to provide solid evidence that they had the ability to get an assignment done. You might try this. But don't expect miracles.

15. I had two meetings with a company about a week apart. Things seemed to be going well. Three weeks have gone by since my last contact with this company, however. Have you any idea what went wrong? And what should I do about the situation?

There are a number of reasons why you may not have heard from this company. They could be minor problems: the person who you are to meet next is out of town; they have had trouble reaching your references. Or they could be major obstacles: the last person who met you didn't like you as well as the first; the company has decided to look at other candidates; one of your references was poor. Just one bad one can knock the best of candidates out of the ball game.

If a company you meet with on several occasions shows a waning interest, why not contact them to find out firsthand what the reason for their silence might be. It's easy to do this if you are working with a recruiter who can act as an intermediary. But what if you met the company directly through an ad? Often, in circumstances like this, candidates decide not to make contact. Their reasoning? They are afraid of hearing bad news, perhaps, or they feel that calling might irritate a possible boss and so jeopardize their chances of getting the job. From my experience, it's a mistake *not* to get in touch with a company if you haven't heard anything in several weeks. If the news is bad—and they're aggressively looking at other candidates—you might as well know it. Recognizing that the job opportunity you were counting on has dried up is important, as it could affect your decisions (and attitude) toward other alternatives you are considering. If the news is good, it could also affect your decisions. In both cases, when you call you let a company know *you* are still interested. Many an employer has chosen one candidate over others because he is the one person who was genuinely interested in the job—interested enough to get back to the company when the others just let things slide.

If, when you call, your prospective boss suggests things aren't going as fast as planned, try to get a date when you might contact him again. And if you find major obstacles in your way after you've given references to the company, find a way to check those references. You can't change a bad reference, but knowing about it gives you an opportunity to blunt the sword. If you tell prospective employers *beforehand* that you do have a bad reference from so and so and give a brief reason why (we didn't see eye to eye), at least it doesn't come as a shock. If the reference is not your immediate supervisor, you might consider eliminating your poor reference and substituting a better reference instead.

16. You make a professionally done job search sound as if it is extremely time-consuming. Would you recommend I quit my current job since it is also time-consuming, in order to go full-time after a new position?

Absolutely not! Being out of work for any reason puts you at a psychological disadvantage with many recruiters and employment agencies. If your search takes longer than you think and your resources start to dry up, being out of work also puts pressures on you to accept jobs that you might not otherwise take. And, most important, it really isn't necessary to do this. *Pace yourself* so that you do not find your job search overburdening. Don't contact all employment agencies and recruiters at once if you can't keep up with the number of interviews that such correspondence generates. Begin answering ads only if recruiters don't seem to have many searches for a person with your background. Conduct a broadcast campaign only if there aren't many ads you can answer, and so on.

17. I'm living in New York now and would really like to move to the West Coast. Have you any advice that would help me conduct my search more effectively?

A number of executives have advised me that they found it extremely difficult to conduct a job search from a distance. Not surprising, since it makes sense for any company to look first at *local* candidates for positions that might be open, rather than to explore opportunities with someone one thousand or two thousand miles away. Keep in mind that if a company *invites* you to fly three thousand miles to meet with them, it has to pick up the tab for your travel expenses. It makes a lot more sense for them to talk to all your competition who can travel to the company on their own, first! If they can't find someone worthwhile, then is the time to search further afield. Given this perspective, the New York jobseeker who responds to opportunities on the West Coast usually finds he does not get many positive replies.

There are several things you can do about this situation, however. One technique that works is to use a *local address* for your long-distance job search. If you have a friend on the West Coast willing to accept mail and calls for you, and who will phone you immediately if anything positive comes up, you can conduct your job search as though you are already a local resident. Of course, a local address has its drawbacks. You are not immediately available for interview. Nonetheless, I've seen this technique used effectively.

Another technique that works is used in conjunction with your broadcast campaign. In this case, you send out one hundred or more letters to companies in the area of the country you wish to work in. Your letter is the same in all respects as the letter described in the chapter on broadcast letters, with one exception: your letter concludes with a statement to the effect that you are planning on a business trip to the area of the country where the company is located on such and such dates, and would particularly like to meet with the recipient of the letter during that period of time, if there is interest on his part. If your broadcast letter has turned on your reader, the final paragraph indicating you are coming from afar can work strongly to your advantage. Quite obviously the reader can't put your letter on the pending file! If he wants to meet you, he knows he must set up an appointment with you while you are in his city. One job-seeker I recommended this technique to wrote one hundred letters—fifty to companies and fifty to executive recruiters and employment agencies in the L.A. area. His efforts netted him fifteen interviews, all in the space of a week, which led to three job offers. His cost: $614 including air fare, motel, and car rental. A small investment versus his return—the job he wanted. And incidentally, the company picked up his moving expenses.

18. From time to time I see ads in the *Wall Street Journal* **and** *The New York Times* **where people describe their abilities in a •Position Wanted* classified section. What do you think of advertising to get yourself another job?**

Over the years, I have met less than fifty people who have tried to get new jobs this way. So my sample might well be biased. Nonetheless, you should know that most of these job-seekers who tried this technique advised me that it was not successful for them. Either they heard from no one with a job that satisfied them or they heard from insurance or encyclopedia companies offering them selling jobs while they were out of work. Some job-seekers reported that they received letters offering to rewrite their resume or to print it for them. There were exceptions. By and large, those job-seekers who were high up on the executive ladder reported the best results, although even in these cases, results weren't all that good. One senior executive advised that he received a number of employment offers but with a catch—he had to invest in the company, or in other words, they were seeking partners, not employees. As usual, there are exceptions to every rule. I've heard of several notable success stories of copywriters securing fantastic new jobs as a result of the ads they placed in *Advertising Age*. This may have been because the ads, themselves, were superb demonstrations of their ability as writers. On the whole, however, I think you're better off putting your money into a direct-mail campaign to those companies that are the most likely prospects for what you have to sell.

19. A few months ago I took a job with a company and things haven't worked out as I thought they would. Thus, I'm in the job market again for the second time in six months. How should I explain this to prospective employers?

The same way you explained it to me. Tell them you made a mistake. And to be sure you don't make a second one, be more careful in any job you accept.

20. Sometimes I see "blind" ads that I really want to answer. Unfortunately, the job descriptions sound as if they might be placed by my own company. Is there anything I can do to make sure someone in my own outfit doesn't receive a response from me to an ad he placed?

Yes. Put your response to such an ad into an envelope marked with the box number of the advertiser. Put this envelope into another, larger envelope, addressed to the manager of the particular classified department. Include a note describing your problem and indicating the specific company or companies you *do not* want the inner envelope to be sent to. The *Wall Street Journal* and *The New York Times* classified departments tell me they will honor your request. No doubt your local paper will honor it as well.

21. I really don't want to leave my company. I've been with them for a number of years and I really like the people. Is there any way you can help me to get a better job within my own company?

While the approach to selling yourself that I recommended is primarily intended for people who want to secure positions with new companies, I know of a number of people who have discovered their worth as a result of this approach, and then gone back to sell their talents within their own company. I recall once receiving an invitation to dinner by a vice-president of one of the largest financial service companies in the world. When I asked why I was invited out of the blue for a night on the town he told me that when he had been competing for the job of vice-president, he was up against a number of other candidates who were more experienced than he was. When it came his turn to meet with the president, he remembered what the first edition of this book had said about selling yourself in a competitive market. As a result, he listened a lot to what the president had to say about the things he expected from his new vice-president, and then talked about the specific things he had *done* for the company during his eight years with it; not one word about his abilities, skills or knowledge. When he was offered the vice-president title, he ascribed it to the fact that he alone knew what the president was looking for and because he knew how to relate himself to these needs in a memorable way.

Another case history makes a telling point about how you can use this book to sell your talents within your present corporate structure. A very bright young engineer with one of the country's leading electronics manufacturers was fired from an internal consultant's position in one of its manufacturing divisions. After taking my course in job search, on a lark he sent his resume to seven or eight other divisions of this enormous firm, and to the corporate headquarters as well. Despite the fact that he had received a pink slip from his division, he was offered a better job at corporate headquarters. He attributed this offer to the fact that he knew his *specific* contributions to the division that was letting him go.

Unforunately, selling your contributions within your present company isn't an easy task most of the time. Other factors are sometimes more important to your superiors than your contributions. Your personality, your relationship with your bosses in the past, and your "image of potential success" all come into play as your management considers your future worth to the company. The old expression "Give a dog a dirty name and it will never change" unfortunately holds back many a capable executive. In some companies, no matter how you personally grow and develop, you are still thought of by management the way you were the day you first joined. If this is your own situation, you're probably better off trying to sell yourself *outside* the company rather than within, even though you had hoped to spend a lifetime with this company.

22. My job search has cost me a lot of money so far. Is any part of this expense tax-deductible?

Yes, all legitimate expenses concerned with getting yourself another job can be deducted from your gross income. Such was not always the case. Until several years ago, the IRS offered no allowance for job-related expenses other than employment agency fees. They lost so many times in tax court, however, that in the early 1970s they finally relented, and now allow a great many search expenses as deductions from your income—to start with, the cost of this book and the three-ring binder you use for your job search.

Other expenses you can deduct include: Your airplane or train ticket and the expense of your motel room if you visit companies in another city and have to pick up the tab yourself. If you drove in your own car to a number of out-of-town companies for interviews, you are entitled to declare 17¢ for each mile you drove to and from your prospective employers' plants. The expenses associated with printing both your resume and broadcast letter are both deductible. In addition, you can deduct the cost of stationery purchased specifically for your search as well as the cost of stamps to mail out your responses to ads and broadcast letters. If you have a professional resume writer develop your resume, you can deduct that, too. Also, the cost of working with a career counseling firm or job-search consultant such as myself are deductible if you need such counsel in getting another job, even if it's not related to what you have done in the past.

You can even deduct your toll calls to prospective employers, and that portion of your basic monthly phone bill that reflects the amount of the phone's use for job-search calls. Unfortunately if this is your first job since school, you're out of luck when it comes to tax time. For some reason, the IRS won't allow you to deduct the expense of securing your first job. But after that, Uncle Sam will help you change jobs to the extent of allowing you not to pay tax on that portion of your income spent in securing a job. For the higher-level executive who runs a first-class campaign, this could mean a considerable saving. So keep receipts of all expenses with notations, and keep a log of your search-related miles, tolls, and parking. And don't destroy those receipts just because you don't locate the right job within the tax year. You're entitled to deduct such expenses whether or not you actually land a job, as long as you can prove that you were making a legitimate attempt.

23. How do I get the salary I want?

Earlier in this book it was recommended that you avoid talking about salaries until you've been offered the job. You should try to convince your prospective boss you're the only person he wants. Then, when you talk salary, you have a much better chance of getting what you want. Sooner or later, however, in every job search you'll have to talk salary. It is, after all, the cement that binds. The real question, then, is this: Will the company that wants you pay what you want to make? In most job situations, you should have a pretty good idea of what the job pays before you arrive on the scene. Executive recruiters and employment agencies are frank about the salary range. Similarly, many ads include salary "up to" statements, although some do not. What you really want to know is how to get paid at the top of the range. There are several things that you can do to help maximize your compensation.

☐ You have already done the first thing by holding off your discussion of specific salaries until the very end. Your prospective boss has resolved to hire you rather than your competition. He has already decided in his mind you are the top person and probably worth the top dollar.

☐ Second, let your prospective boss talk salary specifics before you do. If, after offering you the job, he asks you what you want to make, why not turn the situation around? Why not ask your prospective boss what he has in mind? Put him in a position of trying to make the sale. By the time your prospective boss has offered you a job, he wants you. Put him in the psychological position of trying to get you. Chances are that he'll offer you the maximum dollars in the job's salary range.

☐ If the salary doesn't match up to your needs, use a comparison to help your prospective boss realize the problem. Obviously, the best comparison is a salary offer from a competitive firm. If you're lucky enough to have one, you might let your prospective boss know at this time in a nice way. For example:

> As I told you, I have been talking to several companies. Yours is absolutely my first choice. On the other hand, one of the reasons I'm leaving my current firm is to improve my financial situation. In considering job opportunities, I have to take into account that I have an offer for $5,000 more from that other firm I've been talking to. I'll think the situation over during the next day or so. Maybe there's a way of arranging the budget so that your job could pay more. I certainly would appreciate it if you would let me know. It would make my decision easier!

In addition to letting your prospective boss realize he is in a competitive market, the strategy above does something else that can help your cause: it asks your prospective boss to think the situation over during the next few days. There's no direct confrontation over salary in this meeting. Instead, by letting your prospective boss think the situation over he will realize his alternatives:

☐ He can up the offer to get you.

☐ He can start the search all over again until he gets a candidate as good as you. But that costs him time and effort.

☐ He can settle for his second-best candidate and psychologically that's something he doesn't want to do.

If you are lucky, your prospective boss will come to the conclusion that a few extra thousand dollars is worth it to get the right person *now*.

If you don't have another job in your back pocket, you can still help your boss to see your problem with a comparison to what you're now making. This is the kind of thing you might say:

> Thanks very much for your offer. I'm really glad that I turned out to be your first choice, because, as you know, your company is *my* first choice. But I'll be candid with you and tell you that I do have a problem. When I decided to leave my current firm, I established a goal for myself of securing a job that pays 20 percent more than I now make. Money's really a major reason why I'm leaving. At this point in my job search, I don't think I should move away from this goal. So I have to let you know my problem. I recognize it is really mine. But if perhaps your budget might be adjusted, I hope you will let me know so that we might discuss this further. For now, as much as I appreciate your offer, it's not consistent with my needs. I'll have to think it over during the next few days.

The first half of your strategy is, of course, to make the salary you want seem reasonable. Reasonable by virtue of the competitive situation. Reasonable by virtue of the fact that one normally expects to make more in a move. The second part of your strategy is to give your prospective boss time to think, making it easier for him to rationalize an increase. And chances are greater you'll get what you want.

24. How much time do I have between saying "yes" and joining my new firm?

Most job-seekers expect prospective employers to pressure them into joining a company immediately—to leave their present companies in the lurch, to take no time off before they join their new employer. The amount of pressure that's applied to job-seekers once they've said "yes" is amazing. It's understandable that a company that has been searching for nine months or a year would want you right away. But it's unreasonable. You should be given the opportunity to wind up your business at your present firm; to take a well-deserved vacation. You can easily take six weeks between saying "yes" and joining your new firm—a minimum of four. Two weeks' notice to your current employer, and two weeks for you to unwind and relax. And you really owe it to yourself to do just that. To take a vacation. To look at new surroundings. To think of no work at all. So that when you join your next company your mind is fresh and your senses are keen, and you are ready and willing to tackle the new assignment. As you move up the organization chart, two weeks' notice may be too little. You may want to give four. Hence your prospective employer should expect to wait six weeks.

There is no doubt that this delay will frustrate your prospective boss. He wants you now. He needs you now. But remember, your best opportunity to unwind completely is between jobs. Don't let it slip through your hands. Whatever you do, don't leave your former company on a Friday and start to work at the new company the next Monday. Every executive I know who has done this has regretted it. A weekend is not enough time for yourself. And, since it may be a year or eighteen months before you can get away on a vacation from you new company, take the time between jobs for yourself. Don't succumb to the pressure. You deserve to take a break.

25. What happens if I get a better job offer after I've accepted with one company?

This occurs with greater regularity than you'd think. People accept job offers with one company. Then, if they get a better opportunity with another, they renege on the first. The decision as to whether you renege on a job offer that you've accepted must be yours. It's hardly something that could be recommended in this book. Nonetheless, it might be worthwhile to examine the implications of reneging, in case you find yourself in a situation where you are giving considerable thought to this action.

There are two circumstances that might bring you to a decision to switch your allegiance even before you join a company. The first of these is the situation in which you accept a job simply because you need bread and butter on the table. You know the job isn't what you want. It doesn't conform to your job objective, near- or long-term. After you accept this job, and before you start work, another job appears on the horizon. This one is just what you want. It is in tune with both your short- and long-range goals. I personally think you would be remiss not to take the second opportunity, since it offers you so much more than bread and butter. In this instance, it seems to me that talking frankly to the people at the bread-and-butter company won't be as traumatic as you think. If you refer to the job objective stated on your resume and your long-term goals (if you talked about them in your interview), the people at this company should agree that your change of heart is best for you and for it.

The second reason why you might think about reneging is different. Simply stated, the second company offered you more money. If money is the only differential, and both first and second opportunities satisfy your career goals, think twice before you renege. The people at the first company might well be vindictive. They might try to get in touch with the second company. They most assuredly would get in touch with the recruiting firms they deal with. Your reputation could be tarnished. Even if you disregard the moral issue of reneging after accepting a job offer, it would seem to be in your best interest to join the company you accepted first, even at the loss of a few dollars. Unless it's a question of career objectives being better fulfilled by the second company, I'd think twice before saying "no" once you've said "yes."

At this point you may well ask, "Is there any way in which I can get the first company to up its ante once I get a second job offer that pays more?" The answer to the question is simple: No. Even if you were to speak to the first company concerning the salary offer of the second, and were able to squeeze a few extra dollars from the first, it wouldn't be in your best interests to do so. Chances are your new boss would think a great deal less of you. You would certainly not be starting off on the right foot in your new affiliation. This situation is something like that of the person who sold a house for $65,000 on a Wednesday, and a real estate agent phoned him on Thursday and asked if the house was still for sale. When he told her "No," she said, "Too bad, because I have a buyer who will offer you $70,000 for your house." So be it. The house is no longer yours.

Is there a simple way to avoid the frustration described above? Yes. When you've accepted an offer with one company, forget your job search. Plan your vacation. Finish up your current work. And if you still find yourself with time on your hands, call your next boss. Ask him if there's anything he'd like you to read before joining his company. Get involved with your next job. You won't have any time to be frustrated.

26. When is the best time to talk about fringe benefits and other special arrangements?

Most fringe benefits, such as stock purchase plans and stock options, will be discussed when your boss talks turkey with you concerning your financial package. But there are several extras that might get overlooked. These include a cost-of-living allowance, should your job require you to relocate, six or nine months after you join, to another, more expensive city or to a state or municipality with significantly higher taxes. A second key extra is moving expense. Most companies pay moving expenses of employees who join from a considerable distance. Not all do, however. If you want the company to pay moving expenses, or a cost-of-living allowance, the time to discuss it is when you discuss your financial package. If you haven't made arrangements then, it's a hairy task to reopen the discussion at a later date. A cross-country move could cost your firm $10,000. No one likes a $10,000 surprise. Be sure to write down all the items in your financial package that you want to cover in your negotiations. When the time comes to discuss finances, be sure you touch on each.

27. Is there any need to get back to those recruiters or companies that I talked to, but which haven't come up with job offers at the time I accept a position?

Yes. Be well thought of wherever you go. In the period that follows your acceptance of an offer you might easily forget the companies that didn't offer you a job. Its' not surprising that you would. Trying to finish up your job at your current company, getting organized for a vacation, and getting yourself in the mood to join a new company can keep you hopping. Since many people do forget, one suggestion: Be remembered positively by the companies you didn't join and the professional recruiters who worked with you as you searched for the job you wanted. Send a note, or at the least, a form letter to all those companies, executives recruiters, and agencies who have written to express an interest in you, and particularly to those whom you've met. Let them know where you are going. Express your thanks for their aid. This is obviously a low-priority task. But I'd recommend it to you. Not every new job works out. Not every job that seems better on the surface is really better. And a year or two after you join a company, you may be looking again. Your folder with a thoughtful letter may still be in the active file. When and if you go looking again, you will be very well thought of for the courtesy you showed, since so few people show it. What's more, you never know if a professional recruiter may come up with a great job opportunity and want to see you a year or two after you start your new job. It will give you a nice feeling to know that he knows where to reach you. If there ever is a next time, you'll have a head start in getting your next job.

Appendix #2

A special word
to the job-seeker who
is out of work

If you've ever been fired (and I have) you know that the day it happens is not the most auspicious in your life. Even if you feel you were fired unjustifiably, it stings nonetheless.

The sad fact is that while the day you are fired is a heartache to remember, the days that follow can be even more depressing. Only the numb of mind could fail to feel the financial bind, the sinking feeling that comes when you know that the well must soon run dry, that the usual biweekly replenishing source has been cut off.

And no one, no matter how good he is, can fail to ask himself why he was fired, to assess from time to time what went wrong. What could have been done differently. How things could have worked out, had other ways been tried. Even if your boss tells you it's not your fault (as my boss told me when my position was eliminated), you can't help blaming yourself. The proudest of us feels tarnished on some days; the original luster will never be the same.

Then the loneliness sets in. The office faces and voices, so familiar they have become a subconscious part of you, are suddenly gone. The phone no longer rings. Your secretary is no longer there with coffee and a smile. To many job-seekers, and perhaps to you, the loss of momentum is the source of your greatest frustration. Every day for the past five years, or ten, you've been caught up in a money-making track meet, overcoming obstacles and pushing yourself to meet deadlines. Then, in an instant, the rhythm of business vaporizes. The only pressure left is that which you impose on yourself to get a new job.

And in one way when we've lost a job we amplify the depression for ourselves. The natural batten-down-the-hatches feeling leads most of us to give up dinners out, theater tickets and baby sitters, cleaning help and other commonplace luxuries. The bitter pill of being fired is more bitter for the act of self-preservation.

To those of you who, like me, have been fired, these thoughts:

Don't lose heart

When you are fired, you are automatically initiated into a prestigious club—a club that includes on its rolls some of the most brilliant, successful people the world of commerce has ever known. I know the president of a billion-dollar firm who got the ax. Now he's president of a two-billion-dollar firm. I once worked for a multimillion-dollar corporation whose president proudly told me on the day we first met that he never would have joined his present company if he hadn't been booted from a position with this company's toughest competitor. That president considers his firing to be the luckiest break of his business career. Whatever you do, don't think your situation is unique. If you ask your ten closest friends, chances are good that at least one has pounded the pavements at some point during his business career. In short, no good person ever succumbed fatally to being fired. You won't either. If you still feel down on your luck, remember this: Not more than one in twenty job-seekers takes the time and trouble to prepare himself to get a better job. But you did. You know the rules of the road. You have the inside track. Soon you'll look back on your current circumstances as though they were ancient history. And you'll be all the wiser for them.

Hold on to your office routine

Whatever you do, don't sit at home. For nearly every adult day of your life, you've gone to the office. Keep going. Even if you don't have your old office. Where should you go? It's possible your former employer will let you occupy space somewhere in the recesses of the building, so that you have a place to work out of. If not, a friendly supplier might make room for you. When you join another firm, you'll probably be in the same industry. It would pay a supplier to befriend you now. Later you'll repay his kindness. He knows it. If your list of suppliers doesn't turn up space and a phone, check with your close friends who own their own firms, or who are officers in larger concerns. Chances are you'll come up with desk space, maybe even part-time secretarial assistance, and your name on the telephone list. If you can't find office space, still get out of the house. The public library is public. Occupy a desk every day and keep your files in your briefcase. Don't worry about phone calls. If you check in at home two or three times a day, you can get back to whoever wants you. Don't worry about the delay. Whoever calls will probably think you're out on an interview, and that's better than being thought of as being home in bed. If your spouse works and there's no one at home during the day, that's still no reason to sit at home. Should an executive recruiter or potential employer fail to reach you at home during the day, he'll call at night or send a telegram. No one *expects* you to sit waiting by the telephone.

Two more points regarding office routine:

☐ 1. NO MATTER HOW LITTLE WORK YOU HAVE TO DO, DON'T TAKE A VACATION In the first place you'll lose your job-search momentum. *You're in business for yourself when you're between jobs, and your number-one order of business is to get a new job.* In the second place, you could be away when the very job you want breaks. I know a man who delayed his second interview by a week. When he showed up the next Thursday, he learned the job had been filled on Tuesday. *After* you have a new job, take off. You'll enjoy it more when you have lined up a position, anyhow. And you won't worry how you're going to pay for the vacation.

☐ 2. DRESS AS THOUGH YOU HAD BEEN PROMOTED, NOT FIRED No matter how tight your budget, invest in clean, pressed clothes, and heels that are not run down, even if you have to polish your own shoes. You need to convey an aura of success in order to get the better job you want. Just as important, when you are well dressed you'll feel psychologically at your best. You can't keep your shoulders erect in a slouchy suit. When you're looking, only you should know it.

Keep the pressure on yourself

Until the day the pink slip came, there weren't enough hours in the week to complete all the business tasks you wanted to get done. When you're out looking, you obviously won't feel the same kind of pressure. You might succumb to the well-I-might-as-well-enjoy-my-unemployment-minimum-work pace. Don't. Or your job search may well last longer.

At this point, let me anticipate your inevitable question, "What on earth can I do all day?" Plenty. Let's assume you've written your worthpoint list, your resume, your form letters; that you've developed your list of several hundred companies you want to go after. Even with all that out of the way, there's a great deal you might do. Here are some suggestions:

☐ 1. Develop a second list of another couple of hundred companies that you might work for. If the first list isn't paying off, you should develop new objectives before you start on your second list.

☐ 2. Develop an employment agency follow-up campaign, a short form letter, or postcard, preferably one that will really catch attention. Send a different letter or card each month, asking the agencies what they've done for you lately. You don't want to be forgotten as agencies pursue the placement of newer candidates.

☐ 3. Review your resume critically. After eight weeks of interviews, you may well find elements of your resume that require amplification or deletion. Tighten your resume up. It can't take more than a few hours. And it could save you a few months of searching.

☐ 4. Develop a list of long-forgotten worthpoints. This true story explains why. An advertising executive I know remembered that twelve years before his first agency work he had contributed the basic idea for a direct-mail campaign. Although he hadn't been involved in direct mail since then, he answered an ad seeking a direct-mail advertising manager. He eventually got the job. He never would have applied if he hadn't probed the recesss of his background.

☐ 5. Tape some facsimile interviews. Listen to your voice. You may well want to change your answers or your intonation.

☐ 6. Write an objective memorandum to yourself on how you would have changed your previous job to have made you more successful and avoided your firing. A carefully written memo will help you to define the perimeters of the problem more succintly than daydreaming about what went wrong. If, later on, you read it from time to time, it may actually help you to succeed on your next job—particularly if you own up to how you failed in your relationship to your last boss.

☐ 7. Visit other cities you might work in. Read the last eight weeks' classified sections at a public library. You might find a number of jobs that were not known to you in your current base of operations.

☐ 8. Read other books on job search. They may provide some new ideas that might work for you. And reread this book. The best of us will not recall all the techniques and suggestions in a single reading. A second review may turn up just the thought you needed to make your job campaign quicker and more effective.

☐ 9. Rethink through your career objectives. Maybe being out of work is a blessing in disguise, as it can give you more time to think critically about what you want to do with the rest of your life.

Don't dwell on your weaknesses

Any person who has been fired tends to review what went wrong. It's only natural. How much you think about the past, and how you think about it, however, can affect your ability to sell yourself successfully in person and on paper. If you put yourself in a rotten frame of mind by deciding you were fired because you were no damned good, you can be sure that your depression will work against you in your interviews. Your best bet is to limit the time you think about the past. If, for example, you promise yourself to think about the past only on Monday mornings, turn off your conscious reverie when the past creeps into the crevices of your mind on Tuesday. Instead, work on something productive like a follow-up letter. And when Monday morning's introspective session rolls around, dwell on what went wrong for only a short time. Then get that memo outlined on what you'll do on the next job to avoid the problem again.

Share your search campaign with a friend

Getting a better job is a lonely assignment. This is doubly true if you are out of work. Whatever you do, don't put yourself in needless solitary confinement. Share your progress, your burdens, and your successes with one or more business associates or friends whom you can see on a regular basis (once a week or so) for lunch or during the day. You'll find they enjoy your confidence, are flattered by your asking them for counsel. They are likely to have ideas you haven't explored. Whatever you do, don't place yourself in the role of hermit simply because you are out of a job. Your true friends are your friends, whether you're working or not. When you get a better job, break out the champagne. Your friends will enjoy it more for having helped you along the way.

From the MENTOR Executive Library

Self-Help Books from SIGNET and MENTOR

(0451)

☐ **BORN TO WIN: Transactional Analysis with Gestalt Experiments by Muriel James and Dorothy Jongeward.** This landmark bestseller has convinced millions of readers that they were **Born to Win!** "Enriching, stimulating, rewarding . . . for anyone interested in understanding himself, his relationships with others and his goals."—*Kansas City Times*
(134680—$3.95)*

☐ **UNDERSTANDING YOURSELF by Dr. Christopher Evans.** An interesting collection of questionnaires, tests, quizzes and games, scientifically designed by a team of psychologists to offer a greater self-awareness. Photographs and illustrations included. (111702—$3.50)

☐ **OVERCOMING PROCRASTINATION by Albert Ellis, Ph.D. and William J. Knaus, Ed.D.** The scientifically proven techniques of Rational-Motive Therapy are applied to procrastination (delaying tactics, frustration, and self-disgust). Examines the causes of procrastination, and the links between procrastination and obesity, drugs, depression, and sexual dysfunction, and other personality and health problems.
(127447—$2.95)*

☐ **THE FEAR OF SUCCESS by Leon Tec, M.D.** In this valuable self-help book, a well-known psychiatrist tells why people do not succeed and what they can do about it. The fear of success is identified and traced from birth, and a diagnostic test and role-playing suggestions are provided to help overcome the problem. (123115—$3.50)*

*Prices slightly higher in Canada

Buy them at your local bookstore or use this convenient coupon for ordering.

NEW AMERICAN LIBRARY,
P.O. Box 999, Bergenfield, New Jersey 07621

Please send me the books I have checked above. I am enclosing $_____
(please add $1.00 to this order to cover postage and handling). Send check or money order—no cash or C.O.D.'s. Prices and numbers are subject to change without notice.

Name _____

Address_____

City_____ State_____ Zip Code_____
Allow 4-6 weeks for delivery.
This offer is subject to withdrawal without notice.

Thrilling Fiction from SIGNET

**Buy them at your local
bookstore or use coupon
on next page for ordering.**

World Renowned Authors from SIGNET

(0451)

- ☐ DANIEL MARTIN by John Fowles. (122100—$4.50)†
- ☐ THE EBONY TOWER by John Fowles. (134648—$3.95)*
- ☐ THE FRENCH LIEUTENANT'S WOMAN by John Fowles. (110951—$3.50)*
- ☐ BREAKFAST AT TIFFANY'S by Truman Capote. (120426—$2.50)*
- ☐ THE GRASS HARP and TREE OF NIGHT by Truman Capote.
  (120434—$2.75)*
- ☐ IN COLD BLOOD by Truman Capote. (121988—$3.95)*
- ☐ OTHER VOICES, OTHER ROOMS by Truman Capote. (134516—$2.95)*
- ☐ THE ARMIES OF THE NIGHT by Norman Mailer. (123174—$3.95)
- ☐ THE CHAPMAN REPORT by Irving Wallace. (127102—$3.95)
- ☐ THE PRIZE by Irving Wallace. (123050—$2.95)
- ☐ THE FABULOUS SHOWMAN by Irving Wallace. (113853—$2.95)
- ☐ THE THREE SIRENS by Irving Wallace. (125843—$3.95)*
- ☐ THE SECOND LADY by Irving Wallace. (126602—$3.95)*

*Prices slightly higher in Canada
†Not available in Canada

Buy them at your local bookstore or use this handy coupon for ordering:

NEW AMERICAN LIBRARY,
P.O. Box 999, Bergenfield, New Jersey 07621

Please send me the books I have checked above. I am enclosing $_____
(please add $1.00 to this order to cover postage and handling). Send check
or money order—no cash or C.O.D.'s. Prices and numbers are subject to change
without notice.

Name _____

Address_____

City_____ State_____ Zip Code_____
Allow 4-6 weeks for delivery.
This offer is subject to withdrawal without notice.